# THE HOLY GEETĀ

## Śrīmad Bhagawad Geetā

*Sanskrit & Romanized Text*
*with*
*English Translation*

*Translator*
**PRABHA DUNEJA**



NEW AGE BOOKS
New Delhi (India)

**The Holy Geetā**

**NEW AGE BOOKS**
A-44, Naraina Industrial Area, Phase-I
New Delhi-110 028 (INDIA)
E-mail:nab@newagebooksindia.com
Website: www.newagebooksindia.com

ISBN:978-81-7822-451-0

*First NAB Edition: Delhi,* ***2014***
*First Edition: July, 1998*
*Second Edition: August, 2001*
*Third Edition: January, 2005*



*Printed and published by*
RP Jain for New Age Books
A-44, Naraina Industrial Area
Phase-I, New Delhi 110 028. India

# PUBLISHER'S NOTE

The Publisher feels honoured in presenting the holy sermon of Lord Krsna known as Srimad Bhagawad Geeta in original Sanskrit, a romanized phonetic transliteration and a complete English translation beautifully made by Mrs. Prabha Duneja, an educationist and a devotee of the Lord, spreading the message of Geeta in U.S.A. and other parts of the world.

In Geeta, the Lord Himself addresses the Pandava Prince Arjuna who finds himself in the battlefield mentally agitated and confused. Lord Kṛṣṇa, the Geetacarya initiates him in rediscovering the greater personality in himself, and become enlightened about the significant realities of life. This art of 'self-rediscovery' is the entire theme of Srimad Bhagawad Geeta.

Mrs. Prabha Duneja in her translation brings out clearly this spirit of Geeta. The Publisher would feel immensely rewarded, if the readers are able to catch that spirit and translate into practice the high tenets and subtle advises of Geeta, so as to bring in their day-to-day life a greater stability and peace of mind and more than that, a greater harmony in their personal and social lives.

ŚRĪ KṚṢṆA ARPAṆAM ASTU

त्वदीय गीतं गोविन्दं तुभ्यमेव समर्पये

# YOURS TO YOU

*"... Vasūdeva Sutam Devaṁ*
*Kaṅs Chaṇur Mardanaṁ*
*Devaki Parmanaṅdaṁ*
*Kṛṣṇaṁ Vaṅde Jagatguruṁ..."*

I salute to Lord Kṛṣṇa, the son of Vasūdeva, the destroyer of Kaṅsa and Chanura, the supreme bliss of Devaki and the teacher of the Universe.

# CONTENTS

# ACKNOWLEDGEMENTS

I want to express in few words my heart felt gratitude to the holy sages of past and present and the other several Geeta scholars, whose teachings have inspired me for presenting the Holy Geeta in Sanskrit and Romanized text with English translation. I feel immensely indebted to my husband Amritji and our son Anshuman for their genuine encouragement and sincere support in the completion of this noble work.

I am especially grateful to my respected grandparents Sri & Smt. Ganga Ramji and my parents Dr. & Mrs. Manohar Lalji and my uncle Prof. Nand Lalji, who initiated me into the study of Bhagawad Geeta at the early age of eight. I want to thank sincerely to Mrs. Manorama Iyer, who worked very patiently in typing the preliminary work. Special thanks to Swami Jagdishwaranandji for editing the Sanskrit and romanized text.

—***Prabha Duneja***

# INTRODUCTION

Bhagawad Geeta is the most luminous dialogue in the legacy of Vedic literature. The holy poem has been upheld as one of the *Prasthana-traya*—the three authoritative texts of the *Sanātan Vedic* Religion. The first one is the *Vedic Prasthāna* called the *Upanisadas*, the second is the philosophical *Prasthāna*—the *Brahma Sutra*; the third *Prasthāna* is the Bhagawad Geeta. Bhagawad Geeta is a unique scripture which summarizes almost all the essential teachings of the *Vedic* literature. It has been a perennial source of spiritual inspiration for the entire mankind.

Bhagawad Geeta is one of the most well known and revered text among the other scriptures of the World. It is a compendium of spiritual wisdom and the most appropriate guide for living a harmonious life in all respects

The message of the holy Geeta is indeed phenomenal and timeless. It is an anthology of spiritual wisdom which guides the individual into the mysteries of self-realization and God-realization. It analyses almost all levels of human psychology and trains the person into living a productive, joyful, balanced and creative life. The teachings of Geeta are very intimately connected with the every day life of a man. In the words of Swami Sivananda, "Study of the Geeta alone is sufficient for the purpose of daily *swadhyaya* (scriptural study). You will find a solution here for all your doubts. The more you study with devotion and faith, the more you will get deeper knowledge, penetrative insight and clear right thinking. Even if you live in the spirit of one verse of the Geeta, all your miseries will come to an end and you will attain the goal of life—Immortality and Eternal Peace."

The message of Geeta presents a profound insight into the workings of human nature and provides the most appropriate guidance which is needed in almost every field of life in order to live in perfect harmony with our own self and with others. The dialogue provides an understanding into the mystery of the Supreme-soul and how every individual can restore himself to the Supremacy of his essential nature.

In the words of Dr. Paul Brunton, "The Geeta summarizes various approaches to the Overself and also describes the latter. Srī Kṛṣṇa not only represents the embodied spiritual teacher, but He is ultimately the Overself within man, the God within who can illuminate all dark corners and answer all questions. At the end of the dialogue after hearing all the teachings, the pupil's mind becomes peaceful. He says indeed: "My doubts are dispelled. Destroyed are my illusions". By what magic was this mental change accomplished? Through both the guidance and grace received from his teacher and his own inner growth in striving for insight. The difficulties one meets in modern life can be met and overcome after we gain such insight. Wisdom means the ability to negotiate all the circumstances of life adequately, correctly and with spiritual success. The deep spiritual comfort emanating from the teachings of the Geeta is peculiarly needed at this stage of the world's affairs"

The message of Geeta synthesizes almost all the well known teachings of the ancient scriptures of the world and it is addressed to the entire mankind. In words of Dr. Annie Besant, "Among the priceless teaching that may be found in the great Hindu poem of the Mahabharata, there is none so rare and precious as this "The Lord's song". Since it fell from the divine lips of Srī Kṛṣṇa on the field of battle, and stilled the surging emotions of the disciple and friend, it has quietened and strengthened many troubled hearts, and many weary souls have been led to Him! It is meant to lift the aspirant from the lower levels of renunciation, where objects are renounced, to the loftier heights where desires are dead, and where the Yogi dwells in calm and ceaseless contemplation, while his body and mind are actively employed in discharging the duties that fall to his lot in life. That the spiritual man need not be a recluse, that union with divine life may be achieved and maintained in the midst of worldly affairs, that the obstacles to that union lie, not outside us, within us, such is the central lesson of the Bhagawad Geeta".

Ever since the teachings of Geeta have become known to the people in Europe and America; it has quickly won the interest and admiration of millions. Many philosophical and religious groups in foreign countries hold the same respect for Geeta as the people in India. About the popularity of Geeta, Mahatma Gandhi has written that during one of his visits to England he went to a big library and inquired from the librarian about the most popular religious book, which was in greatest demand. The librarian informed him that it was indeed the Bhagawad Geeta.

The great educationist and philosopher of India Mr. Madan Mohan Malaviya has written about Geeta in these words. "I believe that in all the living languages of the world, there is no book so full of true knowledge, and yet so handy as the Bhagawad Geeta". The well known professor of religion at Oxford University Mr. Zaehner has written about the glory of the sacred song in these words, "Geeta is a first hand guide to the ancient roots of Vedic religion. Although in *Shevatṣvara Upanisad* the transcendence of the personal God has been affirmed to some extent—but with Geeta has come the devotional religion".

The great respect and appreciation for Geeta has been voiced by Warren Hastings the first British Governor General of India in year 1773. He has said, "the work as the Geeta would live long after the British Empire in India has ceased to exist". The song Celestial by Sir Edwin Arnold describes the greatness of Geeta in these words. "In plain but noble language it unfolds a philosophical system which remains to this day the prevailing *Brahmanic* belief, blending as it does the doctrines of *Kapila, Patanjali*, and the Vedas. So lofty are many of its declarations, so sublime its aspirations, and so pure and tender is its piety". Sir Edwin Arnold has called Geeta the incomparable religious classic of India.

Similarly Mr. Von Humboldt, Maxmuller, Emerson, Franklin Edgerton and Aldous Huxely and many other scholars and educationists of the world have taken Geeta as a text for the exposition of their thoughts. In the words of Aldous Huxely, "Bhagawad Geeta is perhaps the most systematic spiritual statement of the perennial philosophy.

The message of the holy dialogue has been held in deep reverence by the sages, philosophers and the learned scholars all over the world. The teachings of Geeta are universal and meant for the welfare of entire creation. There are hundreds of commentaries on Bhagawad Geeta both in Indian and in many foreign languages. This is perhaps the most widely translated scriptural text of the world. In the words of Dr. Radhakrishnan, "for centuries people have found comfort in this great book which sets forth in precise and penetrating words the essential principles of a spiritual religion which are not contingent on ill-founded facts, unscientific dogmas or arbitrary fancies. With a long history of spiritual power, it serves even today as a light to all who will receive illumination from the profundity of its wisdom which insists on a world wider and deeper than wars and revolutions can touch. It is a powerful shaping factor in the renewal of spiritual life and has secured an assured place among the world's greatest scriptures"

The present translation is only a humble addition to the work which has been accomplished earlier by the Geeta scholars. This translation with Romanized Sanskrit verses has been brought forward in order to encourage the modern generation into the study of this ancient scripture. It makes me feel so blessed that the melodious recitation and chanting of Geeta verses, which I have enjoyed sharing with others, is finally going to be presented in Romanized simple form to the admirers of Geeta. This work is meant to help the Indians living in foreign countries and to arouse the interest of foreigners into the recitation of Sanskrit verses and to understand the meaning of Geeta in a simple flexible and comprehensible language. This book is indeed a *prasad* to the readers which will initiate them into the appreciation of the holy dialogue. The entire purpose of composing this pocket book with Romanized Sanskrit verses is to spread the message of Geeta and to pass on the legacy of the Holy sermon to the coming generation.

**Śrī Kṛṣṇa Arpaṇamastu**

***Prabha Duneja***

*2822, Camino Segura*
*Pleasanton, CA 94566, USA, Tel.: 925-484-5411*
*Email: duneja@aol.com, website: holygeeta.org*

## *Chapter One*

# VISHĀDAYOGA

## THE YOGA OF THE DESPONDENCY OF ARJUNA

धृतराष्ट्र उवाच

धर्मक्षेत्रे कुरुक्षेत्रे समवेता युयुत्सवः ।
मामकाः पाण्डवाश्चैव किमकुर्वत सञ्जय ॥ १ ॥

*dharmakṣetre kurukṣetre*
*samavetā yuyutsavaḥ*
*māmakāḥ pāṇḍavāścaiva*
*kimakurvata sañjaya*

**Dhritarashtra said :**

(1) On the holy field of Kurukshetra, assembled together and eager to fight the battle, what did my sons and the sons of Pandu do?, O'Sanjaya.

संजय उवाच

दृष्ट्वा तु पाण्डवानीकं व्यूढं दुर्योधनस्तदा ।
आचार्यमुपसङ्गम्य राजा वचनमब्रवीत् ॥ २ ॥

*dṛṣṭvā tu pāṇḍavānīkaṁ*
*vyūḍhaṁ duryodhanastadā*
*ācāryamupasaṅgamya*
*rājā vacanamabravīt*

**Sanjaya said :**

(2) Having seen the army of the Pandavas arrayed in the battle, Prince Duryodhana then approached his teacher Dronacharya, and spoke these words.

**पश्यैतां पाण्डुपुत्राणामाचार्य महतीं चमूम्।**
**व्यूढां द्रुपदपुत्रेण तव शिष्येण धीमता॥ ३॥**

*paśyaitāṁ pāṇḍuputrāṇām-*
*ācārya mahatīṁ camūm*
*vyūḍhāṁ drupadaputreṇa*
*tava śiṣyeṇa dhīmatā*

(3) Behold O' Teacher, this mighty army of the sons of Pandu, arrayed by the son of King Drupada, thy wise disciple.

**अत्र शूरा महेष्वासा भीमार्जुनसमा युधि।**
**युयुधानो विराटश्च द्रुपदश्च महारथः॥ ४॥**

*atra śūrā maheṣvāsā*
*bhīmārjunasamā yudhi*
*yuyudhāno virāṭaśca*
*drupadaśca mahārathaḥ*

धृष्टकेतुश्चेकितानः काशिराजश्च वीर्यवान्।
पुरुजित्कुन्तिभोजश्च शैब्यश्च नरपुङ्गवः ॥ ५ ॥

*dhṛṣṭaketuścekitānaḥ*
*kāśirājaśca vīryavān*
*purujitkuntibhojaśca*
*śaibyaśca narapuṅgavaḥ*

युधामन्युश्च विक्रान्त उत्तमौजाश्च वीर्यवान्।
सौभद्रो द्रौपदेयाश्च सर्व एव महारथाः ॥ ६ ॥

*yudhāmanyuśca vikrānta*
*uttamaujāśca vīryavān*
*saubhadro draupadeyāśca*
*sarva eva mahārathāḥ*

(4, 5, 6) Here are the heroes, the mighty archers, who are equal in warfare to Bhima and Arjuna—Yuyudhana, Virata and the great chariot-warrior Drupada. Dhristaketu, Cekitana, and the valiant King of Kasi;

Purujit, Kuntibhoja, and Saibya, the best among men; the mighty Yudhamanyu, the valiant Uttamauja, Abhimanyu, the son of Subhadra and the five sons of Draupadi are also there. All of them are the well-known chariot-warriors.

अस्माकं तु विशिष्टा ये तान्निबोध द्विजोत्तम।
नायका मम सैन्यस्य सञ्ज्ञार्थं तान्ब्रवीमि ते॥७॥

*asmākaṁ tu viśiṣṭā ye*
*tānnibodha dvijottama*
*nāyakā mama sainyasya*
*sañjñārthaṁ tānbravīmi te*

(7) Know also O'noblest of the twice-born! the distinguished warriors of our side, the generals of my army. I will name them for your information.

भवान्भीष्मश्च कर्णश्च कृपश्च समितिञ्जयः।
अश्वत्थामा विकर्णश्च सौमदत्तिस्तथैव च॥८॥

*bhavānbhīṣmaśca karṇaśca*
*kṛpaśca samitiñjayaḥ*
*aśvatthāmā vikarṇaśca*
*saumadattistathaiva ca*

(8) Yourself and Bhishma, Karna and also Kripa who is ever victorious in battle; Ashwatthama, Vikarna and Saumadatti, the son of Somadatta.

अन्ये च बहवः शूरा मदर्थे त्यक्तजीविताः ।
नानाशस्त्रप्रहरणाः सर्वे युद्धविशारदाः ॥ ९ ॥

*anye ca bahavaḥ śūrā*
*madarthe tyaktajīvitāḥ*
*nānāśastraprahraṇāḥ*
*sarve yuddhaviśāradāḥ*

(9) And there are many other heroes, who are ready to give up their lives for my sake; they are equipped with many kinds of weapons and all of them are skilled in the strategy of warfare.

अपर्याप्तं तदस्माकं बलं भीष्माभिरक्षितम् ।
पर्याप्तं त्विदमेतेषां बलं भीमाभिरक्षितम् ॥ १० ॥

*aparyāptaṁ tadasmākaṁ*
*balaṁ bhīṣmābhirakṣitam*
*paryāptaṁ tvidameteṣāṁ*
*balaṁ bhīmābhirakṣitam*

(10) This army of ours, which is guarded and marshalled by Bhishma, is insufficient; while their army, which is marshalled by Bhima is sufficient.

अयनेषु च सर्वेषु यथाभागमवस्थिताः ।
भीष्ममेवाभिरक्षन्तु भवन्तः सर्व एव हि ॥ ११ ॥

*ayaneṣu ca sarveṣu*
*yathābhāgamavasthitāḥ*
*bhīṣmamevā'bhirakṣantu*
*bhavantaḥ sarva eva hi*

(11) Therefore, all of you, stationed in your respective positions, in every division, must guard Bhishma in particular by all means.

तस्य सञ्जनयन्हर्षं कुरुवृद्धः पितामहः ।
सिंहनादं विनद्योच्चैः शङ्खं दध्मौ प्रतापवान् ॥ १२ ॥

*tasya sañjanayanharṣaṁ*
*kuruvṛddhaḥ pitāmahaḥ*
*siṁhanādaṁ vinadyoccaiḥ*
*śaṅkhaṁ dadhmau pratāpavān*

(12) Then the revered grandsire Bhishma) the oldest of the Kauravas

roaring like a lion, blew his conch in order to cheer up Duryodhana.

ततः शङ्खाश्च भेर्यश्च पणवानकगोमुखाः ।
सहसैवाभ्यहन्यन्त स शब्दस्तुमुलोऽभवत् ॥ १३ ॥

*tataḥ śaṅkhāśca bheryaśca*
*paṇavānakagomukhāḥ*
*sahasaivābhyahanyanta*
*sa śabdastumulo'bhavat*

(13) Then conches, kettledrums, tabors, drums and cow-horns blared forth all at once and the noise became tumultuous.

ततः श्वेतैर्हयैर्युक्ते महति स्यन्दने स्थितौ ।
माधवः पाण्डवश्चैव दिव्यौ शङ्खौ प्रदध्मतुः ॥ १४ ॥

*tataḥ śvetairhayairyukte*
*mahati syandane sthitau*
*mādhavaḥ pāṇḍvaścaiva*
*divyau śaṅkhau pradadhmatuḥ*

(14) Then seated in the magnificent chariot, yoked with white horses, Srī Kṛṣṇa as well as Arjuna blew their celestial conches.

पाञ्चजन्यं हृषीकेशो देवदत्तं धनञ्जयः।
पौण्ड्रं दध्मौ महाशङ्खं भीमकर्मा वृकोदरः॥ १५॥

*pāñcajanyaṁ hṛṣīkeśo*
*devadattaṁ dhanañjayaḥ*
*pauṇḍraṁ dadhmau mahāśaṅkhaṁ*
*bhīmakarmā vṛkodaraḥ*

(15) Srī Kṛṣṇa blew His conch named Panchajanya, and Arjuna blew his conch called Devadatta, while Bhima the doer of terrific deeds blew his mighty conch, Paundra.

अनन्तविजयं राजा कुन्तीपुत्रो युधिष्ठिरः।
नकुलः सहदेवश्च सुघोषमणिपुष्पकौ॥ १६॥

*anantavijayaṁ rājā*
*kuntīputro yudhiṣṭhiraḥ*
*nakulaḥ sahadevaśca*
*sughoṣamaṇipuṣpakau*

(16) The King Yudhisthira, the son of Kunti, blew his conch Anantavijaya and Nakula and Sahadeva blew their respective conches, the Sughosa and the Manipuspaka.

काश्यश्च परमेष्वासः शिखण्डी च महारथः ।
धृष्टद्युम्नो विराटश्च सात्यकिश्चापराजितः ॥ १७ ॥

*kāśyaśca parameṣvāsaḥ*
*śikhaṇḍī ca mahārathaḥ*
*dhṛṣṭadyumno virāṭaśca*
*sātyakiścāparājitaḥ*

द्रुपदो द्रौपदेयाश्च सर्वशः पृथिवीपते ।
सौभद्रश्च महाबाहुः शङ्खान्दध्मुः पृथक्पृथक् ॥ १८ ॥

*drupado draupadeyāśca*
*sarvaśaḥ pṛthivīpate*
*saubhadraśca mahābāhuḥ*
*śaṅkhāndadhamuḥ pṛthak-pṛthak*

(17, 18) The King of Kasi, an excellent archer; Sikhandi, the great chariot-warrior, Dhristadyumna and Virata and the invincible Satyaki, the King Drupada as well as the five sons of Draupadi and the mighty-armed Abhimanyu, the son of Subhadra, every one of them blew their respective conches.

स घोषो धार्तराष्ट्राणां हृदयानि व्यदारयत्।
नभश्च पृथिवीं चैव तुमुलो व्यनुनादयन्॥ १९॥

*sa ghoṣo dhārtarāṣṭrāṇāṁ*
*hṛdayāni vyadārayat*
*nabhaśca pṛthivīṁ caiva*
*tumulo vyanunādayan*

(19) The tumultuous uproar has pierced the hearts of Dhritrashtra's sons resounding through the heaven and the earth.

अथ व्यवस्थितान्दृष्ट्वा धार्तराष्ट्रान् कपिध्वजः।
प्रवृत्ते शस्त्रसम्पाते धनुरुद्यम्य पाण्डवः॥ २०॥

*atha vyavasthitāndṛṣṭvā*
*dhārtarāṣṭrān kapidhvajaḥ*
*pravṛtte śastrasampāte*
*dhanurudyamya pāndavaḥ*

हृषीकेशं तदा वाक्यमिदमाह महीपते।

*hṛṣīkeśaṁ tadā vākyam-*
*idamāha mahīpate*

(20, 21) Then looking at the people of Dhritrashtra's sons, standing arrayed in battle and about to commence with their weapons; Arjuna, the son of Pandu, whose flag ensign was Hanuman, lifted his bow and said the following words to the Lord of the earth.

अर्जुन उवाच

सेनयोरुभयोर्मध्ये रथं स्थापय मेऽच्युत ॥ २१ ॥

*senayorubhayormadhye*
*rathaṁ sthāpaya me'cyuta*

यावदेतान्निरीक्षेऽहं योद्धुकामानवस्थितान्।
कैर्मया सह योद्धव्यमस्मिन्रणसमुद्यमे ॥ २२ ॥

*yāvadetānnirīkṣe'haṁ*
*yoddhukāmānavasthitān*
*kairmayā saha yoddhavyam-*
*asminraṇasamudyame*

**Arjuna said :**

(21, 22) O'Achyuta (Srī Kṛṣṇa)! Please place my chariot between the two armies, so that I may see all those, who stand here desirous of war with whom I have to fight this battle.

योत्स्यमानानवेक्षेऽहं य एतेऽत्र समागताः।
धार्तराष्ट्रस्य दुर्बुद्धेर्युद्धे प्रियचिकीर्षवः ॥ २३ ॥

*yotsyamānānavekṣehaṁ*
*ya ete'tra samāgatāḥ*
*dhārtarāṣṭrasya durbuddher-*
*yuddhe priyacikīrṣavaḥ*

(23) I want to see those who are assembled here with an intent to fight and are desirous to please in battle, the evil minded son of Dhritrashtra (Duryodhana).

**संजय उवाच**

**एवमुक्तो हृषीकेशो गुडाकेशेन भारत।**
**सेनयोरुभयोर्मध्ये स्थापयित्वा रथोत्तमम्॥ २४॥**

*evamukto hṛṣīkeśo*
*guḍākeśena bhārata*
*senayorubhayormadhye*
*sthāpayitvā rathottamam.*

**भीष्मद्रोणप्रमुखतः सर्वेषां च महीक्षिताम्।**
**उवाच पार्थ पश्यैतान् समवेतान्कुरूनिति॥ २५॥**

*bhīṣmadroṇapramukhataḥ*
*sarveṣāṁ ca mahīkṣitām*
*uvāca pārtha paśyaitān*
*samavetānkurūniti*

**Sanjaya said :**

(24, 25) O'descendant of Bharata (Dhritrashtra), thus addressed by Gudakesa (Arjuna), Hrishikesha (Srī Kṛṣṇa) having placed the magnificent chariot in the middle of the two armies; in front of Bhisma and Drona and all the other kings said, "O'Arjuna, behold these Kurus assembled here."

तत्रापश्यत्स्थितान्पार्थः पितृनथ पितामहान्।

*tatrāpaśyat sthitānpārthaḥ*
*pitṝnatha pitāmahān*

आचार्यान्मातुलान्भ्रातृन्पुत्रान्पौत्रान्सखींस्तथा ॥ २६ ॥
श्वसुरान्सुहृदश्चैव सेनयोरुभयोरपि।

*ācāryānmātulānbhrātṝn-*
*putrānpautrānsakhīnstathā*
*śvasurānsuhṛdaścaiva*
*senayorubhàyorapi*

(26) There, Arjuna beholds, stationed between both the armies; his uncles, granduncles, teachers, maternal uncles, brothers, cousins, sons, grandsons, fathers-in-law and friends as well.

तान्समीक्ष्य स कौन्तेयः सर्वान्बन्धूनवस्थितान्॥ २७॥
कृपया परयाविष्टो विषीदन्निदमब्रवीत्।

*tānsamīkṣya sa kaunteyaḥ*
*sarvānbandhūnavasthitān*
*kṛpayā parayāviṣṭo*
*viṣīdannidamabravīt*

(27) Looking at all the kinsmen, thus assembled there, Arjuna feels overwhelmed with deep compassion and speaks these words.

अर्जुन उवाच

दृष्ट्वेमं स्वजनं कृष्ण युयुत्सुं समुपस्थितम्॥ २८॥

*dṛṣṭvemaṁ svajanaṁ kṛṣṇa*
*yuyutsuṁ samupasthitam*

सीदन्ति मम गात्राणि मुखं च परिशुष्यति।
वेपथुश्च शरीरे मे रोमहर्षश्च जायते॥ २९॥

*sīdanti mama gātrāṇi*
*mukhaṁ ca pariśuṣyati*
*vepathuśca śarīre me*
*romaharṣaśca jāyate*

गाण्डीवं स्रंसते हस्तात्त्वक्चैव परिदह्यते।
न च शक्नोम्यवस्थातुं भ्रमतीव च मे मनः॥ ३०॥

*gāṇḍīvaṁ sraṅsate hastāt*
*tvakcaiva paridahyate*
*na ca śaknomyavasthātuṁ*
*bhramatīva ca me manaḥ*

**Arjuna said :**

(28, 29, 30) O'Kṛṣṇa, at the sight of these kinsmen, thus arrayed here, eager for battle, my limbs have become feeble and my mouth is parched, my whole body quivers and my hair stand on end. The Gandiva is slipping from my hands and my skin is burning all over. I am not able to stand firmly and my mind seems to reel.

निमित्तानि च पश्यामि विपरीतानि केशव।
न च श्रेयोऽनुपश्यामि हत्वा स्वजनमाहवे॥ ३१ ॥

*nimittāni ca paśyāmi*
*viparītāni keśava*
*na ca śreyo'nupaśyāmi*
*hatvā svajanamāhave*

(31) And I see very inauspicious omens, O'Kesava (Srī Kṛṣṇa); I do not

perceive any good in killing my kinsmen in the battle.

न काङ्क्षे विजयं कृष्ण न च राज्यं सुखानि च।
किं नो राज्येन गोविन्द किं भोगैर्जीवितेन वा ॥ ३२ ॥

*na kāṅkṣe vijayaṁ kṛṣṇa*
*na ca rājyaṁ sukhāni ca*
*kiṁ no rājyena govinda*
*kiṁ bhogairjīvitena vā*

(32) O'Kṛṣṇa, I do not desire any victory, nor kingdom, nor pleasures. What is the use of kingdom to us, O'Govinda, or the luxuries or even life itself.

येषामर्थे काङ्क्षितं नो
राज्यं भोगाः सुखानि च।
त इमेऽवस्थिता युद्धे
प्राणांस्त्यक्त्वा धनानि च ॥ ३३ ॥

*yeṣāmarthe kāṅkṣitaṁ no*
*rājyaṁ bhogāḥ sukhāni ca*
*ta ime'vasthitā yuddhe*
*prāṇāṅstyaktvā dhanāni ca*

(33) Those, for whose sake we

desire kingdom, enjoyments and pleasures, are standing poised for battle and ready to give up their lives and wealth.

आचार्याः पितरः पुत्रास्तथैव च पितामहाः।

मातुलाः श्वशुराः पौत्राः श्यालाः सम्बन्धिनस्तथा॥ ३४

*ācāryāḥ pitaraḥ putrās-*
*tathaiva ca pitāmahāḥ*
*mātulāḥ śvaśurāḥ pautrāḥ*
*śyālāḥ sambandhinastathā*

(34) The teachers, uncles, sons and grandfathers, maternal uncles, fathers-in-law, grandsons, brothers-in-law, and other relatives as well.

एतान्न हन्तुमिच्छामि घ्नतोऽपि मधुसूदन।

अपि त्रैलोक्यराज्यस्य हेतोः किं नु महीकृते॥ ३५॥

*etānna hantumicchāmi*
*ghnato'pi madhusūdana*
*api trailokyarājyasya*
*hetoḥ kim nu mahīkṛte*

(35) These, I do not want to kill, even though they may kill me, O'Slayer of Madhu (Kṛṣṇa); even for

the sovereignty of the three worlds—how then just for the sake of the earthly lordship?

निहत्य धार्तराष्ट्रान्नः का प्रीतिः स्याज्जनार्दन।
पापमेवाश्रयेदस्मान्हत्वैतानाततायिनः ॥ ३६ ॥

*nihatya dhārtarāṣṭrānnaḥ*
*kā prītiḥ syājjanārdana*
*pāpamevāśrayedasmān-*
*hatvaitānātatāyinaḥ*

(36) By killing the sons of Dhritrashtra, what pleasure can be ours, O' Kṛṣṇa? Only the sin will accrue to us by slaying these desperadoes.

तस्मान्नार्हा वयं हन्तुं धार्तराष्ट्रान् स्वबान्धवान्।
स्वजनं हि कथं हत्वा सुखिनः स्याम माधव ॥ ३७ ॥

*tasmānnārhā vayaṁ hantuṁ*
*dhārtarāṣṭrān svabāndhavān*
*svajanaṁ hi kathaṁ hatvā*
*sukhinaḥ syāma mādhava*

(37) Therefore, it is not appropriate for us to kill our relatives, the sons of Dhritrashtra. For, if we kill

our kinsmen, how can we be happy, O' Madhva (Kṛṣṇa)?

यद्यप्येते न पश्यन्ति लोभोपहतचेतसः।

कुलक्षयकृतं दोषं मित्रद्रोहे च पातकम्॥ ३८॥

*yadyapyete na paśyanti*
*lobhopahatacetasaḥ*
*kulakṣayakṛtaṁ doṣaṁ*
*mitradrohe ca pātakam*

कथं न ज्ञेयमस्माभिः पापादस्मान्निवर्तितुम्।

कुलक्षयकृतं दोषं प्रपश्यद्भिर्जनार्दन॥ ३९॥

*kathaṁ na jñeyamasmābhiḥ*
*pāpādasmānnivartitum*
*kulakṣayakṛtaṁ doṣaṁ*
*prapaśyadbhirjanārdana*

(38, 39) Although these people, whose minds are blinded by greed, do not perceive evil in the destruction of their own race, and the sin, in treachery to friends; why shouldn't we have the wisdom to turn away from this crime, we can clearly see the sin which is involved in the destruction of the family, O'Janardana (Kṛṣṇa)?

कुलक्षये प्रणश्यन्ति कुलधर्माः सनातनाः।
धर्मे नष्टे कुलं कृत्स्नमधर्मोऽभिभवत्युत ॥ ४० ॥

*kulakṣaye praṇaśyanti*
*kuladharmāḥ sanātanāḥ*
*dharme naṣṭe kulaṁ kṛtsnama-*
*dharmo'bhibhavatyuta*

(40) With the destruction of a family, the ancient religious traditions are destroyed; with the disappearance of the religious traditions, the unrighteousness takes hold of the entire family.

अधर्माभिभवात्कृष्ण प्रदुष्यन्ति कुलस्त्रियः।
स्त्रीषु दुष्टासु वार्ष्णेय जायते वर्णसंकरः ॥ ४१ ॥

*adharmābhibhavātkṛṣṇa*
*praduṣyanti kulastriyaḥ*
*strīṣu duṣṭāsu vārṣṇeya*
*jāyate varṇasaṅkaraḥ*

(41) With the prevalence of unrighteousness, O'Kṛṣṇa, the women of the family become corrupt; when the women become corrupt, O'Varsneya (Kṛṣṇa) there arise the

intermixture of castes.

**संकरो नरकायैव कुलघ्नानां कुलस्य च।**
**पतन्ति पितरो ह्येषां लुप्तपिण्डोदकक्रियाः ॥ ४२ ॥**

*saṅkaro narakāyaiva*
*kulaghnānāṁ kulasya ca*
*patanti pitaro hyeṣāṁ*
*luptapiṇḍodakakriyāḥ*

(42) The confusion of castes leads to hell the entire clan itself and its destroyers; for the spirits of the ancestors fall, deprived of their offerings of rice and water.

**दोषैरेतैः कुलघ्नानां वर्णसङ्करकारकैः।**
**उत्साद्यन्ते जातिधर्माः कुलधर्माश्च शाश्वताः ॥ ४३ ॥**

*doṣairetaiḥ kulaghnānāṁ*
*varṇasaṅkarakārakaiḥ*
*utsādyante jātidharmāḥ*
*kuladharmāśca śāśvatāḥ*

(43) By these evil deeds of the destroyers of the family which create confusion of Varnas, the ancient laws of the caste and family are destroyed.

उत्सन्नकुलधर्माणां मनुष्याणां जनार्दन।
नरकेऽनियतं वासो भवतीत्यनुशुश्रुम ॥ ४४ ॥

*utsannakuladharmāṇāṁ*
*manuṣyāṇāṁ janārdana*
*narake'niyataṁ vāso*
*bhavatītyanuśuśruma*

(44) For those men, in whose families, the ancient religious traditions are destroyed, a place in hell is ordained, O' Kṛṣṇa, we have heard it so.

अहो बत महत्पापं कर्तुं व्यवसिता वयम्।
यद्राज्यसुखलोभेन हन्तुं स्वजनमुद्यताः ॥ ४५ ॥

*aho bata mahatpāpaṁ*
*kartuṁ vyavasitā vayam*
*yadrājyasukhalobhena*
*hantuṁ svajanamudyatāḥ*

(45) Alas! We have resolved to commit a great sin in which we are prepared to kill our own kinsmen, merely out of our desire for sovereignty and enjoyments.

यदि मामप्रतीकारमशस्त्रं शस्त्रपाणयः ।
धार्तराष्ट्रा रणे हन्युस्तन्मे क्षेमतरं भवेत् ॥ ४६ ॥

*yadi māmpratīkāram-*
*aśastraṁ śastrapāṇayaḥ*
*dhārtarāṣṭrā raṇe hanyus-*
*tanme kṣemataraṁ bhavet*

(46) It will be better for me if the well-armed sons of Dhritrashtra do kill me in the battle, while I am unarmed and unresisting.

संजय उवाच

एवमुक्त्वार्जुनः सङ्ख्ये रथोपस्थ उपाविशत् ।
विसृज्य सशरं चापं शोकसंविग्नमानसः ॥ ४७ ॥

*evamuktvārjunaḥ saṅkhye*
*rathopastha upāviśat*
*visṛjya saśaraṁ cāpaṁ*
*śokasaṁvignamānasaḥ*

**Sanjaya said :**

(47) Having spoken thus, in the middle of the battlefield, Arjuna puts away his bow and arrows and sinks

down on the seat of his chariot, with his mind overwhelmed with grief.

ॐ तत्सदिति श्रीमद्भगवद्गीतासूपनिषत्सु ब्रह्मविद्यायां योगशास्त्रे श्रीकृष्णार्जुनसंवादेऽर्जुनविषाद-योगो नाम प्रथमोऽध्यायः ॥ १ ॥

***'Aum' tatsaditi Srīmadbhagawad-geeta supaniṣatsu brahmavidyayam yogasastre Srīkṛṣṇarjunasamvade-Arjuna vishadyogo nama prathamodhyayah***

**'AUM TAT SAT'**—Thus, in the Upanishad of the glorious Bhagawad Geeta, the science of the Brahman (Absolute) the scripture of yoga, the dialogue between Srī Kṛṣṇa and Arjuna—thus, ends the chapter one entitled *"Vishadyoga"*.

इति श्रीमद्भगवद्गीतासु प्रथमोऽध्यायः ॥ १ ॥

# *Chapter Two*

## SĀMKHYAYOGA

## THE YOGA OF TRANSCENDENTAL KNOWLEDGE

संजय उवाच

तं तथा कृपयाविष्टमश्रुपूर्णाकुलेक्षणम्।
विषीदन्तमिदं वाक्यमुवाच मधुसूदनः ॥ १ ॥

*taṁ tathā kṛpayāviṣṭam-*
*aśrupūrṇākulekṣaṇaṁ*
*viṣīdantamidaṁ vākyam-*
*uvāca madhusūdanaḥ*

**Sanjaya said :**

(1) To him, who was thus overwhelmed with pity, whose eyes were filled with tears and was agitated, Madhusudana (Srī Kṛṣṇa) spoke these words.

श्रीभगवानुवाच

कुतस्त्वा कश्मलमिदं विषमे समुपस्थितम्।
अनार्यजुष्टमस्वर्ग्यमकीर्तिकरमर्जुन ॥ २ ॥

*kutastvā kaśmalamidaṁ*
*viṣame samupasthitam*
*anāryajuṣṭamasvargyam-*
*akīrtikaramarjuna*

**The Blessed Lord said :**

(2) From where has come to you this despondency, O'Arjuna in this hour of crisis? It is unfit for a noble man and is indeed very disgraceful. It neither leads to heaven nor to any worldly fame and glory.

क्लैब्यं मा स्म गमः पार्थ नैतत्त्वय्युपपद्यते।
क्षुद्रं हृदयदौर्बल्यं त्यक्त्वोत्तिष्ठ परन्तप॥ ३॥

*klaibyaṁ mā sma gamaḥ pārtha*
*naitattvayyupapadyate*
*kṣudraṁ hṛdayadaurbalyaṁ*
*tyaktvottiṣṭha parantapa*

(3) Yield not to this unmanliness, O'Arjuna. It does not befit you. Shake off this petty faint-heartedness and stand up, O' Scorcher of the enemies.

अर्जुन उवाच

कथं भीष्ममहं सङ्ख्ये द्रोणं च मधुसूदन।
इषुभिः प्रतियोत्स्यामि पूजार्हावरिसूदन॥ ४॥

*katharii bhīṣmamahaṁ saṅkhye*
*droṇaṁ ca madhusūdana*
*iṣubhiḥ pratiyotsyāmi*
*pūjārhāvarisūdana*

**Arjuna said :**

(4) O'Kṛṣṇa, how can I fight in the battle with arrows against Bhishma and Drona? They are worthy of my respect and reverence, O'destroyer of the foes.

गुरूनहत्वा हि महानुभावान्,
श्रेयो भोक्तुं भैक्ष्यमपीह लोके।
हत्वार्थकामांस्तु गुरूनिहैव,
भुञ्जीय भोगान् रुधिरप्रदिग्धान्॥५॥

*gurūnahatvā hi mahānubhāvān*
*śreyo bhoktuṁ bhaikṣyamapīḥ loke*
*hatvārthakāmāṅstu gurūnihaiva*
*bhuṇjīya bhogān rudhirapradigdhān*

(5) It is better to live on alms in this world than to slay these venerable teachers, because even after killing them we will enjoy only bloodstained

wealth, pleasure and worldly enjoyment.

न चैतद्विद्मः कतरन्नो गरीयो
यद्वा जयेम यदि वा नो जयेयुः ।
यानेव हत्वा न जिजीविषाम-
स्तेऽवस्थिताः प्रमुखे धार्तराष्ट्राः ॥ ६ ॥

*na caitadvidmaḥ kataranno garīyo*
*yadvā jayema yadi vā no jayeyuḥ*
*yāneva hatvā na jijīviṣāma-*
*ste'vasthitāḥ pramukhe dhārtarāṣṭrāḥ*

(6) We do not know which is better, whether we should conquer them or they should conquer us. The sons of Dhritarastra, by killing whom, we don't even wish to live, are arrayed against us.

कार्पण्यदोषोपहतस्वभावः
पृच्छामि त्वां धर्मसम्मूढचेताः ।
यच्छ्रेयः स्यान्निश्चितं ब्रूहि तन्मे
शिष्यस्तेऽहं शाधि मां त्वां प्रपन्नम् ॥ ७ ॥

*kārpaṇyadoṣopahatasvabhāvaḥ*
*pṛcchāmi tvāṁ dharmasammūḍhacetāḥ*

*yacchreyaḥ syānniścitaṁ brūhi tanme*

*śiṣyaste'haṁ śādhi māṁ tvāṁ prapannam*

(7) My heart is overpowered by the weakness of pity and my mind is confused about my duty; I request Thee, to tell me for certain, which is decidedly good for me. I am your disciple. Teach me, who has taken refuge in You.

न हि प्रपश्यामि ममापनुद्याद्

यच्छोकमुच्छोषणमिन्द्रियाणाम्।

अवाप्य भूमावसपत्नमृद्धं

राज्यं सुराणामपि चाधिपत्यम्॥८॥

*na hi prapaśyāmi mamāpanudyād*

*yacchokamucchoṣaṇamindriyāṇām.*

*avāpya bhūmāvasapatnamṛddhaṁ*

*rājyaṁ surāṇāmapi cādhipatyam*

(8) I don't see any means, that can dispel this grief which is drying up my senses; even if I attain undisputed sovereignty and an affluent kingdom on this earth or even the Lordship over the gods.

संजय उवाच

**एवमुक्त्वा हृषीकेशं गुडाकेशः परन्तप।**
**न योत्स्य इति गोविन्दमुक्त्वा तूष्णीं बभूव ह॥९॥**

*evamuktvā hṛṣīkeśaṁ*
*guḍākeśaḥ parantapa*
*na yotsya iti govinda-*
*muktvā tūṣṇīṁ babhūva ha*

**Sanjaya said :**

(9) Having thus spoken to Srī Kṛṣṇa, Arjuna the conqueror of sleep and the destroyer of foes said "I will not fight" and became silent.

**तमुवाच हृषीकेशः प्रहसन्निव भारत।**
**सेनयोरुभयोर्मध्ये विषीदन्तमिदं वचः॥१०॥**

*tamuvāca hṛṣīkeśaḥ*
*prahasanniva bhārata*
*senayorubhayormadhye*
*viṣīdantamidaṁ vacaḥ*

(10) Then, O' Dhritarastra, to him who was despondent in the midst of the two armies, Srī Kṛṣṇa spoke the following words with a smile on His face.

श्रीभगवानुवाच

अशोच्यानन्वशोचस्त्वं प्रज्ञावादांश्च भाषसे।
गतासूनगतासूंश्च नानुशोचन्ति पण्डिताः ॥ ११ ॥

*aśocyānanvaśocastvaṁ*
*prajñāvādānśca bhāṣase*
*gatāsūnagatāsūnśca*
*nānuśocanti paṇḍitāḥ*

**The Blessed Lord said :**

(11) O' Arjuna, you grieve for those who should not be grieved for; yet you speak the words of wisdom. The wise men do not grieve for the dead or for the living.

न त्वेवाहं जातु नासं न त्वं नेमे जनाधिपाः।
न चैव न भविष्यामः सर्वे वयमतः परम् ॥ १२ ॥

*na tvevāhaṁ jātu nāsaṁ*
*na tvaṁ neme janādhipāḥ*
*na caiva na bhaviṣyāmaḥ*
*sarve vayamataḥ param*

(12) There was never a time when I or you or these rulers of men did not exist; nor will there be any time in

future when all of us shall cease to be.

देहिनोऽस्मिन्यथा देहे कौमारं यौवनं जरा।
तथा देहान्तरप्राप्तिर्धीरस्तत्र न मुह्यति॥ १३॥

*dehino'sminyathā dehe*
*kaumāraṁ yauvanaṁ jarā*
*tathā dehāntaraprāptir-*
*dhīrastatra na muhyati*

(13) Just as in this body, the embodied-soul, passes through childhood, youth and old age; so too it passes into another body. The man of integral wisdom is not deluded by this.

मात्रास्पर्शास्तु कौन्तेय शीतोष्णसुखदुःखदाः।
आगमापायिनोऽनित्यास्तांस्तितिक्षस्व भारत॥ १४॥

*mātrāsparśāstu kaunteya*
*śītoṣṇasukhaduḥkhadāḥ*
*āgamāpāyino'nityās-*
*tāṅstitikṣasva bhārata*

(14) The contact of the senses with their objects, gives rise to the feeling of cold and heat, pleasure and pain, etc., these are transitory and fleeting. Therefore learn to endure them

patiently, O'Arjuna.

यं हि न व्यथयन्त्येते पुरुषं पुरुषर्षभ।
समदुःखसुखं धीरं सोऽमृतत्वाय कल्पते ॥ १५ ॥

*yaṁ hi na vyathayantyete*
*puruṣaṁ puruṣarṣabha*
*samaduḥkhasukhaṁ dhīraṁ*
*so'mṛtatvāya kalpate*

(15) The man who is not tormented by these, O'Arjuna, to whom the pleasure and pain are alike—that steadfast man becomes eligible for immortality.

नासतो विद्यते भावो नाभावो विद्यते सतः।
उभयोरपि दृष्टोऽन्तस्त्वनयोस्तत्त्वदर्शिभिः ॥ १६ ॥

*nāsato vidyate bhāvo*
*nābhāvo vidyate sataḥ*
*ubhayorapi dṛṣṭo'ntas-*
*tvanayostattvadarśibhiḥ*

(16) The unreal has no existence and the real never ceases to be; the essential truth about both of these, is perceived by the seers of truth.

अविनाशि तु तद्विद्धि येन सर्वमिदं ततम्।
विनाशमव्ययस्यास्य न कश्चित्कर्तुमर्हति॥ १७॥

*avināśi tu tadviddhi*
*yena sarvamidaṁ tatam*
*vināśamavyayasyāsya*
*na kaścitkartumarhati*

(17) Know that to be imperishable by which all this is pervaded. No one can bring about the destruction of the indestructible.

अन्तवन्त इमे देहा नित्यस्योक्ताः शरीरिणः।
अनाशिनोऽप्रमेयस्य तस्माद्युध्यस्व भारत॥ १८॥

*antavanta ime dehā*
*nityasyoktāḥ śarīriṇaḥ*
*anāśino'prameyasya*
*tasmādyudhyasva bhārata*

(18) These bodies of the embodied-self are perishable while the Self is eternal, imperishable and incomprehensible. Therefore O'Arjuna, fight the battle.

य एनं वेत्ति हन्तारं यश्चैनं मन्यते हतम्।
उभौ तौ न विजानीतो नायं हन्ति न हन्यते॥ १९॥

*ya enaṁ vetti hantāraṁ*
*yaścainaṁ manyate hatam*
*ubhau tau na vijānīto*
*nāyaṁ hanti na hanyate*

(19) He who considers the soul to be the slayer and who thinks that this is slain; both of them fail to perceive the truth. The soul neither slays nor is slain.

न जायते म्रियते वा कदाचिन्-
नायं भूत्वा भविता वा न भूयः।
अजो नित्यः शाश्वतोऽयं पुराणो
न हन्यते हन्यमाने शरीरे॥ २०॥

*na jāyate mriyate vā kadācin-*
*nāyaṁ bhūtvā bhavitā vā na bhūyaḥ*
*ajo nityaḥ śāśvato'yaṁ purāṇo*
*na hanyate hanyamāne śarīre*

(20) The soul is neither born nor does it ever die; having come into being once, it never ceases to be. It is

unborn, eternal, permanent and primeval. It is not killed even when the body is killed.

वेदाविनाशिनं नित्यं य एनमजमव्ययम्।
कथं स पुरुषः पार्थ कं घातयति हन्ति कम्॥ २१ ॥

*vedāvināśinaṁ nityaṁ*
*ya enamajamavyayam*
*kathaṁ sa puruṣaḥ pārtha*
*kaṁ ghātayati hanti kam*

(21) He who knows the soul to be indestructible, unborn, unchanging and immutable; how can such a person slay anyone, O'Arjuna or cause any one to slay?

वासांसि जीर्णानि यथा विहाय
नवानि गृह्णाति नरोऽपराणि।
तथा शरीराणि विहाय जीर्णा-
न्यन्यानि संयाति नवानि देही॥ २२ ॥

*vāsāṅsi jīrṇāni yathā vihāya*
*navāni gṛhṇāti naro'parāṇi*
*tathā śarīrāṇi vihāya jīrṇā-*
*nyanyāni saṁyāti navāni dehī*

(22) As a person casts off the worn-out garments and puts on the new ones; likewise the embodied-soul discards the worn out bodies and enters into the new ones.

नैनं छिन्दन्ति शस्त्राणि नैनं दहति पावकः।

न चैनं क्लेदयन्त्यापो न शोषयति मारुतः॥ २३॥

*nainaṁ chindanti śastrāṇi*

*nainaṁ dahati pāvakaḥ*

*na cainaṁ kledayantyāpo*

*na śoṣayati mārutaḥ*

(23) Weapons cannot cut the soul, nor can fire burn it. Water can not wet it nor wind can make it dry.

अच्छेद्योऽयमदाह्योऽयमक्लेद्योऽशोष्य एव च।

नित्यः सर्वगतः स्थाणुरचलोऽयं सनातनः॥ २४॥

*acchedyo'yamadāhyo'yam-*

*akledyo'śoṣya eva ca*

*nityaḥ sarvagataḥ sthāṇu-*

*racalo'yaṁ sanātanaḥ*

(24) The soul is uncleavable and incombustible. It can be neither wetted nor dried. It is eternal, all-pervading,

unchanging, immovable and primordial.

अव्यक्तोऽयमचिन्त्योऽयमविकार्योऽयमुच्यते।
तस्मादेवं विदित्वैनं नानुशोचितुमर्हसि॥ २५॥

*avyakto'yamacintyo'yam-*
*avikāryo'yamucyate*
*tasmādevaṁ viditvai'naṁ*
*nānuśocitumarhasi*

(25) This (soul) is said to be unmanifest, unthinkable and unchanging. Therefore, knowing it as such, you should not grieve.

अथ चैनं नित्यजातं नित्यं वा मन्यसे मृतम्।
तथापि त्वं महाबाहो नैवं शोचितुमर्हसि॥ २६॥

*atha cainaṁ nityajātaṁ*
*nityaṁ vā manyase mṛtam*
*tathāpi tvaṁ mahābāho*
*naivaṁ śocitumarhasi*

(26) Even if you regard the soul as being continually taking birth and continually dying; even then, O'Arjuna, you should not grieve.

जातस्य हि ध्रुवो मृत्युर्ध्रुवं जन्म मृतस्य च।
तस्मादपरिहार्येऽर्थे न त्वं शोचितुमर्हसि॥ २७॥

*jātasya hi dhruvo mṛtyur-*
*dhruvaṁ janma mṛtasya ca*
*tasmādaparihārye'rthe*
*na tvaṁ śocitumarhasi*

(27) For, death is certain of the one who is born, and also the rebirth is certain of the one who is dead; therefore you should not grieve over the inevitable.

अव्यक्तादीनि भूतानि व्यक्तमध्यानि भारत।
अव्यक्तनिधनान्येव तत्र का परिदेवना॥ २८॥

*avyaktādīni bhūtāni*
*vyaktamadhyāni bhārata*
*avyaktanidhnānyeva*
*tatra kā paridevanā*

(28) O'Arjuna, all the beings are unmanifest in their beginnings, they become manifested in the middle state and unmanifested again in the end. What is there in this, for lamentation?

आश्चर्यवत्पश्यति कश्चिदेन-
माश्चर्यवद्वदति तथैव चान्यः।
आश्चर्यवच्चैनमन्यः शृणोति
श्रुत्वाप्येनं वेद न चैव कश्चित्॥ २९॥

*āścaryavatpaśyati kaścidena*
*māścaryavadvadati tathaiva cānyaḥ*
*āścaryavacainamanyaḥ śṛṇoti*
*śrutvāpyenaṁ veda na caiva kaścit*

(29) One perceives the soul in great wonder, likewise another speaks of it in wonder; still another hears of it in great wonder; and even after hearing of it, hardly any one understands it.

देही नित्यमवध्योऽयं देहे सर्वस्य भारत।
तस्मात्सर्वाणि भूतानि न त्वं शोचितुमर्हसि॥ ३०॥

*dehī nityamavadhyo'yaṁ*
*dehe sarvasya bhārata*
*tasmātsarvāṇi bhūtāni*
*na tvaṁ śocitumarhasi*

(30) O'Arjuna, the soul dwelling in the body of every one is eternal and indestructible. Therefore, you should

not grieve for any creature.

स्वधर्ममपि चावेक्ष्य न विकम्पितुमर्हसि।
धर्म्याद्धि युद्धाच्छ्रेयोऽन्यत्क्षत्रियस्य न विद्यते ॥ ३१ ॥

*svadharmamapi cāvekṣya*
*na vikampitumarhasi*
*dharmyāddhi yuddhācchreyo'nyat*
*kṣatriyasya na vidyate*

(31) Besides, in consideration of your own duty as well, it does not befit you to waver. For, to a kshatriya, there is nothing else better than a righteous war.

यदृच्छया चोपपन्नं स्वर्गद्वारमपावृतम्।
सुखिनः क्षत्रियाः पार्थ लभन्ते युद्धमीदृशम् ॥ ३२ ॥

*yadṛcchayā copapannaṁ*
*svargadvāramapāvṛtam*
*sukhinaḥ kṣatriyāḥ pārtha*
*labhante yuddhamīdṛśam*

(32) Happy (fortunate) are the kshatriyas, O'Arjuna, those who are called upon to fight in a battle like this, that comes of itself as an open door to the heaven.

अथ चेत्त्वमिमं धर्म्यं सङ्ग्रामं न करिष्यसि।
ततः स्वधर्मं कीर्तिं च हित्वा पापमवाप्स्यसि॥ ३३॥

*atha cettvamimaṁ dharmyaṁ*
*saṅgrāmaṁ na kariṣyasi*
*tataḥ svadharmaṁ kīrtiṁ ca*
*hitvā pāpamavāpsyasi*

(33) But, if you do not fight this righteous war, you will be turning away from your assigned duty and respectable position. You will definitely incur sin.

अकीर्तिं चापि भूतानि कथयिष्यन्ति तेऽव्ययाम्।
सम्भावितस्य चाकीर्तिर्मरणादतिरिच्यते॥ ३४॥

*akīrtiṁ cāpi bhūtāni*
*kathayiṣyanti te'vyayām*
*sambhāvitasya cākīrtir*
*maraṇādatiricyate*

(34) Besides, people will speak derogatory words about you; and for the one who has been always honoured—dishonour is worse than death.

भयाद्रणादुपरतं मंस्यन्ते त्वां महारथाः।
येषां च त्वं बहुमतो भूत्वा यास्यसि लाघवम्॥ ३५ ॥

*bhayādraṇāduparataṁ*
*maṁsyante tvāṁ mahārathāḥ*
*yeṣāṁ ca tvaṁ bahumato*
*bhūtvā yāsyasi lāghavam*

(35) The great chariot-warriors will think, that you have withdrawn from the battle in fear. Those men, who always held you in high esteem, will also show their disrespect.

अवाच्यवादांश्च बहून्वदिष्यन्ति तवाहिताः।
निन्दन्तस्तव सामर्थ्यं ततो दुःखतरं नु किम्॥ ३६ ॥

*avācyavādāṅśca bahūn-*
*vadiṣyanti tavāhitāḥ*
*nindantastava sāmarthyaṁ*
*tato duḥkhataraṁ nu kim*

(36) Your enemies, slandering your prowess, will speak many disgraceful words. What can be more distressing than that?

हतो वा प्राप्स्यसि स्वर्गं
जित्वा वा भोक्ष्यसे महीम्।

तस्मादुत्तिष्ठ कौन्तेय
युद्धाय कृतनिश्चयः ॥ ३७ ॥

*hato vā prāpsyasi svargaṁ*
*jitvā vā bhokṣyase mahīm*
*tasmāduttiṣṭha kaunteya*
*yuddhāya kṛtaniścayaḥ*

(37) If killed in the battle, you will attain heaven; or, if victorious you will enjoy sovereignty of the earth. Therefore, stand up O'Arjuna, resolved to fight.

सुखदुःखे समे कृत्वा
लाभालाभौ जयाजयौ ।
ततो युद्धाय युज्यस्व
नैवं पापमवाप्स्यसि ॥ ३८ ॥

*sukhaduḥkhe same kṛtvā*
*lābhālābhau jayājayau*
*tato yuddhāya yujyasva*
*naivaṁ pāpamavāpsyasi*

(38) Regarding alike the pleasure and pain, gain and loss, victory and defeat; get ready for the battle. Thus,

you will not incur sin.

एषा तेऽभिहिता साङ्ख्ये
बुद्धिर्योगे त्विमां शृणु।
बुद्ध्या युक्तो यया पार्थ
कर्मबन्धं प्रहास्यसि॥ ३९॥

*eṣā te'bhihitā sāṅkhye*
*buddhiryoge tvimāṁ śṛṇu*
*buddhyā yukto yayā pārtha*
*karmabandhaṁ prahāsyasi*

(39) This which has been declared to you so far is the wisdom of the Samkhya; now listen to the wisdom, in regard to yoga (karmayoga). Endowed with this knowledge, O'Arjuna, you will get freedom from the bondage of karma.

नेहाभिक्रमनाशोऽस्ति प्रत्यवायो न विद्यते।
स्वल्पमप्यस्य धर्मस्य त्रायते महतो भयात्॥ ४०॥

*nehābhikramanāśo'sti*
*pratyavāyo na vidyate*
*svalpamapyasya dharmasya*
*trāyate mahato bhayāt*

(40) In this, there is no loss of effort, nor is there any fear of contrary result. Even a little practice of this discipline (Dharma) protects the individual from great fear.

**व्यवसायात्मिका बुद्धिरेकेह कुरुनन्दन।**
**बहुशाखा ह्यनन्ताश्च बुद्धयोऽव्यवसायिनाम्॥४१॥**

*vyavasāyātmikā buddhir-*
*ekeha kurunandana*
*bahuśākhā hyanantāśca*
*buddhayo'vyavasāyinām*

(41) O'Arjuna, in this path, the resolute intellect is one pointed; whereas the intellect of the irresolute is scattered in many directions and is endlessly diverse.

**यामिमां पुष्पितां वाचं प्रवदन्त्यविपश्चितः।**
**वेदवादरताः पार्थ नान्यदस्तीति वादिनः॥४२॥**

*yāmimāṁ puṣpitāṁ vācaṁ*
*pravadantyavipaścitaḥ*
*vedavādaratāḥ pārtha*
*nānyadastīti vādinaḥ*

(42) Flowery speech is uttered by

the unwise, those who take delight in the eulogizing hymns of Vedas, O' Arjuna, saying, "there is nothing other than this".

कामात्मानः स्वर्गपरा जन्मकर्मफलप्रदाम्।
क्रियाविशेषबहुलां भोगैश्वर्यगतिं प्रति॥ ४३॥

*kāmātmānaḥ svargaparā*
*janmakarmaphalapradām*
*kriyāviśeṣabahulāṁ*
*bhogaiśvaryagatiṁ prati*

(43) Those who are obsessed by desires, who consider heaven as their Supreme goal, they are led to new births as the result of their actions. They perform various rituals for the sake of pleasure and power.

भोगैश्वर्यप्रसक्तानां तयापहृतचेतसाम्।
व्यवसायात्मिका बुद्धिः समाधौ न विधीयते॥ ४४॥

*bhogaiśvaryaprasaktānāṁ*
*tayāpahṛtacetsām*
*vyavasāyātmikā buddhiḥ*
*samādhau na vidhīyate*

(44) Those who are deeply

attached to pleasure and power, whose minds are carried away by such flowery speech; they are unable to develop the resolute will of a concentrated mind in meditation.

त्रैगुण्यविषया वेदा निस्त्रैगुण्यो भवार्जुन।
निर्द्वन्द्वो नित्यसत्त्वस्थो निर्योगक्षेम आत्मवान्॥ ४५॥

*traiguṇyaviṣayā vedā*
*nistraiguṇyo bhavārjuna*
*nirdvandvo nityasattvastho*
*niryogakṣema ātmavān*

(45) The subject matter that deals with the triple attributes of nature in the *Vedas*, be Thou above those three attributes, O' Arjuna. Liberate yourself from the pairs of opposites and ever abide in the Sattva. Being free from the feeling of acquisition and preservation, stay established in the Supreme-self.

यावानर्थ उदपाने सर्वतः सम्प्लुतोदके।
तावान्सर्वेषु वेदेषु ब्राह्मणस्य विजानतः॥ ४६॥

*yāvānartha udapāne*
*sarvataḥ saṁplutodake*

*tāvānsarveṣu vedeṣu*

*brāhmaṇasya vijānataḥ*

(46) To a knower of Brahmana, the *Vedas* are of as much use, as is a small reservoir of water in a place which is flooded with water on all sides.

कर्मण्येवाधिकारस्ते मा फलेषु कदाचन।
मा कर्मफलहेतुर्भूर्मा ते सङ्गोऽस्त्वकर्मणि ॥ ४७ ॥

*karmaṇyevādhikāraste*

*mā phaleṣu kadācana*

*mā karmaphalaheturbhūr-*

*mā te saṅgo'stvakarmaṇi*

(47) Your right is to perform your work only and not at all to its fruit; let not the fruit of action be your motive, nor let your attachment be to inaction.

योगस्थः कुरु कर्माणि

सङ्गं त्यक्त्वा धनञ्जय।

सिद्ध्यसिद्ध्योः समो भूत्वा

समत्वं योग उच्यते ॥ ४८ ॥

*yogasthaḥ kuru karmāṇi*
*saṅgaṁ tyaktvā dhanañjaya*
*siddhyasiddhyoḥ samo bhūtvā*
*samatvaṁ yoga ucyate*

(48) O' Arjuna, perform your actions, being steadfast in Yoga. Renounce all attachments and be balanced in success and failure. Evenness (equanimity) of mind is said to be Yoga.

दूरेण ह्यवरं कर्म बुद्धियोगाद्धनञ्जय।
बुद्धौ शरणमन्विच्छ कृपणाः फलहेतवः ॥४९॥

*dūreṇa hyavaraṁ karma*
*buddhiyogāddhanañjaya*
*buddhau śaraṇamanviccha*
*kṛpaṇāḥ phalahetavaḥ*

(49) Action with attachment is far inferior, O' Arjuna, to that action which is performed with the Yoga of wisdom. Seek refuge in integral wisdom; for pitiful are those who crave for the fruits of their actions.

बुद्धियुक्तो जहातीह उभे सुकृतदुष्कृते।
तस्माद्योगाय युज्यस्व योगः कर्मसु कौशलम् ॥५०॥

*buddhiyukto jahātīha*

*ubhe sukṛtaduṣkṛte*

*tasmādyogāya yujyasva*

*yogaḥ karmasu kauśalam*

(50) Endowed with wisdom, one liberates oneself in this life, from virtues and vices. Therefore devote yourself to yoga. Yoga is skill in action.

कर्मजं बुद्धियुक्ता हि

फलं त्यक्त्वा मनीषिणः।

जन्मबन्धविनिर्मुक्ताः

पदं गच्छन्त्यनामयम् ॥ ५१ ॥

*karmajaṁ buddhiyuktā hi*

*phalaṁ tyaktvā manīṣiṇaḥ*

*janmabandhavinirmuktāḥ*

*padaṁ gacchantyanāmayam*

(51) The wise sages, who are endowed with integral wisdom, having relinquished the fruits of their actions, become liberated from the bondage of rebirth. They attain the blissful Supreme state.

यदा ते मोहकलिलं बुद्धिर्व्यतितरिष्यति।
तदा गन्तासि निर्वेदं श्रोतव्यस्य श्रुतस्य च॥५२॥

*yadā te mohakalilaṁ*
*buddhirvyatitariṣyati*
*tadā gantāsi nirvedaṁ*
*śrotavyasya śrutasya ca*

(52) When your intellect will cross the mire of delusion, then you will gain the indifference to what has been heard and what is yet to be heard.

श्रुतिविप्रतिपन्ना ते यदा स्थास्यति निश्चला।
समाधावचला बुद्धिस्तदा योगमवाप्स्यसि॥५३॥

*śrutivipratipannā te*
*yadā sthāsyati niścalā*
*samādhāvacalā buddhis-*
*tadā yogamavāpsyasi*

(53) When your intellect, which is confused by hearing the conflicting doctrines, will become firm and steadfast in meditation; then you will attain the vision of the Supreme-Self in yoga.

अर्जुन उवाच

स्थितप्रज्ञस्य का भाषा
समाधिस्थस्य केशव।
स्थितधीः किं प्रभाषेत
किमासीत व्रजेत किम्॥५४॥

*sthitaprajñasya kā bhāṣā*
*samādhisthasya keśava*
*sthitadhīḥ kiṁ prabhāṣeta*
*kimāsīta vrajeta kim*

**Arjuna Said :**

(54) O' Kṛṣṇa—what are the marks of the man of steadfast wisdom, who is established in transcendental meditation? How does a man of integral wisdom speak, how does he sit and how does he walk?

श्रीभगवानुवाच

प्रजहाति यदा कामान्सर्वान्पार्थ मनोगतान्।
आत्मन्येवात्मना तुष्टः स्थितप्रज्ञस्तदोच्यते॥५५॥

*prajahāti yadā kāmān-*
*sarvānpārtha manogatān*
*ātmanyevātmanā tuṣṭaḥ*
*sthitaprajñastadocyate*

**The Blessed Lord said :**

(55) When a man abandons all the desires of his mind, O'Arjuna; when he feels satisfied in the Self, by the self, then he is said to be established in transcendental wisdom.

दुःखेष्वनुद्विग्नमनाः सुखेषु विगतस्पृहः।
वीतरागभयक्रोधः स्थितधीर्मुनिरुच्यते॥ ५६॥

*duḥkheṣvanudvignamanāḥ*
*sukheṣu vigataspṛhaḥ*
*vītarāgabhayakrodhaḥ*
*sthitdhīrmunirucyate*

(56) He whose mind remains unperturbed in the midst of sorrows, who has no longing for pleasures, who is free from passion, fear and anger, he is called a sage of steadfast wisdom.

यः सर्वत्रानभिस्नेहस्तत्तत्प्राप्य शुभाशुभम्।
नाभिनन्दति न द्वेष्टि तस्य प्रज्ञा प्रतिष्ठिता॥ ५७॥

*yaḥ sarvatrānabhisnehas-*
*tattatprāpya śubhāśubham*
*nābhinandati na dveṣṭi*
*tasya prajñā pratiṣṭhitā*

(57) He, who is unattached in all

respects, at receiving good or evil, who neither rejoices nor hates, he is surely settled in transcendental wisdom.

**यदा संहरते चायं कूर्मोऽङ्गानीव सर्वशः।**
**इन्द्रियाणीन्द्रियार्थेभ्यस्तस्य प्रज्ञा प्रतिष्ठिता ॥ ५८ ॥**

*yadā saṁharate cāyaṁ*
*kūrmo'ṅgānīva sarvaśaḥ*
*indriyāṇīndriyārthebhyas-*
*tasya prajñā pratiṣṭhitā*

(58) When like a tortoise, which withdraws its limbs from all sides (into the shell), he withdraws his senses from the objects of the senses, then his wisdom becomes firmly set.

**विषया विनिवर्तन्ते निराहारस्य देहिनः।**
**रसवर्जं रसोऽप्यस्य परं दृष्ट्वा निवर्तते ॥ ५९ ॥**

*viṣayā vinivartante*
*nirāhārasya dehinaḥ*
*rasvarjaṁ raso'pyasya*
*paraṁ dṛṣṭvā nivartate*

(59) The objects of the senses, cease to exist for the man who does not enjoy them but the taste for them

persists. This lingering taste also disappears for the man of steadfast mind, on seeing the Supreme.

**यततो ह्यपि कौन्तेय पुरुषस्य विपश्चितः ।**

**इन्द्रियाणि प्रमाथीनि हरन्ति प्रसभं मनः ॥ ६० ॥**

*yatato hyapi kaunteya*
*puruṣasya vipaścitaḥ*
*indriyāṇi pramāthīni*
*haranti prasbhaṁ manaḥ*

(60) O' Arjuna, the turbulent senses, do forcibly carry away the mind of even a wise man, who is practising self-control.

**तानि सर्वाणि संयम्य युक्त आसीत मत्परः ।**

**वशे हि यस्येन्द्रियाणि तस्य प्रज्ञा प्रतिष्ठिता ॥ ६१ ॥**

*tāni sarvāṇi saṁyamya*
*yukta āsīta matparaḥ*
*vaśe hi yasyendriyāṇi*
*tasya prajñā pratiṣṭhitā*

(61) Therefore, having controlled them all, one should remain firm in Yoga, regarding Me as the Supreme;

for he, whose senses are under control, he is surely settled in transcendental wisdom.

ध्यायतो विषयान्पुंसः सङ्गस्तेषूपजायते ।
संगात्सञ्जायते कामः कामात्क्रोधोऽभिजायते ॥ ६२ ॥

*dhyāyato viṣayānpuṁsaḥ*
*saṅgasteṣūpajāyate*
*saṅgātsañjāyate kāmaḥ*
*kāmātkrodho'bhijāyate*

क्रोधाद्भवति सम्मोहः सम्मोहात्स्मृतिविभ्रमः ।
स्मृतिभ्रंशाद् बुद्धिनाशो बुद्धिनाशात्प्रणश्यति ॥ ६३ ॥

*krodhādbhavati sammohaḥ*
*sammohātsmṛtivibhramaḥ*
*smṛtibhraṁśād buddhināśo*
*buddhināśātpraṇaśyati*

(62, 63) The man who broods over the objects of the senses, he develops attachment for them; from attachment springs up desire, the desire (unfulfilled) ensues anger. From anger arises delusion, from delusion the confusion of memory; from the confusion of memory the loss of reason and from the loss of reason, he goes to complete ruin.

रागद्वेषवियुक्तैस्तु विषयानिन्द्रियैश्चरन्।
आत्मवश्यैर्विधेयात्मा प्रसादमधिगच्छति ॥ ६४ ॥

*rāgdveṣaviyuktaistu*
*viṣayānindriyaiścaran*
*ātmavaśyairvidheyātmā*
*prasādamadhigacchati*

(64) But a self-controlled man who moves among the objects of the senses with his senses under control and free from attraction and repulsion; he attains serenity of mind.

प्रसादे सर्वदुःखानां हानिरस्योपजायते।
प्रसन्नचेतसो ह्याशु बुद्धिः पर्यवतिष्ठते ॥ ६५ ॥

*prasāde sarvaduḥkhānāṁ*
*hānirasyopajāyate*
*prasannacetaso hyāśu*
*buddhiḥ paryavatiṣṭhate*

(65) With the attainment of this inner serenity, all his sufferings come to an end; and soon the intellect of such

a person of tranquil mind becomes firmly established in the Bliss of the deepest awareness.

नास्ति बुद्धिरयुक्तस्य न चायुक्तस्य भावना।
न चाभावयतः शान्तिरशान्तस्य कुतः सुखम्॥ ६६॥

*nāsti buddhirayuktasya*
*na cāyuktasya bhāvanā*
*na cābhāvayataḥ śāntir-*
*aśāntasya kutaḥ sukham*

(66) There is no knowledge of the Self for the one who is not united within. The transcendental meditation is not possible for the unsteady, and to the unmeditative there can be no peace. To the man who has no inner peace, how can there be happiness?

इन्द्रियाणां हि चरतां यन्मनोऽनु विधीयते।
तदस्य हरति प्रज्ञां वायुर्नावमिवाम्भसि॥ ६७॥

*indriyāṇāṁ hi caratāṁ*
*yanmano'nu vidhīyate*
*tadasya harati prajñāṁ*
*vāyurnāvamivāmbhasi*

(67) For, when the mind yields to the wandering senses, it carries away the discrimination of the man, just as the wind carries away the ship on the water.

तस्माद्यस्य महाबाहो निगृहीतानि सर्वशः।
इन्द्रियाणीन्द्रियार्थेभ्यस्तस्य प्रज्ञा प्रतिष्ठिता ॥ ६८ ॥

*tasmādyasya mahābāho*
*nigṛhītāni sarvaśaḥ*
*indriyāṇīndriyārthebhyas-*
*tasya prajñā pratiṣṭhitā*

(68) Therefore, O' Arjuna, he, whose senses are withdrawn from their objects, he becomes firmly established in the transcendental wisdom.

या निशा सर्वभूतानां तस्यां जागर्ति संयमी।
यस्यां जाग्रति भूतानि सा निशा पश्यतो मुनेः ॥ ६९ ॥

*yā niśā sarvabhūtānāṁ*
*tasyāṁ jāgarti saṁyamī*
*yasyāṁ jāgrati bhūtāni*
*sā niśā paśyato muneḥ*

(69) That which is night to all

beings, in that state the self-controlled man remains awake. When all beings are awake, that is the night for the muni, who sees.

आपूर्यमाणमचलप्रतिष्ठं
समुद्रमापः प्रविशन्ति यद्वत्।
तद्वत्कामा यं प्रविशन्ति सर्वे
स शान्तिमाप्नोति न कामकामी ॥ ७० ॥

*āpūryamāṇamacalapratiṣṭhaṁ*
*samudramāpaḥ praviśanti yadvat*
*tadvatkāmā yaṁ praviśanti sarve*
*sa śāntimāpnoti na kāmakāmī*

(70) As the water of the rivers enter the ocean which though full, remains undisturbed; likewise the man in whom all desires merge themselves, he attains peace, and not the one who longs after the objects of desire.

विहाय कामान्यः सर्वान्पुमांश्चरति निःस्पृहः।
निर्ममो निरहङ्कारः स शान्तिमधिगच्छति ॥ ७१ ॥

*vihāya kāmānyaḥ sarvān-*
*pumāṁścarati niḥspṛhaḥ*

*nirmamo nirahaṅkāraḥ*
*sa śāntimadhigacchati*

(71) He who has abandoned all his desires, and moves free from attachment and without the feeling of I and Mine, he attains the Supreme peace.

एषा ब्राह्मी स्थितिः पार्थ नैनां प्राप्य विमुह्यति।
स्थित्वास्यामन्तकालेऽपि ब्रह्मनिर्वाणमृच्छति ॥ ७२ ॥

*eṣā brāhmī sthitiḥ pārtha*
*naināṁ prāpya vimuhyati*
*sthitvāsyāmantakāle'pi*
*brahmanirvāṇamṛcchati*

(72) This is the state of transcendental unity *(brahmisthiti)* O'Arjuna. Having attained this, he overcomes the delusion. Being established in this state, even at the time of death, he attains the Supreme Blissful state (Brahma-Nirvana).

ॐ तत्सदिति श्रीमद्भगवद्गीतासूपनिषत्सु ब्रह्मविद्यायां
योगशास्त्रे श्रीकृष्णार्जुनसंवादे सांख्ययोगो
नाम द्वितीयोऽध्यायः ॥ २ ॥

***'Aum' tatsaditi***
***Srīmadbhagawadgeeta supaniṣatsu***
***brahmavidyayam yogaśastre***
***Srīkṛṣṇarjunasamvade***
***samkhyayogo nama dvitiyodhyayah***

**'AUM TAT SAT'**—Thus, in the Upanishad of the glorious Bhagawad Geeta, the science of the Brahman (Absolute) the scripture of yoga, the dialogue between *Srī Kṛṣṇa* and Arjuna thus, ends the chapter two entitled *"Samkhyayoga"*.

इति श्रीमद्भगवद्गीतासु द्वितीयोऽध्यायः ॥ २ ॥

## *Chapter Three*

# THE KARMAYOGA

## THE YOGA OF ACTION

अर्जुन उवाच

ज्यायसी चेत्कर्मणस्ते मता बुद्धिर्जनार्दन।
तत्किं कर्मणि घोरे मां नियोजयसि केशव ॥ १ ॥

*jyāyasī cetkarmaṇaste*
*matā buddhirjanārdana*
*tatkiṁ karmaṇi ghore māṁ*
*niyojayasi keśava*

**Arjuna said :**

(1) If you consider that knowledge is superior to action, O'Kṛṣṇa, then why do you ask me to engage in this terrible action?

व्यामिश्रेणेव वाक्येन बुद्धिं मोहयसीव मे।
तदेकं वद निश्चित्य येन श्रेयोऽहमाप्नुयाम् ॥ २ ॥

*vyāmiśreṇeva vākyena*
*buddhiṁ mohayasīva me*

*tadekaṁ vada niścitya*

*yena śreyo'hamāpnuyām*

(2) With an apparently conflicting statement, you seem to confuse my mind. Therefore, please tell me decisively that 'One', by which I may attain the highest good.

श्रीभगवानुवाच

लोकेऽस्मिन्द्विविधा निष्ठा पुरा प्रोक्ता मयानघ।

ज्ञानयोगेन सांख्यानां कर्मयोगेन योगिनाम्॥ ३॥

*loke'smindvividhā niṣṭhā*

*purā proktā mayānagha*

*jñānayogena sāṅkhyānāṁ*

*karmayogena yoginām*

**The Blessed Lord said :**

(3) O'Arjuna, in this world a twofold path has been declared by Me earlier; the path of knowledge of the Samkhyas and the path of 'Karma-yoga' of the yogins.

न कर्मणामनारम्भान्नैष्कर्म्यं पुरुषोऽश्नुते।

न च सन्न्यसनादेव सिद्धिं समधिगच्छति॥ ४॥

*na karmaṇāmanārambhān-*
*naiṣkarmyaṁ puruṣo'śnute*
*na ca sannyasanādeva*
*siddhiṁ samadhigacchati*

(4) Not by abstention from work, does a man attain liberation from action; nor by mere renunciation does he attain perfection.

न हि कश्चित्क्षणमपि जातु तिष्ठत्यकर्मकृत्।
कार्यते ह्यवशः कर्म सर्वः प्रकृतिजैर्गुणैः ॥ ५ ॥

*na hi kaścitkṣaṇamapi*
*jātu tiṣṭhatyakarmakṛt*
*kāryate hyavaśaḥ karma*
*sarvaḥ prakṛtijairguṇaiḥ*

(5) For no one can remain even for a moment without performing action; everyone is made to act helplessly indeed, forced by the impulses born of nature.

कर्मेन्द्रियाणि संयम्य य आस्ते मनसा स्मरन्।
इन्द्रियार्थान्विमूढात्मा मिथ्याचारः स उच्यते ॥ ६ ॥

*karmendriyāṇi saṁyamya*
*ya āste mansā smaran*

*indriyārthānvimūḍhātmā*

*mithyācāraḥ sa ucyate*

(6) He who controls his organs of actions and sits brooding over the objects of senses, he is said to be a self-deluded hypocrite.

**यस्त्विन्द्रियाणि मनसा नियम्यारभतेऽर्जुन।**

**कर्मेन्द्रियैः कर्मयोगमसक्तः स विशिष्यते॥७॥**

*yastvindriyāṇi manasā*

*niyamyārabhate'rjuna*

*karmendriyaiḥ karmayogam-*

*asktaḥ sa viśiṣyate*

(7) But, he who controls his senses by the mind, O'Arjuna, and engages himself in the Karmayoga; with the organs of action, without any attachment—he definitely excels.

**नियतं कुरु कर्म त्वं कर्म ज्यायो ह्यकर्मणः।**

**शरीरयात्रापि च ते न प्रसिद्ध्येदकर्मणः॥८॥**

*niyataṁ kuru karma tvaṁ*

*karma jyāyo hyakarmaṇaḥ*

*śarīrayātrāpi ca te*

*na prasiddhyedkarmaṇaḥ*

(8) Therefore, you must perform your assigned work, for action is superior to inaction; and even the maintenance of your physical body cannot be possible for you, without action.

यज्ञार्थात्कर्मणोऽन्यत्र लोकोऽयं कर्मबन्धनः।
तदर्थं कर्म कौन्तेय मुक्तसङ्गः समाचर॥ ९॥

*yajñārthātkarmaṇo'nyatra*
*loko'yaṁ karmabandhanaḥ*
*tadarthaṁ karma kaunteya*
*muktasaṅgaḥ samācara*

(9) The world is bound by actions, other than those performed for the sake of sacrifice (selflessly). Therefore, O' Arjuna, perform your work for that sake alone, being free from attachment.

सहयज्ञाः प्रजाः सृष्ट्वा पुरोवाच प्रजापतिः।
अनेन प्रसविष्यध्वमेष वोऽस्त्विष्टकामधुक्॥ १०॥

*sahayajñāḥ prajāḥ sṛṣṭvā*
*puro'vāca prajāpatiḥ*
*anena prasaviṣyadhvam-*
*eṣa vo'stivaṣṭakāmadhuk*

(10) At the beginning of creation the Lord of all beings created mankind along with the sacrifice and said "by this you may prosper"; let this be the milch-cow of your desires.

देवान्भावयतानेन ते देवा भावयन्तु वः ।
परस्परं भावयन्तः श्रेयः परमवाप्स्यथ ॥ ११ ॥

*devānbhāvayatānena*
*te devā bhāvayantu vaḥ*
*parasparaṁ bhāvayantaḥ*
*śreyaḥ paramavāpsyatha*

(11) With this, you foster the gods and may those gods foster you; thus fostering each other, you will attain to the highest good.

इष्टान्भोगान्हि वो देवा दास्यन्ते यज्ञभाविताः ।
तैर्दत्तानप्रदायैभ्यो यो भुङ्क्ते स्तेन एव सः ॥ १२ ॥

*iṣṭānbhogānhi vo devā*
*dāsyante yajñabhāvitāḥ*
*tairdattānapradāyai'bhyo*
*yo bhuṅkte stena eva saḥ*

(12) The gods pleased (nourished) by the sacrifice will surely bestow

upon you the desired enjoyments. He, who enjoys the bounties of the gods without offering them anything in return, is verily a thief.

यज्ञशिष्टाशिनः सन्तो मुच्यन्ते सर्वकिल्बिषैः ।
भुञ्जते ते त्वघं पापा ये पचन्त्यात्मकारणात् ॥ १३ ॥

*yajñaśiṣṭāśinaḥ santo*
*mucyante sarvakilbiṣaiḥ*
*bhuñjate te tvaghaṁ pāpā*
*ye pacantyātmakāraṇāt*

(13) The virtuous, who eat the remnants of the sacrifice (yajña) are released from all sins; but the wicked, who cook food only for their own sake verily eat sin.

अन्नाद्भवन्ति भूतानि पर्जन्यादन्नसम्भवः ।
यज्ञाद्भवति पर्जन्यो यज्ञः कर्मसमुद्भवः ॥ १४ ॥

*annādbhavanti bhūtāni*
*parjanyādannasambhavaḥ*
*yajñādbhavati parjanyo*
*yajñaḥ karmasamudbhavaḥ*

(14) All beings have evolved from food. The food is produced from rain,

the rain ensues from sacrifice, and sacrifice is rooted in action.

कर्म ब्रह्मोद्भवं विद्धि ब्रह्माक्षरसमुद्भवम्।
तस्मात्सर्वगतं ब्रह्म नित्यं यज्ञे प्रतिष्ठितम्॥ १५ ॥

*karma brahmodbhavaṁ viddhi*
*brahmākṣarasamudbhavam*
*tasmātsarvagataṁ brahma*
*nityaṁ yajñe pratiṣṭhitam*

(15) Know that action has its origin in Brahma and Brahma proceeds from the imperishable. Therefore, the all-pervading infinite (God) is always present in the sacrifice (yajña).

एवं प्रवर्तितं चक्रं नानुवर्तयतीह यः।
अघायुरिन्द्रियारामो मोघं पार्थ स जीवति॥ १६ ॥

*evaṁ pravartitaṁ cakraṁ*
*nānuvartayatīha yaḥ*
*aghāyurindriyārāmo*
*moghaṁ pārtha sa jīvati*

(16) He who does not follow the wheel of creation thus set in motion here; leads a sinful life; rejoicing in

the senses. He surely lives in vain, O'Arjuna.

यस्त्वात्मरतिरेव स्यादात्मतृप्तश्च मानवः ।
आत्मन्येव च सन्तुष्टस्तस्य कार्यं न विद्यते ॥ १७ ॥

*yastvātmaratireva syād-*
*ātmatṛptaśca mānavaḥ*
*ātmanyeva ca santuṣṭas*
*tasya kāryaṁ na vidyate*

(17) But the person, who delights only in the Self, who remains satisfied in the consciousness of the Self and is contented in the Self alone; for him there is nothing to be done.

नैव तस्य कृतेनार्थो नाकृतेनेह कश्चन ।
न चास्य सर्वभूतेषु कश्चिदर्थव्यपाश्रयः ॥ १८ ॥

*naiva tasya kṛtenārtho*
*nākṛteneha kaścana*
*na cāsya sarvabhūteṣu*
*kaścidarthavyapāśrayaḥ*

(18) For him there is no interest whatsoever in the performance of an action or its non-performance; nor

does he depend on any creature for any object.

तस्मादसक्तः सततं कार्यं कर्म समाचर।
असक्तो ह्याचरन्कर्म परमाप्नोति पूरुषः ॥ १९ ॥

*tasmādasaktaḥ satataṁ*
*kāryaṁ karma samācara*
*asakto hyācarankarma*
*paramāpnoti pūruṣaḥ*

(19) Therefore, always perform your work, without attachment, which has to be done; for a man who works without attachment he attains the Supreme.

कर्मणैव हि संसिद्धिमास्थिता जनकादयः।
लोकसङ्ग्रहमेवापि सम्पश्यन्कर्तुमर्हसि ॥ २० ॥

*karmaṇaiva hi saṅsiddhim-*
*āsthitā janakādayaḥ*
*lokasaṁgrahamevāpi*
*sampaśyankartumarhasi*

(20) It is through action, that King Janaka and others attained perfection. Even with a view to the maintenance

of the world-order, you must perform action.

यद्यदाचरति श्रेष्ठस्तत्तदेवेतरो जनः।
स यत्प्रमाणं कुरुते लोकस्तदनुवर्तते॥ २१॥

*yadyadācarati śresthas-*
*tattadevetaro janaḥ*
*sa yatpramāṇaṁ kurute*
*lokastadanuvartate*

(21) Whatever a great man does, the others also do the same; whatever standard he sets, the people follow.

न मे पार्थास्ति कर्तव्यं त्रिषु लोकेषु किञ्चन।
नानवाप्तमवाप्तव्यं वर्त एव च कर्मणि॥ २२॥

*na me pārthāsti kartavyaṁ*
*triṣu lokeṣu kiñcana*
*nānavāptamavāptavyaṁ*
*varta eva ca karmaṇi*

(22) There is nothing in all the three worlds, O' Arjuna, that has to be done by Me, nor is there anything unattained that ought to be attained; yet, I engage Myself in action.

यदि ह्यहं न वर्तेयं जातु कर्मण्यतन्द्रितः।
मम वर्त्मानुवर्तन्ते मनुष्याः पार्थ सर्वशः॥ २३॥

*yadi hyahaṁ na varteyaṁ*
*jātu karmaṇyatandritaḥ*
*mama vartmānuvartante*
*manuṣyāḥ pārtha sarvaśaḥ*

उत्सीदेयुरिमे लोका न कुर्यां कर्म चेदहम्।
सङ्करस्य च कर्ता स्यामुपहन्यामिमाः प्रजाः॥ २४॥

*utsīdeyurime lokā*
*na kuryāṁ karma cedaham*
*saṅkarasya ca kartā syām-*
*upahanyāmimāḥ prajāḥ*

(23, 24) For, should I not engage Myself in action unwearied, men would follow My path in all respects, O' Arjuna. These worlds would perish, if I did not perform action; and I would be the cause of confusion, disorder and the destruction of the people.

सक्ताः कर्मण्यविद्वांसो यथा कुर्वन्ति भारत।
कुर्याद्विद्वांस्तथासक्तश्चिकीर्षुर्लोकसङ्ग्रहम्॥ २५॥

*saktāḥ karmaṇyavidvānso*
*yathā kurvanti bhārata*
*kuryādvidvāṅstathāsaktaś-*
*cikīrṣurlokasaṅgraham*

(25) As the ignorant man acts with attachment to action O'Arjuna, so should the wise man act without attachment, desiring the welfare of the world.

न बुद्धिभेदं जनयेदज्ञानां कर्मसङ्गिनाम्।
जोषयेत्सर्वकर्माणि विद्वान्युक्तः समाचरन्॥ २६॥

*na buddhibhedaṁ janayed-*
*ajñānāṁ karmasaṅginām*
*joṣayetsarvakarmāṇi*
*vidvānyuktaḥ samācaran*

(26) The wise man who is established in the Self should not unsettle the mind of the ignorant people who are attached to action; he should get them to perform all their duties, by performing action himself with devotion.

प्रकृतेः क्रियमाणानि गुणैः कर्माणि सर्वशः।
अहङ्कारविमूढात्मा कर्ताहमिति मन्यते॥ २७॥

*prakṛteḥ kriyamāṇāni*
*guṇaiḥ karmāṇi sarvaśaḥ*
*ahaṅkāravimūḍhātmā*
*kartāhamiti manyate*

(27) All actions are performed— in all respects, by the modes of nature. The one whose mind is deluded by egoism, he thinks 'I am the doer'

तत्त्ववित्तु महाबाहो गुणकर्मविभागयोः ।
गुणा गुणेषु वर्तन्त इति मत्वा न सज्जते ॥ २८ ॥

*tattvavittu mahābāho*
*guṇakarmavibhāgayoḥ*
*guṇā guṇeṣu vartanta*
*iti matvā na sajjate*

(28) But he, who knows the truth, about the respective spheres of modes (Gunas) and their functions O' Arjuna, he clearly understands that the Gunas-as-senses move among the Gunas-as-objects; and he does not become attached.

प्रकृतेर्गुणसम्मूढाः सज्जन्ते गुणकर्मसु ।
तानकृत्स्नविदो मन्दान्कृत्स्नविन्न विचालयेत् ॥ २९ ॥

*prakṛterguṇasammūḍhāḥ*
*sajjante guṇakarmasu*
*tānakṛtsnavido mandān-*
*kṛtsnavinna vicālayet*

(29) Those who are deluded by the qualities (gunas) of nature they remain attached to the functions of the gunas. The man of wisdom should not unsettle the minds of the ignorant, who do not know the whole truth.

मयि सर्वाणि कर्माणि सन्न्यस्याध्यात्मचेतसा।
निराशीर्निर्ममो भूत्वा युध्यस्व विगतज्वरः॥ ३०॥

*mayi sarvāṇi karmāṇi*
*sannyasyādhyātmacetsā*
*nirāśīrnirmamo bhūtvā*
*yudhyasva vigatajvaraḥ*

(30) Therefore, dedicating all actions to Me, with your mind focused on the Self, being free from desire, egoism and mental stress, fight the battle.

ये मे मतमिदं नित्यमनुतिष्ठन्ति मानवाः।
श्रद्धावन्तोऽनसूयन्तो मुच्यन्ते तेऽपि कर्मभिः॥ ३१॥

*ye me matamidaṁ nityam-*
*anutiṣṭhanti mānavāḥ*
*śraddhāvanto'nasūyanto*
*mucyante te'pi karmabhiḥ*

(31) Those men who constantly follow this teaching of Mine with faith and without cavilling, they are also liberated from the bondage of actions.

ये त्वेतदभ्यसूयन्तो नानुतिष्ठन्ति मे मतम्।
सर्वज्ञानविमूढांस्तान्विद्धि नष्टानचेतसः ॥ ३२ ॥

*ye tvetadabhyasūyanto*
*nānutiṣṭhanti me matam*
*sarvajñānavimūḍhāṅstān-*
*viddhi naṣṭānacetsaḥ*

(32) But those who cavil at My teaching and do not follow it, know them to be absolutely ignorant, devoid of all knowledge and lost.

सदृशं चेष्टते स्वस्याः प्रकृतेर्ज्ञानवानपि।
प्रकृतिं यान्ति भूतानि निग्रहः किं करिष्यति ॥ ३३ ॥

*sadṛśaṁ ceṣṭate svasyāḥ*
*prakṛterjñānavānapi*

*prakṛtiṁ yānti bhūtāni*
*nigrahaḥ kiṁ kariṣyati*

(33) Even the man of wisdom acts in accordance with his own nature; all beings follow their nature, what can restrain accomplish?

इन्द्रियस्येन्द्रियस्यार्थे रागद्वेषौ व्यवस्थितौ।
तयोर्न वशमागच्छेत्तौ ह्यस्य परिपन्थिनौ ॥ ३४॥

*indriyasyendriyasyārthe*
*rāgadveṣau vyavasthitau*
*tayorna vaśamāgacchettau*
*hyasya paripanthinau*

(34) Attachment and aversion for the objects of senses abide in the senses; one should not come under their sway, because they are his enemies.

श्रेयान्स्वधर्मो विगुणः परधर्मात्स्वनुष्ठितात्।
स्वधर्मे निधनं श्रेयः परधर्मो भयावहः ॥ ३५॥

*śreyānsvadharmo viguṇaḥ*
*paradharmātsvanuṣṭhitāt*
*svadharme nidhanaṁ śreyaḥ*
*paradharmo bhayāvahaḥ*

(35) Better is one's own duty, though devoid of merit, than the duty of another well performed. Even the death becomes blessed (gracious), in the performance of one's own duty; the duty of another is fraught with fear.

अर्जुन उवाच

अथ केन प्रयुक्तोऽयं पापं चरति पूरुषः।
अनिच्छन्नपि वार्ष्णेय बलादिव नियोजितः ॥ ३६ ॥

*atha kena prayukto'yaṁ*
*pāpaṁ carati pūruṣaḥ*
*anicchannapi vārṣṇeya*
*balādiva niyojitaḥ*

**Arjuna said :**

(36) But impelled by what, O'Kṛṣṇa, does a man commit sin, even against his will, as though driven by force?

श्रीभगवानुवाच

काम एष क्रोध एष रजोगुणसमुद्भवः।
महाशनो महापाप्मा विद्ध्येनमिह वैरिणम्॥ ३७ ॥

*kāma eṣa krodha eṣa*
*rajoguṇasamudbhavaḥ*

*mahāśano mahāpāpmā*
*vidhyenamiha vairiṇam*

**The Blessed Lord said :**

(37) It is desire, it is anger born of the mode of passion; which is insatiable and most sinful. Know this to be the enemy in this respect.

**धूमेनाव्रियते वह्निर्यथादर्शो मलेन च।**
**यथोल्बेनावृतो गर्भस्तथा तेनेदमावृतम्॥ ३८॥**

*dhūmenāvriyate vahnir-*
*yathādarśo malena ca*
*yatholbenāvṛto garbhas-*
*tathā tenedaṃāvṛtam*

(38) As the flame is enveloped by the smoke, as a mirror by the dust and as an embryo by the amnion, so is this (knowledge) covered by that (desire).

**आवृतं ज्ञानमेतेन ज्ञानिनो नित्यवैरिणा।**
**कामरूपेण कौन्तेय दुष्पूरेणानलेन च॥ ३९॥**

*āvṛtaṁ jñānametena*
*jñānino nityavairiṇā*
*kāmarūpeṇa kaunteya*
*duṣpūreṇānalena ca*

(39) O' Arjuna, the wisdom stands enveloped by this constant enemy of the wise in the form of desire, which is insatiable like fire.

**इन्द्रियाणि मनो बुद्धिरस्याधिष्ठानमुच्यते।**
**एतैर्विमोहयत्येष ज्ञानमावृत्य देहिनम्॥ ४० ॥**

*indriyāṇi mano buddhir-*
*aśyādhiṣṭhānamucyate*
*etairvimohayatyeṣa*
*jñānamāvṛtya dehinam*

(40) The senses, the mind and the intellect are said to be its seat; through these it deludes the embodied-self—by enveloping his wisdom.

**तस्मात्त्वमिन्द्रियाण्यादौ नियम्य भरतर्षभ।**
**पाप्मानं प्रजहि ह्येनं ज्ञानविज्ञाननाशनम्॥ ४१ ॥**

*tasmāttvamindriyāṇyādau*
*niyamya bharatarṣabha*
*pāpmānaṁ prajahi hyenaṁ*
*jñānavijñānanāśanam*

(41) Therefore, O' Arjuna, control thy senses from the very beginning and kill this sinful destroyer of knowledge

and experiential wisdom.

इन्द्रियाणि पराण्याहुरिन्द्रियेभ्यः परं मनः।
मनसस्तु परा बुद्धिर्यो बुद्धेः परतस्तु सः॥४२॥

*indriyāṇi parāṇyāhur-*
*indriyebhyaḥ paraṁ manaḥ*
*manasastu parā buddhiryo*
*buddheḥ paratastu saḥ*

(42) Senses are said to be superior (to the body), superior to senses is the mind; but higher than mind is the intellect and higher than the intellect is indeed the indwelling-Self.

एवं बुद्धेः परं बुद्ध्वा संस्तभ्यात्मानमात्मना।
जहि शत्रुं महाबाहो कामरूपं दुरासदम्॥४३॥

*evaṁ buddheḥ paraṁ buddhvā*
*saṅstabhyātmānamātmanā*
*jahi śatruṁ mahābāho*
*kāmarūpaṁ durāsadam*

(43) Thus, knowing the indwelling-Self to be higher than the intellect and controlling the mind by the Self, O'Arjuna kill this enemy in

the form of desire, which is very difficult to conquer.

ॐ तत्सदिति श्रीमद्भगवद्गीतासूपनिषत्सु ब्रह्मविद्यायां
योगशास्त्रे श्रीकृष्णार्जुनसंवादे कर्मयोगो
नाम तृतीयोऽध्यायः ॥ ३ ॥

***'Aum' tatsaditi Srīmadbhāgawadgītā supaniṣatsu brahmavidyāyām yogaśāstre Srīkṛṣṇārjunasamvāde karmayogo nāma tṛtityodhyayaḥ***

**'AUM TAT SAT'**—Thus, in the Upanishad of the glorious Bhagawad Geeta, the science of the Brahman (Absolute) the scripture of yoga, the dialogue between Srī Kṛṣṇa and Arjuna—thus, ends the chapter three entitled *"Karmayoga"*

इति श्रीमद्भगवद्गीतासु तृतीयोऽध्यायः ॥ ३ ॥

# *Chapter Four*

# JÑĀNA-KARMAYOGA

## THE YOGA OF ACTION AND KNOWLEDGE

श्रीभगवानुवाच

इमं विवस्वते योगं प्रोक्तवानहमव्ययम्।
विवस्वान्मनवे प्राह मनुरिक्ष्वाकवेऽब्रवीत्॥ १ ॥

*imaṁ vivasvate yogaṁ*
*proktavānahamavyayam*
*vivasvānmanave prāha*
*manurikṣvākave'bravīt*

**The Blessed Lord said :**

(1) I taught this imperishable Yoga to Vivasvan (sun-god). Vivasvan taught it to Manu; and Manu taught to Ikshvaku.

एवं परम्पराप्राप्तमिमं राजर्षयो विदुः।
स कालेनेह महता योगो नष्टः परन्तप॥ २ ॥

*evaṁ paramparāprāpta-*
*mimaṁ rājarṣayo viduḥ*

*sa kāleneha mahatā*

*yogo naṣṭaḥ parantapa*

(2) Thus, handed down in regular succession, the royal sages knew this. But, through the long lapse of time, this yoga became lost to the world, O'Arjuna.

स एवायं मया तेऽद्य योगः प्रोक्तः पुरातनः ।

भक्तोऽसि मे सखा चेति रहस्यं ह्येतदुत्तमम् ॥ ३ ॥

*sa evāyaṁ mayā te'dya*

*yogaḥ proktaḥ purātanaḥ*

*bhakto'si me sakhā ceti*

*rahasyaṁ hyetaduttamam*

(3) This same ancient Yoga has been declared to you by Me today; for you are My devotee and My friend. This is the Supreme secret.

अर्जुन उवाच

अपरं भवतो जन्म परं जन्म विवस्वतः ।

कथमेतद्विजानीयां त्वमादौ प्रोक्तवानिति ॥ ४ ॥

*aparaṁ bhavato janma*

*paraṁ janma vivasvataḥ*

*kathametad vijānīyāṁ*

*tvamādau proktavāniti*

**Arjuna said :**

(4) Later on, was Thy birth and earlier to it was the birth of Vivasvan (sun-god). How can I understand this; that You ever taught this yoga in the beginning?

श्रीभगवानुवाच

बहूनि मे व्यतीतानि जन्मानि तव चार्जुन।

तान्यहं वेद सर्वाणि न त्वं वेत्थ परन्तप॥५॥

*bahūni me vyatītāni*

*janmāni tava cā'rjuna*

*tānyahaṁ veda sarvāṇi*

*na tvaṁ vettha parantapa*

**The Blessed Lord said :**

(5) Many births of Mine have passed as well as of yours, O'Arjuna. I know them all, but you do not know them. O'scorcher of the foes.

अजोऽपि सन्नव्ययात्मा भूतानामीश्वरोऽपि सन्।

प्रकृतिं स्वामधिष्ठाय सम्भवाम्यात्ममायया॥६॥

*ajo'pi sannavyayātmā*
*bhūtānāmīśvaro'pi san*
*prakṛtiṁ svāmadhiṣṭhāya*
*saṁbhavāmyātmamāyayā*

(6) Though I am unborn, of imperishable nature and the Lord of all beings, yet, governing My own Nature, I come into being through My power. (Yoga Maya).

यदा यदा हि धर्मस्य ग्लानिर्भवति भारत।
अभ्युत्थानमधर्मस्य तदात्मानं सृजाम्यहम्॥ ७॥

*yadā yadā hi dharmasya*
*glānirbhavati bhārata*
*abhyutthānamadharmasya*
*tadātmānaṁ sṛjāmyaham*

(7) Whenever there is decline of righteousness, (Dharma) and rise of unrighteousness, O'Arjuna, then I manifest Myself.

परित्राणाय साधूनां विनाशाय च दुष्कृताम्।
धर्मसंस्थापनार्थाय सम्भवामि युगे युगे॥ ८॥

*paritrāṇāya sādhūnāṁ*
*vināśāya ca duṣkṛtām*

*dharmasaṅsthāpanārthāya*
*saṁbhavāmi yuge yuge*

(8) For the protection of the virtuous, for the destruction of the wicked, and for the establishment of righteousness (Dharma) I come into being from age to age.

जन्म कर्म च मे दिव्यमेवं यो वेत्ति तत्त्वतः ।
त्यक्त्वा देहं पुनर्जन्म नैति मामेति सोऽर्जुन ॥ ९ ॥

*janma karma ca me divya-*
*mevaṁ yo vetti tattvataḥ*
*tyaktvā dehaṁ punarjanma*
*naiti māmeti so'rjuna*

(9) He who, thus understands My divine birth and actions in essence; having abandoned the body, he is not born again. He comes to Me, O'Arjuna.

वीतरागभयक्रोधा मन्मया मामुपाश्रिताः ।
बहवो ज्ञानतपसा पूता मद्भावमागताः ॥ १० ॥

*vītarāgabhayakrodhā*
*manmayā māmupāśritāḥ*
*bahavo jñānatapasā*
*pūtā madbhāvamāgatāḥ*

(10) Liberated from desire, fear and anger with the mind absorbed in Me, taking refuge in Me, purified by the austerity of wisdom, many have attained to My state of being.

ये यथा मां प्रपद्यन्ते तांस्तथैव भजाम्यहम्।
मम वर्त्मानुवर्तन्ते मनुष्याः पार्थ सर्वशः ॥ ११ ॥

*ye yathā māṁ prapadyante*
*tāṅstathaiva bhajāmyaham*
*mama vartmānuvartante*
*manuṣyāḥ pārtha sarvaśaḥ*

(11) In whatever way, men approach Me, so do I accept them; for all men follow My path in every way, O'Arjuna.

काङ्क्षन्तः कर्मणां सिद्धिं यजन्त इह देवताः।
क्षिप्रं हि मानुषे लोके सिद्धिर्भवति कर्मजा ॥ १२ ॥

*kāṅkṣantaḥ karmaṇāṁ siddhiṁ*
*yajanta iha devatāḥ*
*kṣipraṁ hi mānuṣe loke*
*siddhirbhavati karmajā*

(12) Those who desire the fruits of their actions, worship the gods in

this world, because the success is quickly attained by men, through action.

चातुर्वर्ण्यं मया सृष्टं गुणकर्मविभागशः।
तस्य कर्तारमपि मां विद्ध्यकर्तारमव्ययम्॥ १३॥

*cāturvarṇyaṁ mayā sṛṣṭaṁ*
*guṇakarmavibhāgaśaḥ*
*tasya kartāramapi māṁ*
*viddhyakartāramavyayam*

(13) The fourfold work order has been created by Me according to the differentiation of Guna and Karma. Though I am the creator, know Me as non-doer and immutable.

न मां कर्माणि लिम्पन्ति न मे कर्मफले स्पृहा।
इति मां योऽभिजानाति कर्मभिर्न स बध्यते॥ १४॥

*na māṁ karmāṇi limpanti*
*na me karmaphale spṛhā*
*iti māṁ yo'bhijānāti*
*karmabhirna sa badhyate*

(14) Actions do not contaminate Me, because I have no desire for the

fruit of actions. He who understands Me thus (in essence) is not bound by actions.

एवं ज्ञात्वा कृतं कर्म पूर्वैरपि मुमुक्षुभिः ।
कुरु कर्मैव तस्मात्त्वं पूर्वैः पूर्वतरं कृतम् ॥ १५ ॥

*evaṁ jñātvā kṛtaṁ karma*
*pūrvairapi mumukṣubhiḥ*
*kuru karmaiva tasmāttvaṁ*
*pūrvaiḥ pūrvataraṁ kṛtam*

(15) Having known this, the seekers of liberation from ancient times have also performed their actions. Therefore, do thou also perform action as the ancients did in their times.

किं कर्म किमकर्मेति कवयोऽप्यत्र मोहिताः ।
तत्ते कर्म प्रवक्ष्यामि यज्ज्ञात्वा मोक्ष्यसेऽशुभात् ॥ १६ ॥

*kiṁ karma kimakarmeti*
*kavayo'pyatra mohitāḥ*
*tatte karma pravakṣyāmi*
*yajjñātvā mokṣyase'śubhāt*

(16) What is action? What is

inaction?—Even men of wisdom are confused about it. Therefore, I must explain to you about action; by knowing which, you will be liberated from its evil effect.

कर्मणो ह्यपि बोद्धव्यं बोद्धव्यं च विकर्मणः ।
अकर्मणश्च बोद्धव्यं गहना कर्मणो गतिः ॥ १७ ॥

*karmaṇo hyapi boddhavyaṁ*
*boddhavyaṁ ca vikarmaṇaḥ*
*akarmaṇaśca boddhavyaṁ*
*gahanā karmaṇo gatiḥ*

(17) One must understand the truth about action, and the truth about the prohibited action. Likewise, the truth about inaction should also be known; for, mysterious is the nature of action.

कर्मण्यकर्म यः पश्येदकर्मणि च कर्म यः ।
स बुद्धिमान्मनुष्येषु स युक्तः कृत्स्नकर्मकृत् ॥ १८ ॥

*karmaṇyakarma yaḥ paśyed-*
*akarmaṇi ca karma yaḥ*
*sa buddhimānmanuṣyeṣu*
*sa yuktaḥ kṛtsnakarmakṛt*

(18) He, who sees inaction in action, and also action in inaction, he is wise among men. He is a yogi, and a true performer of all actions.

**यस्य सर्वे समारम्भाः कामसङ्कल्पवर्जिताः।**

**ज्ञानाग्निदग्धकर्माणं तमाहुः पण्डितं बुधाः॥१९॥**

*yasya sarve samārambhāḥ*
*kāmasaṅkalpavarjitāḥ*
*jñānāgnidagdhakarmāṇaṁ*
*tamāhuḥ paṇḍitaṁ budhāḥ*

(19) He whose undertakings are all free from self-centred personal desires, whose actions have been purified in the fire of wisdom—him, the wise call a sage.

**त्यक्त्वा कर्मफलासङ्गं नित्यतृप्तो निराश्रयः।**

**कर्मण्यभिप्रवृत्तोऽपि नैव किञ्चित्करोति सः॥२०॥**

*tyaktvā karmaphalāsaṅgaṁ*
*nityatṛpto nirāśrayaḥ*
*karmaṇyabhipravṛtto'pi*
*naiva kiñcitkaroti saḥ*

(20) Renouncing attachment to the

fruits of action, ever contented and free from all kinds of dependence, he does not do anything, though fully engaged in action.

निराशीर्यतचित्तात्मा त्यक्तसर्वपरिग्रहः।
शारीरं केवलं कर्म कुर्वन्नाप्नोति किल्बिषम्॥ २१॥

*nirāśīryatacittātmā*
*tyaktasarvaparigrahaḥ*
*śārīraṁ kevalaṁ karma*
*kurvannāpnoti kilbiṣam*

(21) Having no desires, with his mind and body fully controlled, who has given up the desire for all sorts of possessions and performs only the necessary actions for the body; he is not tainted by sin (he is not subject to evil).

यदृच्छालाभसन्तुष्टो द्वन्द्वातीतो विमत्सरः।
समः सिद्धावसिद्धौ च कृत्वापि न निबध्यते॥ २२॥

*yadṛcchālābhasantuṣṭo*
*dvandvātīto vimatsaraḥ*
*samaḥ siddhāvasiddhau ca*
*kṛtvāpi na nibadhyate*

(22) Fully contented with whatever comes along, who is free from the pairs of opposites and envy, balanced in success and failure, even though he acts, he is not bound.

**गतसङ्गस्य मुक्तस्य ज्ञानावस्थितचेतसः ।**
**यज्ञायाचरतः कर्म समग्रं प्रविलीयते ॥ २३ ॥**

*gatasaṅgasya muktasya*
*jñānāvasthitacetasaḥ*
*yajñāyācarataḥ karma*
*samagraṁ pravilīyate*

(23) He, who is totally unattached and liberated, whose mind is established in transcendental knowledge, who performs all his work in the spirit of yajña (selflessly)—his actions are entirely dissolved.

**ब्रह्मार्पणं ब्रह्म हविर्ब्रह्माग्नौ ब्रह्मणा हुतम् ।**
**ब्रह्मैव तेन गन्तव्यं ब्रह्मकर्मसमाधिना ॥ २४ ॥**

*brahmārpaṇaṁ brahma havir-*
*brahmāgnau brahmaṇā hutam*
*brahmaiva tena gantavyaṁ*
*brahmakarmasamādhinā*

(24) For him, the act of offering is Brahman (God), the melted butter and oblation is Brahman. The oblation is offered by Brahman into the fire, which is Brahman. Thus, Brahman alone is to be reached by him, who meditates on Brahman in his work.

दैवमेवापरे यज्ञं योगिनः पर्युपासते।

ब्रह्माग्नावपरे यज्ञं यज्ञेनैवोपजुह्वति॥ २५॥

*daivamevāpare yajñaṁ*

*yoginaḥ paryupāsate*

*brahmāgnāvapare yajñaṁ*

*yajñenaivopajuhvati*

(25) Some yogis perform sacrifice (yajña) to the gods alone; while others offer sacrifice (selfless action) by the sacrifice itself, into the fire of Brahman.

श्रोत्रादीनीन्द्रियाण्यन्ये संयमाग्निषु जुह्वति।

शब्दादीन्विषयानन्य इन्द्रियाग्निषु जुह्वति॥ २६॥

*śrotrādīnīndriyāṇyanye*

*saṁyamāgniṣu juhvati*

*śabdādīnviṣayānanya*
*indriyāgniṣu juhvati*

(26) Some offer hearing and other senses as sacrifice into the fire of self-restraint; Others offer sound and the object of senses as sacrifice into the fire of the senses.

सर्वाणीन्द्रियकर्माणि प्राणकर्माणि चापरे।
आत्मसंयमयोगाग्नौ जुह्वति ज्ञानदीपिते ॥ २७ ॥

*sarvāṇīndriyakarmāṇi*
*prāṇakarmāṇi cāpare*
*ātmasaṁyamayogāgnau*
*juhvati jñānadīpite*

(27) Some others offer the functions of the senses and the activity of the vital force (prana) into the fire of the yoga of self-control, lighted by the flame of knowledge.

द्रव्ययज्ञास्तपोयज्ञा योगयज्ञास्तथापरे।
स्वाध्यायज्ञानयज्ञाश्च यतयः संशितव्रताः ॥ २८ ॥

*dravyayajñāstapoyajñā*
*yogayajñāstathāpare*
*svādhyāyajñānayajñāśca*
*yatayaḥ saṅśitavratāḥ*

(28) Some others offer their material possessions (wealth), austerity and yoga as sacrifice; while others of self-restraint and rigid vows offer the scriptural studies and knowledge as sacrifice.

अपाने जुह्वति प्राणं प्राणेऽपानं तथापरे।
प्राणापानगती रुद्ध्वा प्राणायामपरायणाः ॥ २९ ॥

*apāne juhvati prāṇaṁ*
*prāṇe'pānaṁ tathāpare*
*prāṇāpānagatī ruddhvā*
*prāṇāyāmaparāyaṇāḥ*

(29) Yet others, who are devoted to the breath control, sacrifice the outgoing breath into incoming and the incoming into outgoing, by restraining the movement of both.

अपरे नियताहाराः प्राणान्प्राणेषु जुह्वति।
सर्वेऽप्येते यज्ञविदो यज्ञक्षपितकल्मषाः ॥ ३० ॥

*apare niyatāhārāḥ*
*prāṇānprāṇeṣu juhvati*
*sarve'pyete yajñavido*
*yajñakṣapitakalmaṣāḥ*

(30) Others, who regulate their diet, they pour as sacrifice their life-breath into the life-breath. All these are the knowers of sacrifice, whose sins have been destroyed by sacrifice.

यज्ञशिष्टामृतभुजो यान्ति ब्रह्म सनातनम्।
नायं लोकोऽस्त्ययज्ञस्य कुतोऽन्यः कुरुसत्तम ॥ ३१ ॥

*yajñaśiṣṭāmṛtabhujo*
*yānti brahma sanātanam*
*nā'yaṁ loko'styayajñasya*
*kuto'nyaḥ kurusattama*

(31) Those who eat the sacred remnants of the sacrifice, which is like nectar, they attain to the eternal Absolute. Even this world is not for him, who does not perform sacrifice (selfless action)—how then the other, O'Arjuna?

एवं बहुविधा यज्ञा वितता ब्रह्मणो मुखे।
कर्मजान्विद्धि तान्सर्वानेवं ज्ञात्वा विमोक्ष्यसे ॥ ३२ ॥

*evaṁ bahuvidhā yajñā*
*vitatā brahmaṇo mukhe*
*karmajānviddhi tānsarvān-*
*evaṁ jñātvā vimokṣyase*

(32) Many forms of sacrifices are spread out before the Brahman (set forth as means of attaining Brahman in Vedas). Know them all as born of action; knowing thus, you will be liberated.

श्रेयान्द्रव्यमयाद्यज्ञाज्ज्ञानयज्ञः परन्तप।
सर्वं कर्माखिलं पार्थ ज्ञाने परिसमाप्यते॥ ३३॥

*śreyāndravyamayādyajñāj-*
*jñānayajñaḥ parantapa*
*sarvaṁ karmākhilaṁ pārtha*
*jñāne parisamāpyate*

(33) Superior is sacrifice of wisdom to the sacrifice of material objects, O'Arjuna. All actions in their entirety culminate in wisdom.

तद्विद्धि प्रणिपातेन परिप्रश्नेन सेवया।
उपदेक्ष्यन्ति ते ज्ञानं ज्ञानिनस्तत्त्वदर्शिनः॥ ३४॥

*tadviddhi praṇipātena*
*paripraśnena sevayā*
*upadekṣyanti te jñānaṁ*
*jñāninastattvadarśinaḥ*

(34) Attain this knowledge by

prostration (humble reverence) by asking questions and by service. The men of wisdom, who have realized the truth will instruct you in knowledge.

यज्ज्ञात्वा न पुनर्मोहमेवं यास्यसि पाण्डव।
येन भूतान्यशेषेण द्रक्ष्यस्यात्मन्यथो मयि ॥ ३५ ॥

*yajjñātvā na punarmoham-*
*evaṁ yāsyasi pāṇḍava*
*yena bhūtānyaśeṣeṇa*
*drakṣyasyātmanyatho mayi*

(35) Knowing that, O' Arjuna, you will not again get deluded like this—by that knowledge you will see all beings without exception within yourself and then in Me.

अपि चेदसि पापेभ्यः सर्वेभ्यः पापकृत्तमः।
सर्वं ज्ञानप्लवेनैव वृजिनं सन्तरिष्यसि ॥ ३६ ॥

*api cedasi pāpebhyaḥ*
*sarvebhyaḥ pāpakṛttamaḥ*
*sarvaṁ jñānaplavenaiva*
*vṛjinaṁ santariṣyasi*

(36) Even if you are the most sinful of all sinners, you will surely

cross all the sins by the boat of knowledge alone.

यथैधांसि समिद्धोऽग्निर्भस्मसात्कुरुतेऽर्जुन।
ज्ञानाग्निः सर्वकर्माणि भस्मसात्कुरुते तथा॥ ३७॥

*yathaidhāṁsi samiddho'gnir-*
*bhasmasātkurute'rjuna*
*jñānāgniḥ sarvakarmāṇi*
*bhasmasātkurute tathā*

(37) Just as the blazing fire reduces the fuel to ashes, O'Arjuna, similarly the fire of knowledge reduces all actions to ashes.

न हि ज्ञानेन सदृशं पवित्रमिह विद्यते।
तत्स्वयं योगसंसिद्धः कालेनात्मनि विन्दति॥ ३८॥

*na hi jñānena sadṛśaṁ*
*pavitramiha vidyate*
*tatsvayaṁ yogasaṅsiddhaḥ*
*kālenātmani vindati*

(38) Certainly, there is no purifier in this world like the 'transcendental knowledge'. He who becomes perfected in yoga, he experiences this, in his own-self, in due course of time.

श्रद्धावाँल्लभते ज्ञानं तत्परः संयतेन्द्रियः।
ज्ञानं लब्ध्वा परां शान्तिमचिरेणाधिगच्छति ॥ ३९ ॥

*śraddhāvānllabhate jñānaṁ*
*tatparaḥ saṅyatendriyaḥ*
*jñānaṁ labdhvā parāṁ śāntim-*
*acireṇādhigacchati*

(39) He, who is endowed with faith and who is devoted to it, who has disciplined his senses, he obtains knowledge. Having attained knowledge, he immediately attains Supreme-peace.

अज्ञश्चाश्रद्दधानश्च संशयात्मा विनश्यति।
नायं लोकोऽस्ति न परो न सुखं संशयात्मनः ॥ ४० ॥

*ajñaścāśraddadhānaśca*
*saṅśayātmā vinaśyati*
*nāyaṁ loko'sti na paro*
*na sukhaṁ saṁśayātmanaḥ*

(40) The man who is ignorant, who has no faith, who is sceptical, he goes to destruction. For the suspicious man there is neither this world, nor the world beyond, nor any happiness.

योगसन्न्यस्तकर्माणं ज्ञानसञ्छिन्नसंशयम्।
आत्मवन्तं न कर्माणि निबध्नन्ति धनञ्जय॥ ४१॥

*yogasannyastakarmāṇaṁ*
*jñānasañchinnasaṅśayam*
*ātmavantaṁ na karmāṇi*
*nibadhnanti dhanañjaya*

(41) He who has renounced actions by unity in yoga, whose doubts have been destroyed by knowledge, and who is settled in the Self—actions do not bind him, O' Arjuna.

तस्मादज्ञानसम्भूतं हृत्स्थं ज्ञानासिनात्मनः।
छित्त्वैनं संशयं योगमातिष्ठोत्तिष्ठ भारत॥ ४२॥

*tasmādajñānasambhūtaṁ*
*hṛtsthaṁ jñānāsinātmanaḥ*
*chittvainaṁ saṅśayaṁ yogam-*
*ātiṣṭhottiṣṭha bhārata*

(42) Therefore, with the sword of knowledge, cut asunder the doubt in your heart, which is born of ignorance. Take refuge in Yoga and stand up, O' Arjuna.

ॐ तत्सदिति श्रीमद्भगवद्गीतासूपनिषत्सु ब्रह्मविद्यायां योगशास्त्रे श्रीकृष्णार्जुनसंवादे ज्ञानकर्मसंन्यास-
योगो नाम चतुर्थोऽध्यायः ॥ ४ ॥

***'Aum' tatsaditi Srīmadbhagawadgeeta supaniṣatsu brahmavidyayam yogaśāstre Srīkṛṣṇarjunasamvade jñana-karmayogo nama caturthodhyayah***

**'AUM TAT SAT'**—Thus, in the Upanishad of the glorious Bhagawad Geeta, the science of the Brahman (Absolute) the scripture of yoga, the dialogue between Srī Kṛṣṇa and Arjuna—thus, ends the chapter four entitled *"Jñanakarmayoga"*.

इति श्रीमद्भगवद्गीतासु चतुर्थोऽध्यायः ॥ ४ ॥

## *Chapter Five*

# KARMA-SANNYĀSAYOGA

## THE YOGA OF ACTION AND RENUNCIATION

अर्जुन उवाच

संन्यासं कर्मणां कृष्ण पुनर्योगं च शंससि ।
यच्छ्रेय एतयोरेकं तन्मे ब्रूहि सुनिश्चितम् ॥ १ ॥

*sannyāsaṁ karmaṇāṁ kṛṣṇa*
*punaryogaṁ ca śaṁsasi*
*yacchreya etayorekaṁ*
*tanme brūhi suniścitam*

**Arjuna said :**

(1) O' Kṛṣṇa, you praise the renunciation of actions and then again the practice of Yoga; (the performance of selfless action)—tell me for certain, which one of these two is decidedly better.

श्रीभगवानुवाच

संन्यासः कर्मयोगश्च निःश्रेयसकरावुभौ।
तयोस्तु कर्मसंन्यासात्कर्मयोगो विशिष्यते॥ २॥

*sannyāsaḥ karmayogaśca*
*niḥśreyasakarāvubhau*
*tayos tu karmasannyāsāt*
*karmayogo viśiṣyate*

**The Blessed Lord said :**

(2) Renunciation and the yoga of action both lead to the highest Bliss; but of the two, yoga of action is superior to the renunciation of action.

ज्ञेयः स नित्यसंन्यासी यो न द्वेष्टि न काङ्क्षति।
निर्द्वन्द्वो हि महाबाहो सुखं बन्धात्प्रमुच्यते॥ ३॥

*jñeyaḥ sa nityasannyāsī*
*yo na dveṣthi nā kāṅkṣati*
*nirdvandvo hi mahābāho*
*sukham bandhātpramucyate*

(3) He should be known as a perpetual renouncer, who neither hates nor desires and who is free from all dualities. O' Arjuna, he is indeed easily liberated from bondage.

साङ्ख्ययोगौ पृथग्बालाः प्रवदन्ति न पण्डिताः।
एकमप्यास्थितः सम्यगुभयोर्विन्दते फलम्॥ ४॥

*sāṅkhyayogau pṛathag bālāḥ*
*pravadaṅti na paṅditāḥ*
*ekamapyāsthitaḥ samyag-*
*ubhayorvindate phalam*

(4) Children, not the learned, speak of knowledge (Samkhya) and the Yoga of action as distinct. He who is truly established in either, attains the fruits of both.

यत्साङ्ख्यैः प्राप्यते स्थानं तद्योगैरपि गम्यते।
एकं साङ्ख्यं च योगं च यः पश्यति स पश्यति॥ ५॥

*yatsāṅkhyaiḥ prāpyate sthānaṁ*
*tad yagairapi gamyate*
*ekaṁ sāṅkhyaṁ ca yogaṁ ca*
*yaḥ paśyati sa paśyati*

(5) The spiritual status which is obtained with the yoga of knowledge is also achieved with the yoga of action. He truly sees, who sees the knowledge and the yoga of action as one.

संन्यासस्तु महाबाहो दुःखमाप्तुमयोगतः ।
योगयुक्तो मुनिर्ब्रह्म नचिरेणाधिगच्छति ॥ ६ ॥

*sannyāṣastu māhabāho*
*duḥkhamāptumayogataḥ*
*yogayukto munirbrahma*
*nacireṇādhigacchati*

(6) O'Arjuna, renunciation is indeed difficult to attain without yoga. The sage who is established in yoga, he definitely reaches the Brahman very quickly.

योगयुक्तो विशुद्धात्मा विजितात्मा जितेन्द्रियः ।
सर्वभूतात्मभूतात्मा कुर्वन्नपि न लिप्यते ॥ ७ ॥

*yogayukto viśuddhātmā*
*vijitātmā jitendriyaḥ*
*sarvabhūtātmabhūtāṭmā*
*kurvannapi na lipyate*

(7) He, who is united with the Self in yoga, who is pure at heart, whose body and senses are under his control, who realizes his own Self, as the Self in all beings, he is not tainted by actions, while he performs.

नैव किञ्चित्करोमीति युक्तो मन्येत तत्त्ववित्।
पश्यञ्शृण्वन्स्पृशञ्जिघ्रन्नश्नन्गच्छन्स्वपञ्श्वसन्॥ ८॥

*naiva kiñcit karomīti*
*yukto manyeta tattvavit*
*paśyaṇ śṛṇvan spṛsañ jighrann-*
*aśnan gacchan śvapan śvasan*

प्रलपन्विसृजन्गृह्णन्नुन्मिषन्निमिषन्नपि।
इन्द्रियाणीन्द्रियार्थेषु वर्तन्त इति धारयन्॥ ९॥

*pralapan visṛjan gṛhṇann-*
*unmiṣan nimiṣannapi*
*indriyāṇīndriyārtheṣu*
*vartanta iti dhārayan*

(8, 9) The knower of truth, who is united within, he believes 'I am not doing anything' even while—seeing, hearing, touching, smelling, eating, walking, sleeping, breathing, speaking, excreting, grasping, opening and closing the eyelids. He always remains convinced that the senses operate among the sense objects.

ब्रह्मण्याधाय कर्माणि सङ्गं त्यक्त्वा करोति यः।
लिप्यते न स पापेन पद्मपत्रमिवाम्भसा॥ १०॥

*brahmaṇyādhāya karmāṇi*
*saṅgaṁ tyaktvā karoti yaḥ*
*lipyate na sa pāpena*
*padmapatramivāmbhasā*

(10) He who performs all his actions, offering them to the Divine and abandons all attachment, he is not touched by sin, just as the lotus leaf is not tainted by water.

कायेन मनसा बुद्ध्या केवलैरिन्द्रियैरपि।
योगिनः कर्म कुर्वन्ति सङ्गं त्यक्त्वात्मशुद्धये॥ ११॥

*kāyena manasā buddhyā*
*kevalairindriyairapi*
*yoginaḥ karma kurvanti*
*saṅgaṁ tyaktvātmaśuddhaye*

(11) The yogins perform their actions merely with the body, the mind, the intellect and the senses, without any attachment—for the

purification of the self (heart).

युक्तः कर्मफलं त्यक्त्वा शान्तिमाप्नोति नैष्ठिकीम्।
अयुक्तः कामकारेण फले सक्तो निबध्यते॥१२॥

*yuktaḥ karmaphalaṁ tyaktvā*
*śāntimāpnoti naiṣṭhikīm*
*ayuktaḥ kāmakāreṇa*
*phale sakto nibadhyate*

(12) He who is united within, having renounced the fruits of actions, attains the highest peace; but the disintegrated man being impelled by desire, remains attached to the fruits and becomes bound.

सर्वकर्माणि मनसा संन्यस्यास्ते सुखं वशी।
नवद्वारे पुरे देही नैव कुर्वन्न कारयन्॥१३॥

*sarvakarmāṇi manasā*
*sannyasyāste sukhaṁ vaśī*
*navadvāre pure dehī*
*naiva kurvanna kārayan*

(13) Mentally, renouncing the doership of all actions, the self-controlled embodied-self (Jivatma), rests peacefully in the city of nine

gates, neither acting nor causing others to act.

न कर्तृत्वं न कर्माणि लोकस्य सृजति प्रभुः ।
न कर्मफलसंयोगं स्वभावस्तु प्रवर्तते ॥ १४ ॥

*na kartṛtvaṁ na karmāṇi*
*lokasya sṛjati prabhuḥ*
*na karmaphalasaṅyogaṁ*
*svabhāvastu pravartate*

(14) The Lord does not create the agency nor the actions for the world; nor does he connect actions with their fruits. It is only the innate nature that operates.

नादत्ते कस्यचित्पापं न चैव सुकृतं विभुः ।
अज्ञानेनावृतं ज्ञानं तेन मुह्यन्ति जन्तवः ॥ १५ ॥

*nādatte kasyacit pāpāṁ*
*na caiva sukṛtaṁ vibhuḥ*
*ajñānenāvṛtaṁ jñānaṁ*
*tena muhyanti jantavaḥ*

(15) The Omnipresent Lord takes neither the sin nor the virtue of any; the knowledge is enveloped by

ignorance, therefore creatures are bewildered.

ज्ञानेन तु तदज्ञानं येषां नाशितमात्मनः ।
तेषामादित्यवज्ज्ञानं प्रकाशयति तत्परम् ॥ १६ ॥

*jñānena tu tadajñānaṁ*
*yeṣāṁ nāśitamātmanaḥ*
*teṣāmādityavajjñānaṁ*
*prakāśayati tat param*

(16) To those, whose ignorance has been dispelled by the knowledge of the Self, for them, the knowledge reveals the Supreme Brahman like the Sun.

तद्बुद्धयस्तदात्मानस्तन्निष्ठास्तत्परायणाः ।
गच्छन्त्यपुनरावृत्तिं ज्ञाननिर्धूतकल्मषाः ॥ १७ ॥

*tadbuddhayastadātmānas*
*tanniṣṭhās tatparāyaṇāḥ*
*gacchantyapunarāvṛttiṁ*
*jñānanirdhūtakalmaṣāḥ*

(17) Those, whose mind and intellect are totally merged in God, who remain established in unity, and consider that as their Supreme goal

they reach the state from which there is no return—their sins being dispelled by knowledge.

विद्याविनयसम्पन्ने ब्राह्मणे गवि हस्तिनि।
शुनि चैव श्वपाके च पण्डिताः समदर्शिनः ॥ १८ ॥

*vidyāvinayasampanne*
*brāhmaṇe gavi hastini*
*śuni caiva śvapāke ca*
*paṇḍitāḥ samadarśinaḥ*

(18) The man of wisdom looks with equanimity upon the Brahmin endowed with learning and humility, a cow, an elephant, and even a dog and a pariah.

इहैव तैर्जितः सर्गो येषां साम्ये स्थितं मनः।
निर्दोषं हि समं ब्रह्म तस्माद् ब्रह्मणि ते स्थिताः ॥ १९ ॥

*ihaiva tairjitaḥ sargo*
*yeṣāṁ sāmye sthitaṁ manaḥ*
*nirdoṣaṁ hi samaṁ brahma*
*tasmād brahmaṇi te sthitāḥ*

(19) Even here the world is conquered by those, whose mind is

established in equality. Brahman is indeed flawless and the same everywhere, therefore, they are established in Brahman.

न प्रहृष्येत्प्रियं प्राप्य नोद्विजेत्प्राप्य चाप्रियम्।
स्थिरबुद्धिरसम्मूढो ब्रह्मविद् ब्रह्मणि स्थितः ॥ २० ॥

*na prahṛṣyetpriyaṁ prāpya*
*nodvijet prāpya cāpriyam*
*sthirabuddhirasaṁmūḍho*
*brahmavid brahmaṇi sthitaḥ*

(20) He who neither rejoices on receiving what is pleasant nor grieves on receiving the unpleasant; who is firm of understanding and undeluded; such a knower of Brahman is established in Brahman.

बाह्यस्पर्शेष्वसक्तात्मा विन्दत्यात्मनि यत्सुखम्।
स ब्रह्मयोगयुक्तात्मा सुखमक्षयमश्नुते ॥ २१ ॥

*bāhyasparśeṣvasaktātmā*
*vindatyātmani yat sukham*
*sa brahmayogayuktātmā*
*sukham akṣayam aśnute*

(21) When the embodied-self is not attached to the external objects of the senses, and finds happiness within the Self—he becomes united with Brahman in yoga and enjoys the eternal Bliss.

ये हि संस्पर्शजा भोगा दुःखयोनय एव ते।

आद्यन्तवन्तः कौन्तेय न तेषु रमते बुधः ॥ २२ ॥

*ye hi saṅsparaśajā bhoga*

*duḥkhayonaya eva te*

*ādyantavantaḥ Kaunteya*

*na teṣu ramate budhaḥ*

(22) The enjoyments that are born of contacts with the sense objects are the source of pain; they have a beginning and an end, O'Arjuna. The wise man does not rejoice in them.

शक्नोतीहैव यः सोढुं प्राक्शरीरविमोक्षणात्।

कामक्रोधोद्भवं वेगं स युक्तः स सुखी नरः ॥ २३ ॥

*śaknotīhaiva yaḥ soḍhuṁ*

*prākśarīravimokṣaṇāt*

*kāmakrodhodbhavaṁ vegaṁ*

*sa yuktaḥ sa sukhī naraḥ*

(23) He who in this world is able to resist the impulse, born out of desire and anger, before he gives up his body—he is indeed a yogi, he is a happy man.

योऽन्तःसुखोऽन्तरारामस्तथान्तर्ज्योतिरेव यः।
स योगी ब्रह्मनिर्वाणं ब्रह्मभूतोऽधिगच्छति॥ २४॥

*yo'ntaḥsukho'ntarārāmas*
*tathāntarjyotireva yaḥ*
*sa yogī brahmanirvāṇaṁ*
*brahmabhūto'dhigacchati*

(24) He who finds his happiness within, who rejoices within himself, who is illuminated from within—that yogi attains absolute liberation (Brahman Nirvana); because of his firm identification with Brahman.

लभन्ते ब्रह्मनिर्वाणमृषयः क्षीणकल्मषाः।
छिन्नद्वैधा यतात्मानः सर्वभूतहिते रताः॥ २५॥

*labhante brahmanirvāṇam*
*ṛṣayaḥ kṣīṇakalmaṣāḥ*
*chinnadvaidhā yatātmānaḥ*
*sarvabhūtahite ratāḥ*

(25) The Rishis obtain absolute freedom—whose sins have been destroyed and whose dualities are torn asunder. Who are self-controlled and always devoted to the welfare of all beings.

कामक्रोधवियुक्तानां यतीनां यतचेतसाम्।
अभितो ब्रह्मनिर्वाणं वर्तते विदितात्मनाम्॥ २६॥

*kāmakrodhaviyuktānaṁ*
*yatīnāṁ yatacetasām*
*abhito brahmanirvāṇaṁ*
*vartate viditātmanām*

(26) The ascetics those are free from desire and anger, who have controlled their mind and have realized the Self; for them the eternal Bliss (Brahmic Bliss) exists on all sides.

स्पर्शान्कृत्वा बहिर्बाह्यांश्चक्षुश्चैवान्तरे भ्रुवोः।
प्राणापानौ समौ कृत्वा नासाभ्यन्तरचारिणौ॥ २७॥

*sparśān kṛtvā bahir bāhyāṅś*
*cakṣuś caivāntare bhruvoḥ*
*prāṇāpānau samau kṛtvā*
*nāsābhyantaracāriṇau*

यतेन्द्रियमनोबुद्धिर्मुनिर्मोक्षपरायणः ।
विगतेच्छाभयक्रोधो यः सदा मुक्त एव सः ॥ २८ ॥

*yatendriyamanobuddhir*
*munirmokṣaparāyaṇaḥ*
*vigatecchābhayakrodho*
*yaḥ sadā mukta eva saḥ*

(27, 28) Shutting out the external sensory contacts, fixing the vision between the two eyebrows, controlling the outgoing and incoming breath flow, with the senses, mind and intellect fully restrained, and free from desire, fear and anger—the sage who aims at liberation, as his highest goal, he is verily liberated for ever.

भोक्तारं यज्ञतपसां सर्वलोकमहेश्वरम् ।
सुहृदं सर्वभूतानां ज्ञात्वा मां शान्तिमृच्छति ॥ २९ ॥

*bhoktākaraṁ yajñatapasāṁ*
*sarvalokamaheśvaram*
*suhṛdaṁ sarvabhūtānāṁ*
*jñātvā māṁ śāntimṛcchati*

(29) Knowing Me as the enjoyer of all sacrifices and austerities, the

great Lord of all the worlds and the well-wisher (friend) of all beings, one attains peace.

ॐ तत्सदिति श्रीमद्भगवद्गीतासूपनिषत्सु ब्रह्मविद्यायां

योगशास्त्रे श्रीकृष्णार्जुनसंवादे कर्मसंन्यासयोगो

नाम पञ्चमोऽध्यायः ॥५॥

***'Aum' tatsaditi Srīmadbhagawadgeeta supaniṣatsu brahmavidyayam yogaśāstre Srīkṛṣṇarjunasamvade karmasannyasayogo nama pancamodhyayah***

**'AUM TAT SAT'**—Thus, in the Upanishad of the glorious Bhagawad Geeta, the science of the Brahman (Absolute) the scripture of yoga, the dialogue between Srī Kṛṣṇa and Arjuna—thus, ends the chapter five entitled *"Karma-sannyasayoga"*.

इति श्रीमद्भगवद्गीतासु पञ्चमोऽध्यायः ॥५॥

## *Chapter Six*

# DHYĀNAYOGA

## THE YOGA OF MEDITATION

श्रीभगवानुवाच

अनाश्रितः कर्मफलं कार्यं कर्म करोति यः।
स संन्यासी च योगी च न निरग्निर्न चाक्रियः॥ १॥

*anāśritaḥ karmaphalaṁ*
*kāryaṁ karma karoti yaḥ*
*sa sannyāsī ca yogī ca*
*na niragnir na cākriyaḥ*

**The Blessed Lord said :**

(1) He who performs obligatory duties without depending upon the fruits of actions—he is a true renunciate (Sannyasi) and a yogi; not the one who has renounced the sacred fire and the performance of action.

यं संन्यासमिति प्राहुर्योगं तं विद्धि पाण्डव।
न ह्यसंन्यस्तसङ्कल्पो योगी भवति कश्चन॥ २॥

*yaṁ sannyāsamiti prāhur*
*yogaṁ taṁ viddhi pāṇḍava*
*na hy asannyastasaṅkalpo*
*yogī bhavati kaścana*

(2) That which is called renunciation know that to be the yoga, O' Arjuna; for no one can become a yogi, without renouncing the selfish desires of the world.

**आरुरुक्षोर्मुनेर्योगं कर्म कारणमुच्यते।**
**योगारूढस्य तस्यैव शमः कारणमुच्यते॥ ३॥**

*ārurukṣor muner yogaṁ*
*karma kāraṇamucyate*
*yogārūḍhasya tasyaiva*
*śamaḥ kāraṇamucyate*

(3) Action is considered to be the means for the sage who aspires to ascend in yoga; when he is established in yoga, tranquillity of mind is said to be the means.

**यदा हि नेन्द्रियार्थेषु न कर्मस्वनुषज्जते।**
**सर्वसङ्कल्पसंन्यासी योगारूढस्तदोच्यते॥ ४॥**

*yadā hi nendriyārtheṣu*
*na karmasvanuṣajjate*
*sarvasaṅkalpasannyāsī*
*yogārūḍhasta docyate*

(4) When one becomes detached from the objects of senses and from actions, and has renounced all personal desires, then he is said to have ascended in Yoga.

उद्धरेदात्मनात्मानं नात्मानमवसादयेत्।
आत्मैव ह्यात्मनो बन्धुरात्मैव रिपुरात्मनः ॥५॥

*uddharedātmanātmānaṁ*
*nātmānamavasādayet*
*ātmai'va hyātmano bandhur-*
*ātmaiva ripurātmanaḥ*

(5) Let a man lift himself by his Self, Let him not degrade himself; for he himself is his own friend and he himself is his own enemy.

बन्धुरात्मात्मनस्तस्य येनात्मैवात्मना जितः।
अनात्मनस्तु शत्रुत्वे वर्तेतात्मैव शत्रुवत्॥६॥

*bandhurātmatmanastasya*
*yenātmaivātmanā jitaḥ*
*anātmanastu śatrutve*
*vartetātmaiva śatruvat*

(6) To him who has conquered his lower-self by the Higher-Self, his Self becomes a friend; but for him who has not conquered his lower-self his own Self acts as an enemy.

जितात्मनः प्रशान्तस्य परमात्मा समाहितः ।
शीतोष्णसुखदुःखेषु तथा मानापमानयोः ॥ ७ ॥

*jitātmanaḥ praśāntasya*
*paramātmā samāhitaḥ*
*śītoṣṇasukhaduḥkheṣu*
*tathā mānāpamānayoḥ*

(7) The self-controlled man, whose mind is perfectly serene and settled in the Supreme-Self, becomes balanced in cold and heat, in pleasure and pain, in honour and dishonour.

ज्ञानविज्ञानतृप्तात्मा कूटस्थो विजितेन्द्रियः ।
युक्त इत्युच्यते योगी समलोष्टाश्मकाञ्चनः ॥ ८ ॥

*jñānavijñānatṛptātmā*
*kūtastho vijitendriyaḥ*
*yukta ityucyate yogī*
*samaloṣṭāśmakāñcanaḥ*

(8) Who is satisfied with the knowledge and the experiential wisdom of the Self, who is steadfast and self-controlled, who considers a clod, a stone and a piece of gold alike; he is said to be established in yoga.

**सुहृन्मित्रार्युदासीनमध्यस्थद्वेष्यबन्धुषु।**
**साधुष्वपि च पापेषु समबुद्धिर्विशिष्यते॥ ९॥**

*suhṛnmitrāryudāsīna-*
*madhyasthadveṣyabandhuṣu*
*sādhuṣvapi ca pāpeṣu*
*sambuddhirviśiṣyate*

(9) He who regards the well-wishers, friends, enemies, indifferent, neutral, hateful, relatives, saint and the sinner alike, is indeed balanced and stands distinguished.

**योगी युञ्जीत सततमात्मानं रहसि स्थितः।**
**एकाकी यतचित्तात्मा निराशीरपरिग्रहः॥ १०॥**

*yogī yuñjīta satatam-*
*ātmānaṁ rahasi sthitaḥ*
*ekākī yatacittātmā*
*nirāśīraparigrahaḥ*

(10) The yogi should constantly engage his mind in meditation, while living alone in solitude. Having controlled his mind and body and being free from the sense of possession and desire.

**शुचौ देशे प्रतिष्ठाप्य स्थिरमासनमात्मनः ।**
**नात्युच्छ्रितं नातिनीचं चैलाजिनकुशोत्तरम् ॥ ११ ॥**

*śucau deśe pratiṣṭhāpya*
*sthiramāsanamātmanaḥ*
*nātyucchritaṁ nātinīcaṁ*
*cailājinakuśottaram*

(11) On a clean spot, having established for himself a firm seat which is neither too high nor too low, and covered with a cloth, deer skin, and kusha-grass, one over the other.

**तत्रैकाग्रं मनः कृत्वा यतचित्तेन्द्रियक्रियः ।**
**उपविश्यासने युञ्ज्याद्योगमात्मविशुद्धये ॥ १२ ॥**

*tatraikāgraṁ manaḥ kṛtvā*
*yatacittendriyakriyaḥ*
*upaviśyāsane yuñjyād*
*yogamātmaviśuddhaye*

(12) Sitting there, on his seat with one-pointed mind; controlling the functions of mind and senses; he should practise yoga for the purification of the self.

समं कायशिरोग्रीवं धारयन्नचलं स्थिरः।
सम्प्रेक्ष्य नासिकाग्रं स्वं दिशश्चानवलोकयन्॥ १३॥

*samaṁ kāyaśirogrīvaṁ*
*dhārayannacalaṁ sthiraḥ*
*samprekṣya nāsikāgraṁ svaṁ*
*diśaścānavalokayan*

(13) Holding the trunk, head and neck straight, steady and still; he should fix the gaze on the tip of his nose, without looking in any other direction.

प्रशान्तात्मा विगतभीर्ब्रह्मचारिव्रते स्थितः।
मनः संयम्य मच्चित्तो युक्त आसीत मत्परः॥ १४॥

*praśāntātmā vigatabhīr-*
*brahmacārivrate sthitaḥ*

*manaḥ saṅyamya maccitto*
*yukta āsīta matparaḥ*

(14) Peaceful and fearless, steadfast in the vow of celibacy, with mind fully disciplined and concentrated on Me; he should sit in yogic meditation—having Me as the Supreme goal.

युञ्जन्नेवं सदात्मानं योगी नियतमानसः ।
शान्तिं निर्वाणपरमां मत्संस्थामधिगच्छति ॥ १५ ॥

*yuñjannevaṁ sadā'tamānaṁ*
*yogī niyatamānasaḥ*
*śāntiṁ nirvāṇaparamāṁ*
*matsaṅsthāmadhigacchati*

(15) Thus constantly uniting his mind with Me, the yogi of disciplined mind, attains peace; the Supreme Nirvana, which abides in Me.

नात्यश्नतस्तु योगोऽस्ति न चैकान्तमनश्नतः ।
न चातिस्वप्नशीलस्य जाग्रतो नैव चार्जुन ॥ १६ ॥

*nātyaśnatastu yogo'sti*
*na caikāntamanaśnataḥ*
*na cāti svapnaśīlasya*
*jāgrato naiva cārjuna*

(16) Yoga is not for him who eats too much, nor for him who does not eat at all; it is not for him who sleeps too much, nor for him who is ever awake, O' Arjuna.

युक्ताहारविहारस्य युक्तचेष्टस्य कर्मसु।
युक्तस्वप्नावबोधस्य योगो भवति दुःखहा॥ १७॥

*yuktāhāravihārasya*
*yuktaceṣṭasya karmasu*
*yuktasvapnāvabodhasya*
*yogo bhavati duḥkhahā*

(17) The man who is regulated in diet and recreation, disciplined in the performance of work, who is regulated in sleep and wakefulness, for him the Yoga becomes the destroyer of pain.

यदा विनियतं चित्तमात्मन्येवावतिष्ठते।
निःस्पृहः सर्वकामेभ्यो युक्त इत्युच्यते तदा॥ १८॥

*yadā viniyataṁ cittām*
*atmanyevāvatiṣṭhate*
*niḥspṛhaḥ sarvakāmebhyo*
*yukta ityucyate tadā*

(18) When the perfectly disciplined mind rests in the Self alone, and is free from the yearning for the objects of desires, one is said to be united in Yoga.

यथा दीपो निवातस्थो नेङ्गते सोपमा स्मृता।

योगिनो यतचित्तस्य युञ्जतो योगमात्मनः॥ १९॥

*yathā dīpo nivātastho*

*neṅgate sopamā smṛtā*

*yogino yatacittasya*

*yuñjato yogāmatmanaḥ*

(19) As a lamp placed in a windless spot does not flicker, is the simile used for a yogi of subdued mind, who is practising to unite in Yoga with the Self.

यत्रोपरमते चित्तं निरुद्धं योगसेवया।

यत्र चैवात्मनात्मानं पश्यन्नात्मनि तुष्यति॥ २०॥

*yatroparamate cittaṁ*

*niruddhaṁ yogasevayā*

*yatra caivātmanātmānaṁ*

*paśyannātmani tuṣyati*

(20) Where the mind becomes peaceful and restrained by the practice of Yoga, wherein one beholds the Self within the self, one rejoices in the Self alone.

सुखमात्यन्तिकं यत्तद्बुद्धिग्राह्यमतीन्द्रियम्।
वेत्ति यत्र न चैवायं स्थितश्चलति तत्त्वतः॥ २१॥

*sukhamātyantikaṁ yat tad*
*buddhigrāhymatīndriyam*
*vetti yatra na caivāyaṁ*
*sthitaścalati tattvataḥ*

(21) Where one experiences transcendental bliss, which is perceived only by the subtle intellect, and which is beyond the grasp of the senses, established in that state, one never moves from the essential truth.

यं लब्ध्वा चापरं लाभं मन्यते नाधिकं ततः।
यस्मिन्स्थितो न दुःखेन गुरुणापि विचाल्यते॥ २२॥

*yaṁ labdhvā cāparaṁ lābhaṁ*
*manyate nādhikaṁ tataḥ*
*yasminsthito na duḥkhena*
*guruṇāpi vicālyate*

(22) Having obtained that which one considers nothing else superior to it; wherein established, the individual is not shaken even by the deepest sorrow.

तं विद्याद्दुःखसंयोगवियोगं योगसंज्ञितम्।

स निश्चयेन योक्तव्यो योगोऽनिर्विण्णचेतसा ॥ २३ ॥

*taṁ vidyād duḥkhasaṅyoga-*

*viyogaṁ yogasamjñitam*

*sa niścayena yoktavyo*

*yogo'nirvinnacetasā*

(23) This state is known by the name of Yoga which is free from the contacts of sorrow. This Yoga should be practised with determination and concentration of mind.

सङ्कल्पप्रभवान्कामांस्त्यक्त्वा सर्वानशेषतः।

मनसैवेन्द्रियग्रामं विनियम्य समन्ततः ॥ २४ ॥

*saṅkalpaprabhavān kāmāṅs*

*tyaktvā sarvānaśeṣataḥ*

*manasaivendriyagrāmaṁ*

*viniyamya samantataḥ*

शनैः शनैरुपरमेद् बुद्ध्या धृतिगृहीतया।
आत्मसंस्थं मनः कृत्वा न किंचिदपि चिन्तयेत्॥ २५ ॥

*śanaiḥ śanairuparamed*
*bhuddhayā dhṛtigṛhītayā*
*ātmasaṁsthaṁ manaḥ kṛtvā*
*na kiñcidapi cintayet*

(24, 25) Abandoning all desires which arise from the thoughts of the world and fully controlling the mind from the entire group of senses, let him gradually attain tranquillity, with the intellect held in firmness; having made the mind established in the Self, let him not think about anything else.

यतो यतो निश्चरति मनश्चञ्चलमस्थिरम्।
ततस्ततो नियम्यैतदात्मन्येव वशं नयेत्॥ २६ ॥

*yato-yato niścarati*
*manaścañcalam asthiram*
*tatas-tato niyamyaitad*
*ātmanyeva vaśaṁ nayet*

(26) For whatever reason, when the restless mind wanders away, he should restrain it and bring it under the control of Self alone.

प्रशान्तमनसं ह्येनं योगिनं सुखमुत्तमम्।
उपैति शान्तरजसं ब्रह्मभूतमकल्मषम्॥ २७॥

*praśāntamanasaṁ hyenaṁ*
*yoginaṁ sukhamuttamam*
*upaiti śāntarajasaṁ*
*brahmabhūtamakalmaṣam*

(27) The Supreme Bliss comes to the yogi whose mind is at peace, whose passion (rajas) has been subdued, who is sinless and has become identified with the Brahman.

युञ्जन्नेवं सदात्मानं योगी विगतकल्मषः।
सुखेन ब्रह्मसंस्पर्शमत्यन्तं सुखमश्नुते॥ २८॥

*yuñjannevaṁ sadātmānaṁ*
*yogī vigatakalmaṣaḥ*
*sukhena brahmasaṁsparśam*
*atyantaṁ sukhamaśnute*

(28) Thus constantly uniting the mind with the Self, the yogi becomes free from sins and easily attains the infinite Bliss of oneness with Brahman.

सर्वभूतस्थमात्मानं सर्वभूतानि चात्मनि।
ईक्षते योगयुक्तात्मा सर्वत्र समदर्शनः ॥ २९ ॥

*sarvabhūtasthamātmānaṁ*
*sarvabhūtāni cātmani*
*īkṣate yogayuktātmā*
*sarvatra samadarśanaḥ*

(29) He whose self is established in Yoga, he beholds the self abiding in all beings and all beings in the Self. He sees equality everywhere.

यो मां पश्यति सर्वत्र सर्वं च मयि पश्यति।
तस्याहं न प्रणश्यामि स च मे न प्रणश्यति ॥ ३० ॥

*yo māṁ paśyati sarvatra*
*sarvaṁ ca mayi paśyati*
*tasyā'haṁ na praṇaśyāmi*
*sa ca me na praṇaśyati*

(30) He who sees Me everywhere and sees everything existing in Me, I am never out of sight for him, nor is he ever out of My sight.

सर्वभूतस्थितं यो मां भजत्येकत्वमास्थितः।
सर्वथा वर्तमानोऽपि स योगी मयि वर्तते ॥ ३१ ॥

*sarvabhūtasthitaṁ yo māṁ*
*bhajatyekatvamāsthitaḥ*
*sarvathā vartamānopi*
*sa yogī mayi vartate*

(31) He who, being established in oneness, worships Me dwelling in all beings, that yogi ever resides in Me, though engaged in all forms of activities.

आत्मौपम्येन सर्वत्र समं पश्यति योऽर्जुन।
सुखं वा यदि वा दुःखं स योगी परमो मतः॥ ३२॥

*ātmaupamyena sarvatra*
*samaṁ paśyati yo'rjuna*
*sukhaṁ vā yadi vā duḥkhaṁ*
*sa yogī parmo mataḥ*

(32) He who, through the reflections of his own-self, sees equality everywhere, be it pleasure or pain, he is considered a perfect yogi., O'Arjuna.

अर्जुन उवाच

योऽयं योगस्त्वया प्रोक्तः साम्येन मधुसूदन।
एतस्याहं न पश्यामि चञ्चलत्वात्स्थितिं स्थिराम्॥ ३३॥

*yo'yaṁ yogastvayā proktaḥ*
*sāmyena madhūsudana*
*etasyāhaṁ na paśyāmi*
*cañcalatvātsthitiṁ sthirām*

**Arjuna said :**

(33) This Yoga of equanimity, which has been declared by you, O' Kṛṣṇa, I don't see that it can be steady and lasting because of the instability of the mind.

**चञ्चलं हि मनः कृष्ण प्रमाथि बलवद् दृढम्।**
**तस्याहं निग्रहं मन्ये वायोरिव सुदुष्करम्॥ ३४॥**

*cañcalaṁ hi manaḥ kṛṣṇa*
*pramāthi balavad dṛḍham*
*tasyāhaṁ nigrahaṁ manye*
*vāyoriva suduṣkaram*

(34) Mind is very restless O'Kṛṣṇa,—turbulent, powerful and very stubborn. I believe that it is as difficult to control as the wind.

**श्रीभगवानुवाच**

**असंशयं महाबाहो मनो दुर्निग्रहं चलम्।**
**अभ्यासेन तु कौन्तेय वैराग्येण च गृह्यते॥ ३५॥**

*asaṅśayaṁ mahābāho*
*mano durnigrahaṁ calam*
*abhyāsena tu kaunteya*
*vairāgyeṇa ca gṛhyate*

**The blessed Lord said :**

(35) Without doubt, O'mighty-armed (Arjuna), the mind is restless, very hard to control; but by practice and by dispassion O' son of Kunti, it can be controlled.

**असंयतात्मना योगो दुष्प्राप इति मे मतिः।**
**वश्यात्मना तु यतता शक्योऽवाप्तुमुपायतः॥ ३६॥**

*asaṅyatātmanā yogo*
*duṣprāpa iti me matiḥ*
*vaśyātmanā tu yatatā*
*śakyo'vāptumupāyataḥ*

(36) The yoga is indeed very difficult to attain for a person of unrestrained mind—this is My opinion. But the self-controlled one, who strives ceaselessly, it becomes possible through proper practice.

**अर्जुन उवाच**

**अयतिः श्रद्धयोपेतो योगाच्चलितमानसः।**
**अप्राप्य योगसंसिद्धिं कां गतिं कृष्ण गच्छति॥ ३७॥**

*ayatiḥ śraddhayopeto*
*yogāccalitamānsaḥ*
*aprāpya yogasaṅsiddhiṁ*
*kāṁ gatiṁ kṛṣṇa gacchati*

**Arjuna said :**

(37) He who is endowed with full faith, but is undisciplined and whose mind slips away from yogic communion, having failed to attain perfection in yoga,—where does he go? O' Kṛṣṇa.

कच्चिन्नोभयविभ्रष्टश्छिन्नाभ्रमिव नश्यति।
अप्रतिष्ठो महाबाहो विमूढो ब्रह्मणः पथि॥ ३८॥

*kaccinnobhayavibhraṣṭaś*
*chinnābhramiva naśyati*
*apratiṣṭho māhābāho*
*vimūḍho brahmaṇaḥ pathi*

(38) Thus, fallen from both, doesn't he perish like a dissipated cloud, O' Kṛṣṇa; lacking firm support and bewildered in the path that leads to the Brahman.

एतन्मे संशयं कृष्ण छेत्तुमर्हस्यशेषतः।
त्वदन्यः संशयस्यास्य छेत्ता न ह्युपपद्यते॥ ३९॥

*etanme saṅśayaṁ kṛṣṇa*
*chetturmahasyaśeṣataḥ*
*tvadanyaḥ saṅśayasyāsya*
*chettā na hyupapadyate*

(39) This doubt of mine, O' Kṛṣṇa, Thou shouldst dispel completely; for no one else except You can clear this doubt.

श्रीभगवानुवाच

पार्थ नैवेह नामुत्र विनाशस्तस्य विद्यते।
न हि कल्याणकृत्कश्चिद्दुर्गतिं तात गच्छति॥ ४०॥

*pārtha nāiveha nāmutra*
*vināśastasya vidyate*
*na hi kalyāṇakṛtkaścid*
*durgatiṁ tāta gacchati*

**The Blessed Lord said :**

(40) O'Arjuna, neither in this world nor hereafter there is any chance of destruction for him; for no one, who does the virtuous deeds ever comes to grief.

प्राप्य पुण्यकृतां लोकानुषित्वा शाश्वतीः समाः।
शुचीनां श्रीमतां गेहे योगभ्रष्टोऽभिजायते॥ ४१॥

*prāpya puṇyakṛtāṁ lokān-*
*uṣitvā śāśvatīḥ samaḥ*
*śucīnāṁ śrīmatāṁ gehe*
*yogabhraṣṭo'bhijāyate*

(41) Having attained to the world of the righteous, and having lived there for countless years; he who has fallen from yoga, is reborn in the family of the virtuous and prosperous.

अथवा योगिनामेव कुले भवति धीमताम्।
एतद्धि दुर्लभतरं लोके जन्म यदीदृशम्॥ ४२॥

*athavā yogināmeva*
*kule bhavati dhīmatām*
*etaddhi durlabhataraṁ*
*loke janma yadīdṛśam*

(42) Or he is born in a family of the enlightened yogins, although this type of birth is very difficult to obtain in this world.

तत्र तं बुद्धिसंयोगं लभते पौर्वदेहिकम्।
यतते च ततो भूयः संसिद्धौ कुरुनन्दन॥ ४३॥

*tatra taṁ buddhisaṁyogaṁ*
*labhate paurvadehikam*

*yatate ca tato bhūyaḥ*
*saṅsiddhau kurunandana*

(43) There, he regains with increased intuition, the knowledge of his previous birth and strives much more than before for perfection, O' Arjuna.

पूर्वाभ्यासेन तेनैव ह्रियते ह्यवशोऽपि सः ।
जिज्ञासुरपि योगस्य शब्दब्रह्मातिवर्तते ॥ ४४ ॥

*pūrvābhyāsena tenaiva*
*hriyate hyavaśo'pi saḥ*
*jijñāsurapi yogasya*
*śabdabrahmātivartate*

(44) Initiated by the force of his former practice, he is carried on irresistibly. Even if he merely strives to know about yoga, he transcends the Sabad brahman.

प्रयत्नाद्यतमानस्तु योगी संशुद्धकिल्बिषः ।
अनेकजन्मसंसिद्धस्ततो याति परां गतिम् ॥ ४५ ॥

*prayatnādyatamānastu*
*yogī saṅśuddhakilbiṣaḥ*
*anekajanmasaṅsiddhas-*
*tato yāti parām gatim*

(45) The yogi who strives earnestly, he becomes purified from all sins, perfected gradually through many births, he reaches the supreme state.

तपस्विभ्योऽधिको योगी ज्ञानिभ्योऽपि मतोऽधिकः ।
कर्मिभ्यश्चाधिको योगी तस्माद्योगी भवार्जुन ॥ ४६ ॥

*tapasvibhyo'dhiko yogī*
*jñānibhyo'pi mato'dhikaḥ*
*karmibhyaścādhiko yogī*
*tasmādyogī bhavā'rjuna*

(46) The yogi is thought to be more revered than the ascetic, he is considered to be greater than the man of knowledge; yogi is indeed superior 'to those who perform ritualistic actions. Therefore, Arjuna you be a yogi.

योगिनामपि सर्वेषां मद्गतेनान्तरात्मना ।
श्रद्धावान्भजते यो मां स मे युक्ततमो मतः ॥ ४७ ॥

*yogināmapi sarveṣāṁ*
*madgatenāntarātmanā*
*śraddhāvānbhajate yo māṁ*
*sa me yuktatamo mataḥ*

(47) Among all the yogis, he who worships Me with full faith and devotion, with his mind focused on Me, I consider him to be the most devout yogi.

ॐ तत्सदिति श्रीमद्भगवद्गीतासूपनिषत्सु ब्रह्मविद्यायां
योगशास्त्रे श्रीकृष्णार्जुनसंवादे आत्मसंयमयोगो
नाम षष्ठोऽध्यायः ॥ ६ ॥

***'Aum' tatsaditi Srīmadbhagawadgeetasupanisatsu brahmavidyayam yogasastre Srīkṛṣṇarjunasamvade ātmasanyamyogo nama sasthodhyayah***

**'AUM TAT SAT'**—Thus, in the Upanishad of the glorious Bhagawad Geeta, the science of the Brahman (Absolute) the scripture of yoga, the dialogue between Srī Kṛṣṇa and Arjuna—thus, ends the chapter six entitled *"Dhyānayoga"*.

इति श्रीमद्भगवद्गीतासु षष्ठोऽध्यायः ॥ ६ ॥

# *Chapter Seven*

# JÑĀNAVIJÑĀNAYOGA

## THE YOGA OF WISDOM AND KNOWLEDGE

श्रीभगवानुवाच

मय्यासक्तमनाः पार्थ योगं युञ्जन्मदाश्रयः ।
असंशयं समग्रं मां यथा ज्ञास्यसि तच्छृणु ॥ १ ॥

*mayyāsaktamanāḥ pārtha*
*yogaṁ yuñjan madāsrayaḥ*
*asaṅśayaṁ samagraṁ māṁ*
*yathā jñasyasi tacchṛṇu*

**The Blessed Lord Said :**

(1) With your mind focused on Me, O' Arjuna, and taking refuge in Me through the practice of yoga— listen, how you can know Me, for sure in My entirety.

ज्ञानं तेऽहं सविज्ञानमिदं वक्ष्याम्यशेषतः ।
यज्ज्ञात्वा नेह भूयोऽन्यज्ज्ञातव्यमवशिष्यते ॥ २ ॥

*jñānaṁ te'haṁ savijñānam-*
*idaṁ vakṣyāmyaśeṣataḥ*
*yajjñātvā ne'ha bhūyo'nya-*
*jjñātavyam avaśiṣyate*

(2) I shall teach you in detail the wisdom along with the experiential knowledge which makes it distinguished; having known which nothing else remains to be known.

मनुष्याणां सहस्रेषु कश्चिद्यतति सिद्धये।
यततामपि सिद्धानां कश्चिन्मां वेत्ति तत्त्वतः॥ ३॥

*manuṣyānāṁ sahasreṣu*
*kaścid yatati siddhaye*
*yatatāmapi siddhānāṁ*
*kaścinmāṁ vetti tattvataḥ*

(3) Among thousands of men, scarcely one strives for perfection; and those who strive and attain perfection, scarcely there is one, who knows Me in essence.

भूमिरापोऽनलो वायुः खं मनो बुद्धिरेव च।
अहङ्कार इतीयं मे भिन्ना प्रकृतिरष्टधा॥ ४॥

*bhūmirāpo'nalo vāyuḥ*
*khaṁ mano buddhireva ca*

*ahaṅkāra itīyaṁ me*
*bhinnā, prakṛtiraṣṭadhā*

अपरेयमितस्त्वन्यां प्रकृतिं विद्धि मे पराम्।
जीवभूतां महाबाहो ययेदं धार्यते जगत्॥ ५॥

*apareyam itastvanyāṁ*
*prakṛtiṁ viddhi me parām*
*jīvabhūtāṁ mahābāho*
*yayedaṁ dhāryate jagat*

(4, 5) Earth, Water, Fire, Air, Ether, Mind, Intellect and Ego, this is the division of My eight-fold Prakrti (Nature). This is My lower Nature, and other than this is My transcendental Nature. It is the life-element, O'Arjuna, by which this universe is sustained.

एतद्योनीनि भूतानि सर्वाणीत्युपधारय।
अहं कृत्स्नस्य जगतः प्रभवः प्रलयस्तथा॥ ६॥

*etad yonīni bhūtāni*
*sarvāṇītyupadhāraya*
*ahaṁ kṛtsnasya jagataḥ*
*prabhavaḥ pralayastathā*

(6) Know, that all the created beings have evolved from this twofold nature. I am the origin of the whole universe, as well as the dissolution.

मत्तः परतरं नान्यत्किञ्चिदस्ति धनञ्जय।
मयि सर्वमिदं प्रोतं सूत्रे मणिगणा इव॥७॥

*mattaḥ parataraṁ nānyat*
*kiñcid asti dhanañjaya*
*mayi sarvamidaṁ protaṁ*
*sūtre maṇigaṇā iva*

(7) There is nothing else besides Me, O'Arjuna. Everything is strung on Me, like the clusters of gems on a string.

रसोऽहमप्सु कौन्तेय प्रभाऽस्मि शशिसूर्ययोः।
प्रणवः सर्ववेदेषु शब्दः खे पौरुषं नृषु॥८॥

*raso'hamapsu kaunteya*
*prabhā'smi śaśisūryayoḥ*
*praṇavaḥ sarvavedeṣu*
*śabdaḥ khe pauruṣaṁ nṛṣu*

(8) I am the taste in water, O'Arjuna. I am the radiance in the

moon and in the sun. I am the sacred syllable 'AUM' in all the Vedas; sound in the ether and virility in men.

पुण्यो गन्धः पृथिव्यां च तेजश्चास्मि विभावसौ ।
जीवनं सर्वभूतेषु तपश्चास्मि तपस्विषु ॥ ९ ॥

*puṇyo gandhaḥ pṛthivyāṁ ca*
*tejaścāsmi vibhāvasau*
*jīvanaṁ sarvabhūteṣu*
*tapasca'śmi tapasviṣu*

(9) I am the pure fragrance in the earth and the brilliance in the fire. I am the life in all beings, and austerity in ascetics.

बीजं मां सर्वभूतानां विद्धि पार्थ सनातनम् ।
बुद्धिर्बुद्धिमतामस्मि तेजस्तेजस्विनामहम् ॥ १० ॥

*bījaṁ māṁ sarvabhūtānāṁ*
*viddhi pārtha sanātanam*
*buddhir buddhimatāmasmi*
*tejas tejasvināmaham*

(10) Know Me, to be the eternal seed of all beings, O'Arjuna. I am the intelligence of the intelligent and the

brilliance of the brilliant.

बलं बलवतां चाहं कामरागविवर्जितम्।

धर्माविरुद्धो भूतेषु कामोऽस्मि भरतर्षभ॥ ११॥

*balaṁ balavatāṁ cāhaṁ*

*kāmarāgavivarjitam*

*dharmāviruddho bhūteṣu*

*kāmo'smi bhartarṣabha*

(11) Of the strong, I am the strength, which is devoid of passion and attachment; in all beings I am that desire, which is not opposed by Dharma (righteousness) O'Arjuna.

ये चैव सात्त्विका भावा राजसास्तामसाश्च ये।

मत्त एवेति तान्विद्धि न त्वहं तेषु ते मयि॥ १२॥

*ye cai'va sātvikā bhāvā*

*rājasāstāmasāśca ye*

*matta eve'ti tān viddhi*

*na tvahaṁ teṣu te mayi*

(12) Know that all those states of *sattva, rajas* and *tamas* originate from Me alone. I am not in them yet, they are in Me.

त्रिभिर्गुणमयैर्भावैरेभिः सर्वमिदं जगत्।
मोहितं नाभिजानाति मामेभ्यः परमव्ययम्॥१३॥

*tribhir guṇamayair bhāvai-*
*rebhiḥ sarvamidaṁ jagat*
*mohitaṁ nābhijānāti*
*māmebhyaḥ paramavyayam*

(13) The whole world is deluded by these three qualities originating from the Prakirti (Nature), and fails to recognize Me; who is beyond them and imperishable.

दैवी ह्येषा गुणमयी मम माया दुरत्यया।
मामेव ये प्रपद्यन्ते मायामेतां तरन्ति ते॥१४॥

*daivī hyeṣā guṇamayī*
*mama māyā duratyayā*
*māmeva ye prapadyante*
*māyām etāṁ taranti te*

(14) The Divine illusion (Maya) of Mine consisting of three qualities *(gunas)* of nature is very difficult to transcend. However, those who take refuge in Me alone, cross over this illusion (Maya).

न मां दुष्कृतिनो मूढाः प्रपद्यन्ते नराधमाः ।
माययापहृतज्ञाना आसुरं भावमाश्रिताः ॥ १५ ॥

*na māṁ duṣkṛtino mūḍhāḥ*
*prapadyante narādhamāḥ*
*māyayāphṛtajñānā*
*āsuraṁ bhāvamāsritāḥ*

(15) The evil-doers, deluded and the lowest among men do not seek refuge in Me; being deluded by the illusive nature (Maya), they lack proper knowledge and follow the ways of the demons.

चतुर्विधा भजन्ते मां जनाः सुकृतिनोऽर्जुन।
आर्तो जिज्ञासुरर्थार्थी ज्ञानी च भरतर्षभ ॥ १६ ॥

*caturvidhā bhajante māṁ*
*janāḥ sukṛtino'rjuna*
*ārto jijñāsurarthārthī*
*jñānī ca bharatarṣabha*

(16) Four kinds of virtuous men worship Me, O'Arjuna. These are the distressed, the seeker of knowledge, the seeker of wealth, and the man of wisdom O'Bharata.

तेषां ज्ञानी नित्ययुक्त एकभक्तिर्विशिष्यते।
प्रियो हि ज्ञानिनोऽत्यर्थमहं स च मम प्रियः॥ १७॥

*teṣāṁ jñānī nityayukta*
*ekabhaktir viśiṣyate*
*priyo hi jñānino'tyartham-*
*ahaṁ sa ca mama priyaḥ*

(17) Of these, the man of wisdom, who is ever united with Me in yoga, through single minded-devotion, is the foremost. I am extremely dear to the man of wisdom and he too is very dear to Me.

उदाराः सर्व एवैते ज्ञानी त्वात्मैव मे मतम्।
आस्थितः स हि युक्तात्मा मामेवानुत्तमां गतिम्॥ १८॥

*udārāḥ sarva evaite*
*jñānī tvātmaiva me matam*
*āsthitaḥ sa hi yuktātmā*
*māmevānuttamāṁ gatim*

(18) All these are noble indeed, but the man of wisdom I regard to be My very Self; for he is steadfast, ever united in the Self, and has resorted to Me alone as the Supreme goal.

बहूनां जन्मनामन्ते ज्ञानवान्मां प्रपद्यते।
वासुदेवः सर्वमिति स महात्मा सुदुर्लभः ॥ १९ ॥

*bahūnāṁ janmanām ante*
*jñānavān māṁ prapadyate*
*vāsudevaḥ sarvamiti*
*sa mahātmā sudurlabhaḥ*

(19) At the end of many births, the man of wisdom seeks refuge in Me alone, realizing that 'Vasudeva is all.' It is indeed very difficult to find such a great soul (Mahatma).

कामैस्तैस्तैर्हृतज्ञानाः प्रपद्यन्तेऽन्यदेवताः।
तं तं नियममास्थाय प्रकृत्या नियताः स्वया॥ २० ॥

*kāmais tais-tair hṛtajñānāḥ*
*prapadyante 'nyadevatāḥ*
*taṁ-taṁ niyamamāsthāya*
*prakṛtyā niyatāḥ svayā*

(20) Those whose wisdom has been distorted by desires, resort to other gods, observing this or that rite; swayed by their own inherent nature.

यो यो यां यां तनुं भक्तः श्रद्धयार्चितुमिच्छति।
तस्य तस्याचलां श्रद्धां तामेव विदधाम्यहम्॥ २१॥

*yo-yo yāṁ-yāṁ tanuṁ bhaktaḥ*
*śraddhayārcitumicchati*
*tasya-tasyācalāṁ śraddhāṁ*
*tāmeva vidadhāmyaham*

(21) Whatever form a devotee seeks to worship with faith—I make his faith in that firm and unflinching.

स तया श्रद्धया युक्तस्तस्याराधनमीहते।
लभते च ततः कामान्मयैव विहितान्हि तान्॥ २२॥

*sa tayā śraddhayā yuktas*
*tasyā'rādhanamīhate*
*labhate ca tataḥ kāmān*
*mayaiva vihitānhi tān*

(22) Endowed with steadfast faith, he engages in the worship of that form and obtains the objects of his desire, verily granted in reality by Me alone.

अन्तवत्तु फलं तेषां तद्भवत्यल्पमेधसाम्।
देवान्देवयजो यान्ति मद्भक्ता यान्ति मामपि॥ २३॥

*antavattu phalaṁ teṣāṁ*

*tad bhavaty alpamedhasām*

*devān devāyajo yānti*

*madbhaktā yānti māmapi*

(23) The rewards attained by these people of limited understanding are temporary. The worshippers of gods go to gods, but My devotees come to Me.

अव्यक्तं व्यक्तिमापन्नं मन्यन्ते मामबुद्धयः।

परं भावमजानन्तो ममाव्ययमनुत्तमम्॥ २४॥

*avyaktaṁ vyaktimāpannaṁ*

*manyante māmabuddhayaḥ*

*param bhavamajānanto*

*mamāvyayamanuttamam*

(24) The ignorant regard Me, the unmanifest, as having manifestation, they do not know My Supreme Nature, which is unchanging and unsurpassed.

नाहं प्रकाशः सर्वस्य योगमायासमावृतः।

मूढोऽयं नाभिजानाति लोको मामजमव्ययम्॥ २५॥

*nāhaṁ prakāśaḥ sarvasya*
*yogamāyāsamāvṛtaḥ*
*mūḍho'yaṁ nābhijānāti*
*loko mām ajamavyayam*

(25) I am not revealed to all, veiled by My Yoga-Maya (divine potency). The deluded ones in this world, do not recognize Me as the unborn and the imperishable Supreme spirit.

वेदाहं समतीतानि वर्तमानानि चार्जुन।
भविष्याणि च भूतानि मां तु वेद न कश्चन॥ २६ ॥

*vedāhaṁ samatītāni*
*vartamānāni cā'rjuna*
*bhaviṣyāṇi ca bhūtāni*
*māṁ tu veda na kaścana*

(26) I know all the beings of the past, the present, O'Arjuna and even the future, but no one knows Me.

इच्छाद्वेषसमुत्थेन द्वन्द्वमोहेन भारत।
सर्वभूतानि सम्मोहं सर्गे यान्ति परन्तप॥ २७ ॥

*icchādveṣasamutthena*
*dvandvamohena bhārata*
*sarvabhūtāni saṁmohaṁ*
*sarge yānti parantapa*

(27) Through the delusion of the pairs of opposites, arising from desire and aversion, O'Arjuna, all the creatures become subject to delusion at birth, O'Parantapa.

येषां त्वन्तगतं पापं जनानां पुण्यकर्मणाम्।
ते द्वन्द्वमोहनिर्मुक्ता भजन्ते मां दृढव्रताः ॥ २८ ॥

*yeṣāṁ tvantagataṁ pāpaṁ*
*jnānāṁ puṇyakarmaṇām*
*te dvandvamohanirmuktā*
*bhajante māṁ dṛḍhavratāḥ*

(28) But the men of virtuous deeds, whose sins have come to an end, those are liberated from the delusion of the pairs of opposites, they worship Me, with firm resolve.

जरामरणमोक्षाय मामाश्रित्य यतन्ति ये।
ते ब्रह्म तद्विदुः कृत्स्नमध्यात्मं कर्म चाखिलम् ॥ २९ ॥

*jarāmaraṇamokṣāya*
*māmāśritya yatanti ye*
*te brahma tadviduḥ kṛtsnam-*
*adhyātmaṁ karma cākhilam*

(29) Those who take refuge in Me and strive for deliverance from old age and death, they know all about the absolute Brahman, the Self and the entire field of actions.

साधिभूताधिदैवं मां साधियज्ञं च ये विदुः ।
प्रयाणकालेऽपि च मां ते विदुर्युक्तचेतसः ॥ ३० ॥

*sādhibhūtādhidaivaṁ māṁ*
*sadhiyajnaṁ ca ye viduḥ*
*prayāṇakāle'pi ca māṁ*
*te vidur yuktacetasaḥ*

(30) Those who realize Me within the Adhibuta, in the Adhidaiva and in the Adhiyajña, also realize Me at the time of death with their minds united in Yoga.

ॐ तत्सदिति श्रीमद्भगवद्गीतासूपनिषत्सु
ब्रह्मविद्यायां योगशास्त्रे श्रीकृष्णार्जुनसंवादे
ज्ञानविज्ञानयोगो नाम सप्तमोऽध्यायः ॥ ७ ॥

***'Aum' tatsaditi Srīmadbhagawadgeetasupanisatsu brahmavidyayam yogasastre Srīkṛṣṇarjunasamvade jñanavijñanayogo nama saptamodhyayah.***

'AUM TAT SAT'—Thus, in the Upanishad of the glorious Bhagawad Geeta, the science of the Brahman (Absolute) the scripture of yoga, the dialogue between Srī Kṛṣṇa and Arjuna—thus, ends the chapter seven entitled *"Jñanavijñanayoga"*.

इति श्रीमद्भगवद्गीतासु सप्तमोऽध्यायः ॥७॥

# *Chapter Eight*

# AKṢARABRAHMAYOGA

## THE YOGA OF THE IMPERISHABLE BRAHMAN

अर्जुन उवाच

किं तद् ब्रह्म किमध्यात्मं किं कर्म पुरुषोत्तम ।
अधिभूतं च किं प्रोक्तमधिदैवं किमुच्यते ॥ १ ॥

*kiṁ tad brahma kim adhyātmaṁ*
*kiṁ karma puroṣottama*
*adhibhūtaṁ ca kiṁ proktam*
*adhidaivaṁ kim ucyate*

**Arjuna Said :**

(1) What is Brahman? What is *adhyatma*? What is action? O'Supreme person. What is called *adhibuta*? And what is said to be *adhidaiva*?

अधियज्ञः कथं कोऽत्र देहेऽस्मिन्मधुसूदन ।
प्रयाणकाले च कथं ज्ञेयोऽसि नियतात्मभिः ॥ २ ॥

*adhiyajñaḥ kathaṁ ko'tra*
*dehe'smin madhusūdana*
*prayāṇakāle ca kathaṁ*
*jñeyo'si niyatātmabhiḥ*

(2) Who and how is Adhiyajña here in this body, O'Kṛṣṇa? And how You are to be realized at the time of death by the self-controlled?

श्रीभगवानुवाच

अक्षरं ब्रह्म परमं स्वभावोऽध्यात्ममुच्यते।
भूतभावोद्भवकरो विसर्गः कर्मसंज्ञितः ॥ ३ ॥

*akṣaraṁ brahma paramaṁ*
*svabhāvo'dhyātmamucyate*
*bhūtabhāvodbhavakaro*
*visargaḥ karmasaṁjñitaḥ*

**The Blessed Lord said :**

(3) The Supreme imperishable is Brahman; Its essential nature is known as *adhyatma.* The creative force which brings forth the existence of beings is called Karma (action).

अधिभूतं क्षरो भावः पुरुषश्चाधिदैवतम्।
अधियज्ञोऽहमेवात्र देहे देहभृतां वर ॥ ४ ॥

*adhibhūtaṁ kṣaro bhāvaḥ*

*puruṣaś cādhidaivatam*

*adhiyajño'ham evātra*

*dehe dehabhṛtāṁ vara*

(4) *Adhibuta* pertains to My perishable nature; and the conscious principle Purusha is the *adhidaiva.* I am the *adhiyajña* here in this body, O' Arjuna.

अन्तकाले च मामेव स्मरन्मुक्त्वा कलेवरम्।

यः प्रयाति स मद्भावं याति नास्त्यत्र संशयः ॥५॥

*antakāle ca māmeva*

*smaran muktvā kalevaram*

*yaḥ prayāti sa madbhāvaṁ*

*yāti nāstyatra saṅśayaḥ*

(5) At the time of death, he who departs from the body thinking of Me alone, he attains to My essential nature, there is no doubt of this.

यं यं वापि स्मरन्भावं त्यजत्यन्ते कलेवरम्।

तं तमेवैति कौन्तेय सदा तद्भावभावितः ॥६॥

*yaṁ-yaṁ vāpi smaran bhāvaṁ*

*tyajatyante kalevaram*

*taṁ-tamevaiti kaunteya*
*sadā tadbhāvabhāvitaḥ*

(6) Whatever a person thinks at the time of his death while leaving his body, to that only he goes, O' Kaunteya, because of his being constantly absorbed in that thought.

**तस्मात्सर्वेषु कालेषु मामनुस्मर युध्य च।**
**मय्यर्पितमनोबुद्धिर्मामेवैष्यस्यसंशयम्॥ ७॥**

*tasmāt sarveṣu kāleṣu*
*māmanusmara yudhya ca*
*mayyarpitamanobuddhir*
*māmevaiṣyasyasaṅśayam*

(7) Therefore at all times, think of Me alone and fight the battle. With your mind and intellect thus fixed on Me, Thou shall surely come to Me alone.

**अभ्यासयोगयुक्तेन चेतसा नान्यगामिना।**
**परमं पुरुषं दिव्यं याति पार्थानुचिन्तयन्॥ ८॥**

*abhyāsayogayuktena*
*cetasā nānyagāminā*
*paramaṁ puruṣaṁ divyaṁ*
*yāti pārthānucintayan*

(8) He who is established in the yogic meditation through constant practice, and does not let his mind wander after anything else, he surely attains the Supreme resplendent Divine Purusha, O' Arjuna.

कविं पुराणमनुशासितार-
मणोरणीयांसमनुस्मरेद्यः।
सर्वस्य धातारमचिन्त्यरूप-
मादित्यवर्णं तमसः परस्तात्॥ ९॥

*kaviṁ purāṇamanuśāsitāra-*
*maṇoraṇīyānsamanusmared yaḥ*
*sarvasya dhātāramacintyarūpa*
*mādityavarṇaṁ tamasaḥ parastāt*

(9) He, who contemplates on the Omniscient, the Primordial, the Ruler, subtler than an atom, the sustainer of all, the inconceivable, effulgent like the sun and beyond the darkness of ignorance.

प्रयाणकाले मनसाऽचलेन,
भक्त्या युक्तो योगबलेन चैव।
भ्रुवोर्मध्ये प्राणमावेश्य सम्यक्,
स तं परं पुरुषमुपैति दिव्यम्॥ १०॥

*prayāṇkāle manasā'calena*

*bhaktyā yukto yogabalena caiva*

*bhruvormadhye prāṇamāveśya samyak*

*sa taṁ paraṁ puruṣamupaiti divyam*

(10) At the time of death with a steadfast mind, endowed with devotion and the power of Yoga, who can firmly hold the life-breath in the middle of the two eyebrows, he surely reaches that resplendent supreme purusha.

यदक्षरं वेदविदो वदन्ति,

विशन्ति यद्यतयो वीतरागाः ।

यदिच्छन्तो ब्रह्मचर्यं चरन्ति,

तत्ते पदं संग्रहेण प्रवक्ष्ये ॥ ११ ॥

*yad akṣaraṁ vedavido vadanti*

*viśanti yad yatayo vītarāgaḥ*

*yad icchanto brahmacaryaṁ caranti*

*tatte padaṁ saṅgraheṇa pravakṣye*

(11) That state which the knowers of Vedas call eternal, where in the ascetics enter, being free from attachment and desiring which they

practise continence—that goal I must declare to you briefly.

सर्वद्वाराणि संयम्य मनो हृदि निरुध्य च।
मूर्ध्न्याधायात्मनः प्राणमास्थितो योगधारणाम्॥ १२॥

*sarvadvārāṇi saṁyamya*
*mano hṛdi nirudhya ca*
*mūrdhanyādhāyātmanaḥ prāṇa-*
*māsthito yogadhāraṇām*

ओमित्येकाक्षरं ब्रह्म व्याहरन्मामनुस्मरन्।
यः प्रयाति त्यजन्देहं स याति परमां गतिम्॥ १३॥

*omityekākṣaraṁ brahma*
*vyāharan mām anusmaran*
*yaḥ prayāti tyajan dehaṁ*
*sa yāti paramāṁ gatim*

(12, 13) Having closed all the doors of senses and firmly restoring the mind in the heart and the life-breath in the crown of the head; established in the yogic concentration he who utters the single syllable AUM the Supreme Brahman and remembers Me while departing from his body, he certainly attains the Supreme Goal.

अनन्यचेताः सततं यो मां स्मरति नित्यशः।
तस्याहं सुलभः पार्थ नित्ययुक्तस्य योगिनः॥ १४॥

*ananyacetāḥ satataṁ*
*yo māṁ smarati nityaśaḥ*
*tasyā'haṁ sulabhaḥ pārtha*
*nityayuktasya yoginaḥ*

(14) He who constantly remembers Me with undivided attention, to him I am easily attainable, O'Partha, since he is ever united in Yoga.

मामुपेत्य पुनर्जन्म दुःखालयमशाश्वतम्।
नाप्नुवन्ति महात्मानः संसिद्धिं परमां गताः॥ १५॥

*mām upetya punarjanma*
*duḥkhālayamaśāśvatam*
*nāpnuvanti mahātmānaḥ*
*saṁsiddhiṁ paramāṁ gatāḥ*

(15) Having come to Me, these great souls are not born again (here) which is the abode of sorrow and is transitory, for they have reached the highest perfection.

आब्रह्मभुवनाल्लोकाः पुनरावर्तिनोऽर्जुन।
मामुपेत्य तु कौन्तेय पुनर्जन्म न विद्यते॥ १६ ॥

*ābrahmabhuvanāllokāḥ*
*punarāvartino'rjuna*
*māmupetya tu kaunteya*
*punarjanma na vidyate*

(16) From the realm of the Supreme creator, all the worlds are subject to return again and again, O' Arjuna. But having attained Me, O' son of Kunti, there is no rebirth.

सहस्रयुगपर्यन्तमहर्यद्ब्रह्मणो विदुः।
रात्रिं युगसहस्रान्तां तेऽहोरात्रविदो जनाः॥ १७ ॥

*sahasrayugaparyantam-*
*aharyad brahmaṇo viduḥ*
*rātriṁ yugasahasrāntāṁ*
*te'horātravido janāḥ*

(17) Those who know that the day of Brahma extends to a thousand epochs (yugas) and also the night extends to a thousand epochs, they are the knowers of the day and night (reality about time).

अव्यक्ताद्व्यक्तयः सर्वाः प्रभवन्त्यहरागमे।
रात्र्यागमे प्रलीयन्ते तत्रैवाव्यक्तसंज्ञके॥ १८॥

*avyaktād vyaktayaḥ sarvāḥ*
*prabhavanty aharāgame*
*rātryāgame pralīyante*
*tatraivāvyaktasañjñake*

(18) From the unmanifested, all the manifestations emerge at the commencement of the Brahma's day; at the coming of the night, they merge verily into that alone, which is called unmanifested.

भूतग्रामः स एवायं भूत्वा भूत्वा प्रलीयते।
रात्र्यागमेऽवशः पार्थ प्रभवत्यहरागमे॥ १९॥

*bhūtagrāmaḥ sa evāyaṁ*
*bhūtvā-bhūtvā pralīyate*
*rātryāgame'vaśaḥ pārtha*
*prabhavatyaharāgame*

(19) The multitude of beings, being born again and again, are dissolved helplessly at the coming of the night, O' Partha. It comes forth again at the beginning of the day.

परस्तस्मात्तु भावोऽन्योऽव्यक्तोऽव्यक्तात्सनातनः।
यः स सर्वेषु भूतेषु नश्यत्सु न विनश्यति॥ २०॥

*parastasmāttu bhāvo'nyo-*
*'vyakto'vyaktāt sanātanaḥ*
*yaḥ sa sarveṣu bhūteṣu*
*naśyatsu na vinaśyati*

(20) Beyond this unmanifested, verily there is another unmanifested, Eternal, which does not perish even when all existence perish.

अव्यक्तोऽक्षर इत्युक्तस्तमाहुः परमां गतिम्।
यं प्राप्य न निवर्तन्ते तद्धाम परमं मम॥ २१॥

*avyakto'kṣara ityuktas-*
*tamāhuḥ paramāṁ gatim*
*yaṁ prāpya na nivartante*
*taddhāma paramaṁ mama*

(21) This Unmanifested and Imperishable is said to be the highest goal, upon attaining which, there is no return. That is My Supreme Abode.

पुरुषः स परः पार्थ भक्त्या लभ्यस्त्वनन्यया।
यस्यान्तःस्थानि भूतानि येन सर्वमिदं ततम्॥ २२॥

*puruṣaḥ sa paraḥ pārtha*
*bhaktyā labhyastvananyayā*
*yasyāntaḥsthāni bhūtāni*
*yena sarvamidaṁ tatam*

(22) That Supreme transcendent Purusha, O'Arjuna, is attainable by undivided devotion; within whom all the beings reside and by whom all this is pervaded.

**यत्र काले त्वनावृत्तिमावृत्तिं चैव योगिनः ।**
**प्रयाता यान्ति तं कालं वक्ष्यामि भरतर्षभ ॥ २३ ॥**

*yatra kāle tvanāvṛttim-*
*āvṛttiṁ caiva yoginaḥ*
*prayātā yānti taṁ kālaṁ*
*vakṣyāmi bharatarṣabha*

(23) The time in which the yogis do not return after they depart and also the time when they do return again, of that, I shall tell you, O' best of the Bharatas (Arjuna).

**अग्निर्ज्योतिरहः शुक्लः षण्मासा उत्तरायणम् ।**
**तत्र प्रयाता गच्छन्ति ब्रह्म ब्रह्मविदो जनाः ॥ २४ ॥**

*agnir jyotirahaḥ śuklaḥ*
*ṣaṇmāsā uttrāyaṇam*

*tatra prayātā gacchanti*
*brahma brahmavido janāḥ*

(24) Fire, light, the day time, the moonlit fortnight, the six months of the sun's northern course—departing in that time; the men who know Brahman go to Brahman.

धूमो रात्रिस्तथा कृष्णः षण्मासा दक्षिणायनम्।
तत्र चान्द्रमसं ज्योतिर्योगी प्राप्य निवर्तते ॥ २५ ॥

*dhūmo rātristathā kṛṣṇaḥ*
*ṣaṇmāsā dakṣināyanam*
*tatra cāndramasaṁ jyotir-*
*yogī prāpya nivartate*

(25) Smoke, the night time, the dark lunar fortnight, the six months of the sun's southern course—having obtained the lunar light, the yogi returns (to the world of mortals).

शुक्लकृष्णे गती ह्येते जगतः शाश्वते मते।
एकया यात्यनावृत्तिमन्ययावर्तते पुनः ॥ २६ ॥

*śuklakṛṣṇe gatī hyete*
*jagataḥ śāśvate mate*
*ekayā yāty anāvṛtti*
*manyayā'vartate punaḥ*

(26) The bright and the dark paths of the world are verily thought to be perennial. By the one a person leaves not to return, while by the other he returns again.

**नैते सृती पार्थ जानन्योगी मुह्यति कश्चन।**

**तस्मात्सर्वेषु कालेषु योगयुक्तो भवार्जुन॥ २७॥**

*naite sṛtī pārtha jānan*
*yogī muhyati kaścana*
*tasmāt sarveṣu kāleṣu*
*yogayukto bhavārjuna*

(27) Knowing these two paths, O'Arjuna, the yogi is not deluded. Therefore, at all times, stay united in Yoga, O'Arjuna.

**वेदेषु यज्ञेषु तपःसु चैव**
**दानेषु यत्पुण्यफलं प्रदिष्टम्।**
**अत्येति तत्सर्वमिदं विदित्वा**
**योगी परं स्थानमुपैति चाद्यम्॥ २८॥**

*vedeṣu yajñeṣu tapaḥsu caiva*
*dāneṣu yat puṇyaphalaṁ pradiṣṭam*
*atyeti tat sarvamidaṁ viditvā*
*yogī paraṁ sthānamupaiti cādyam*

(28) The yogi, who realizes this profound truth, he transcends all the rewards of the meritorious deeds attached to the study of the Vedas, performance of sacrifices, austerities, and charities—he attains the Supreme primal status.

ॐ तत्सदिति श्रीमद्भगवद्गीतासूपनिषत्सु ब्रह्मविद्यायां योगशास्त्रे श्रीकृष्णार्जुनसंवादे अक्षरब्रह्मयोगो नाम अष्टमोऽध्यायः ॥ ८ ॥

***Aum tatsaditi Srīmadbhagawadgeeta supanisatsu brahmavidyayam yogasastre Srīkṛṣṇarjunasamvade aksarabrahmayogo nama astmodhyayah***

**'AUM TAT SAT'**—Thus, in the Upanishad of the glorious Bhagawad Geeta, the science of the Brahman (Absolute) the scripture of yoga, the dialogue between Srī Kṛṣṇa and Arjuna—thus, ends the chapter eight entitled "Aksarabrahmayoga".

इति श्रीमद्भगवद्गीतासु अष्टमोऽध्यायः ॥ ८ ॥

## *Chapter Nine*

# RAJAVIDYA RAJAGUHYAYOGA

## THE YOGA OF THE SOVEREIGN SCIENCE AND SOVEREIGN SECRET

श्रीभगवानुवाच

इदं तु ते गुह्यतमं प्रवक्ष्याम्यनसूयवे।

ज्ञानं विज्ञानसहितं यज्ज्ञात्वा मोक्ष्यसेऽशुभात्॥ १ ॥

*idaṁ tu te guhyatamaṁ*

*pravakṣyāmy anasūyave*

*jñānaṁ vijñānasahitaṁ*

*yajjñātvā mokṣyase'śubhāt*

**The Blessed Lord said :**

(1) To thee, who does not cavil, I shall now unfold the most profound secret of wisdom combined with the experiential knowledge, by knowing which you will be released from evil.

राजविद्या राजगुह्यं पवित्रमिदमुत्तमम्।
प्रत्यक्षावगमं धर्म्यं सुसुखं कर्तुमव्ययम्॥ २ ॥

*rājavidyā rājaguhyaṁ*
*pavitramidamuttamam*
*pratyakṣāvagamaṁ dharmyaṁ*
*susukhaṁ kartumavyayam*

(2) This is the sovereign wisdom, the sovereign mystery, the most purifying excellent and easy to comprehend by direct experience. It is in accordance with the Dharma (righteousness) and renders happiness. It is easy to accomplish and imperishable.

अश्रद्दधानाः पुरुषा धर्मस्यास्य परन्तप।
अप्राप्य मां निवर्तन्ते मृत्युसंसारवर्त्मनि॥ ३ ॥

*aśraddadhānāḥ puruṣā*
*dharmasyā'sya parantapa*
*aprāpya māṁ nivartante*
*mṛtyusaṁsārvartmani*

(3) Persons lacking faith and reverence in the sacred doctrine (Dharma) O' Arjuna, fail to attain Me.

They revolve in the path of the world of death.

**मया ततमिदं सर्वं जगदव्यक्तमूर्तिना।**

**मत्स्थानि सर्वभूतानि न चाहं तेष्ववस्थितः ॥ ४ ॥**

*mayā tatamidaṁ sarvaṁ*

*jagadavyaktamūrtinā*

*matsthāni sarvabhūtāni*

*na cāhaṁ teṣvavasthitaḥ*

(4) This whole universe is pervaded by Me, in My unmanifest aspect. All the beings exist in Me, but I do not dwell in them.

**न च मत्स्थानि भूतानि पश्य मे योगमैश्वरम्।**

**भूतभृन्न च भूतस्थो ममात्मा भूतभावनः ॥ ५ ॥**

*na ca matsthāni bhūtāni*

*paśya me yogamaiśvaram*

*bhutabhṛanna ca bhūtastho*

*mamātmā bhūtabhāvanaḥ*

(5) Nor do the beings exist in Me; behold My divine Yoga! I Myself am the creator and sustainer of all beings, yet I do not dwell in them.

यथाकाशस्थितो नित्यं वायुः सर्वत्रगो महान्।
तथा सर्वाणि भूतानि मत्स्थानीत्युपधारय॥ ६ ॥

*yathākāśasthito nityam*
*vāyuḥ sarvatrago mahān*
*tathā sarvāni bhūtāni*
*matsthānītyupadhāraya*

(6) As the mighty wind, always rests in the ether, while it moves everywhere; likewise know thou, that all created beings rest in Me.

सर्वभूतानि कौन्तेय प्रकृतिं यान्ति मामिकाम्।
कल्पक्षये पुनस्तानि कल्पादौ विसृजाम्यहम्॥ ७ ॥

*sarvabhūtāni kaunteya*
*prakṛtiṁ yānti māmikām*
*kalpakṣaye punastāni*
*kalpādau visṛjāmyaham*

(7) All beings, O' Kaunteya (Arjuna), go into My Nature, at the end of each *kalpa* and again at the beginning of the next *kalpa*, I send them forth again.

प्रकृतिं स्वामवष्टभ्य विसृजामि पुनः पुनः ।
भूतग्राममिमं कृत्स्नमवशं प्रकृतेर्वशात् ॥ ८ ॥

*prakṛtiṁ svamavaṣṭabhya*

*visṛjāmi punaḥ-punaḥ*

*bhūtagrāmamimaṁ kṛtsnam*

*avaśaṁ prakṛter vaśāt*

(8) Having hold on My nature, I send forth again and again the multitude of beings, subject to the helplessness of their own nature.

न च मां तानि कर्माणि निबध्नन्ति धनञ्जय ।
उदासीनवदासीनमसक्तं तेषु कर्मसु ॥ ९ ॥

*na ca māṁ tāni karmāṇi*

*nibadhnanti dhanañjaya*

*udāsīnavadāsīnam-*

*asaktaṁ teṣu karmasu*

(9) These actions do not bind Me, O'Dhananjaya (Arjuna), for I remain seated like the one unconcerned and unattached in those actions.

मयाध्यक्षेण प्रकृतिः सूयते सचराचरम् ।
हेतुनानेन कौन्तेय जगद्विपरिवर्तते ॥ १० ॥

*mayādhyakṣeṇa prakṛtiḥ*
*sūyate sacarācaram*
*hetunānena kaunteya*
*jagad viparivartate*

(10) Under My supervision, Nature gives birth to all, the moving and the unmoving—by this means O' Kaunteya (Arjuna) the world revolves.

अवजानन्ति मां मूढा मानुषीं तनुमाश्रितम्।
परं भावमजानन्तो मम भूतमहेश्वरम्॥ ११॥

*avajānanti māṁ mūḍhā*
*mānuṣīṁ tanumāśritam*
*paraṁ bhāvamajānanto*
*mama bhūtamaheśvaram*

मोघाशा मोघकर्माणो मोघज्ञाना विचेतसः।
राक्षसीमासुरीं चैव प्रकृतिं मोहिनीं श्रिताः॥ १२॥

*moghāśā moghakarmāṇo*
*moghajñānā vicetasaḥ*
*rākṣasīmāsurīṁ caiva*
*prakṛtiṁ mohinīṁ śritāḥ*

(11,12) The fools disregard Me, dwelling in human form. They do not know My transcendental nature, as the great Lord of all beings. With vain hopes, vain actions, and with vain knowledge they senselessly become possessed of the deceitful nature of demons and monsters.

**महात्मानस्तु मां पार्थ दैवीं प्रकृतिमाश्रिताः ।**

**भजन्त्यनन्यमनसो ज्ञात्वा भूतादिमव्ययम् ॥ १३ ॥**

*mahātmānastu māṁ pārtha*
*daivīṁ prakṛtim āśritāḥ*
*bhajantyananyamanaso*
*jñātvā bhūtādimavyayam*

(13) But the great souls, O' Partha (Arjuna), resorting to the divine nature, devote themselves to Me, with undistracted mind; knowing Me as the source of entire creation and imperishable.

**सततं कीर्तयन्तो मां यतन्तश्च दृढव्रताः ।**

**नमस्यन्तश्च मां भक्त्या नित्ययुक्ता उपासते ॥ १४ ॥**

*satataṁ kīrtayanto māṁ*
*yatantaś ca dṛḍhavratāḥ*
*namasyantaś ca māṁ bhaktyā*
*nityayuktā upāsate*

(14) Always singing My glories and endeavouring with determined vows, prostrating before Me with love and humility, they worship Me with steadfast devotion.

ज्ञानयज्ञेन चाप्यन्ये यजन्तो मामुपासते।
एकत्वेन पृथक्त्वेन बहुधा विश्वतोमुखम्॥ १५॥

*jñānayajñena cāpyanye*
*yajanto māmupāsate*
*ekatvena pṛthaktvena*
*bahudhā viśvatomukham*

(15) Others worship Me through their offerings of integral knowledge, as the One, as distinct and as manifold; facing in all directions.

अहं क्रतुरहं यज्ञः स्वधाहमहमौषधम्।
मन्त्रोऽहमहमेवाज्यमहमग्निरहं हुतम्॥ १६॥

*ahaṁ kraturahaṁ yajñaḥ*
*svadhāhamahamauṣadham*
*mantro'ham ahamevājyam*
*ahamagniraham̐ hutam*

(16) I am the Vaidika ritual and also the yajña, I am the offering given

to ancestors, I am the medicinal herb of oblation. I am the sacred hymn, I am the clarified butter, I am the fire, I am the act of offering the oblation.

पिताहमस्य जगतो माता धाता पितामहः।
वेद्यं पवित्रमोङ्कार ऋक्साम यजुरेव च॥ १७॥

*pitāhamasya jagato*
*mātā dhātā pitāmahaḥ*
*vedyaṁ pavitramoṅkāra*
*ṛksāma yajureva ca*

गतिर्भर्ता प्रभुः साक्षी निवासः शरणं सुहृत्।
प्रभवः प्रलयः स्थानं निधानं बीजमव्ययम्॥ १८॥

*gatir bhartā prabhuḥ sākṣī*
*nivāsaḥ śaraṇaṁ suhṛt*
*prabhavaḥ pralayaḥ sthānaṁ*
*nidhānaṁ bījamavyayam*

(17,18) I am the Father of this world and also the Mother, the sustainer and the Grandfather. I am the object of sacred knowledge, I am the purifier and the sacred syllable 'Aum.' I am *Rigveda, Samveda* and also the *Yajurveda.* I am the goal, the supporter, the Lord, the witness, the abode, the refuge, and the well-wisher. I am the origin and the dissolution, the resting place, the store-house and the imperishable seed of the universe.

तपाम्यहमहं वर्षं निगृह्णाम्युत्सृजामि च।
अमृतं चैव मृत्युश्च सदसच्चाहमर्जुन॥ १९॥

*tapāmyahamaham varṣam*
*nigṛhṇāmyutsṛjāmi ca*
*amṛtam caiva mṛtyuś ca*
*sadasaccāhmarjuna*

(19) I radiate heat, I withhold and send forth the rain, I am immortality as well as death, I am being as well as non-being, O'Arjuna (existence and non-existence).

त्रैविद्या मां सोमपाः पूतपापा,
यज्ञैरिष्ट्वा स्वर्गतिं प्रार्थयन्ते।
ते पुण्यमासाद्य सुरेन्द्रलोक-
मश्नन्ति दिव्यान्दिवि देवभोगान्॥ २०॥

*traividyā mām somapāḥ pūtapāpā*
*yajñairiṣṭvā svargatim prārthayante*

*te puṇyāmāsādya surendrālokam*
*aśnanti divyān divi devabhogān*

(20) The knowers of the three *Vedas*, who partake *soma* and are purified of all sins, who perform yajña seeking to reach the heaven; they surely obtain the holy world of the Lord of gods, and enjoy the celestial pleasures of the gods.

ते तं भुक्त्वा स्वर्गलोकं विशालं,
क्षीणे पुण्ये मर्त्यलोकं विशन्ति।
एवं त्रयीधर्ममनुप्रपन्ना,
गतागतं कामकामा लभन्ते ॥ २१ ॥

*te taṁ bhuktvā svargalokaṁ viśālaṁ*
*kṣīṇe puṇye martyalokaṁ viśanti*
*evaṁ trayīdharmamanuprapannā*
*gatāgataṁ kāmakāmā labhante*

(21) Having enjoyed the extensive heavenly world, they enter again into the world of mortals upon the exhaustion of their virtuous deeds. Thus confirming to the doctrine enjoined in the three *Vedas* and desirous of worldly enjoyments, they repeatedly come and go.

अनन्याश्चिन्तयन्तो मां ये जनाः पर्युपासते।
तेषां नित्याभियुक्तानां योगक्षेमं वहाम्यहम्॥ २२ ॥

*ananyāścintayanto māṁ*
*ye janaḥ paryupāsate*
*teṣāṁ nityābhiyuktānāṁ*
*yogakṣemaṁ vahāmyaham*

(22) The men who worship Me alone with undivided devotion, to those ever united in thought with Me, I bring full security and personally attend to their needs.

येऽप्यन्यदेवताभक्ता यजन्ते श्रद्धयान्विताः।
तेऽपि मामेव कौन्तेय यजन्त्यविधिपूर्वकम्॥ २३ ॥

*ye'pyanyadevatābhaktā*
*yajante śraddhāyanvitāḥ*
*te'pi māmeva kaunteya*
*yajantyavidhipūrvakam*

(23) Even those who are the devotees of other gods and worship them with faithful reverence, even they O' Kaunteya, worship Me alone in essence, though not in accordance with the right approach.

अहं हि सर्वयज्ञानां भोक्ता च प्रभुरेव च।
न तु मामभिजानन्ति तत्त्वेनातश्च्यवन्ति ते॥ २४॥

*ahaṁ hi sarvayajñānāṁ*
*bhoktā ca prabhureva ca*
*na tu mām abhijānanti*
*tattvenātaścyavanti te*

(24) I alone am the receiver of all offerings and I alone am the Lord; but they do not know Me in essence, hence they fall.

यान्ति देवव्रता देवान्पितॄन्यान्ति पितृव्रताः।
भूतानि यान्ति भूतेज्या यान्ति मद्याजिनोऽपि माम्॥ २५॥

*yānti devavratā devān*
*pitṝn yānti pitṛvratāḥ*
*bhūtāni yānti bhūtejyā*
*yānti madyājino'pi mām*

(25) The worshippers of gods go to the gods, the worshippers of manes reach the manes and of the evil spirits (Bhuta) go to the evil spirits. Those who worship Me alone, they surely come to Me.

पत्रं पुष्पं फलं तोयं यो मे भक्त्या प्रयच्छति।
तदहं भक्त्युपहृतमश्नामि प्रयतात्मनः॥ २६॥

*patraṁ puṣpaṁ phalaṁ toyaṁ*
*yo me bhaktyā prayacchati*
*tadahaṁ bhaktyupahṛtam-*
*aśnāmi prayatātmanaḥ*

(26) A leaf, flower, fruit, water; whoever offers Me with loving devotion, I accept the pious offering of the pure minded with great joy.

यत्करोषि यदश्नासि यज्जुहोषि ददासि यत्।
यत्तपस्यसि कौन्तेय तत्कुरुष्व मदर्पणम्॥ २७॥

*yatkaroṣi yad aśnāsi*
*yajjuhoṣi dadāsi yat*
*yat tapasyasi kaunteya*
*tat kuruṣva madarpaṇam*

(27) Whatever you do, whatever you eat, whatever you offer in sacrifice (yajña), whatever you give as charity, whatever austerity you practice O' Kaunteya—perform that as an offering to Me.

शुभाशुभफलैरेवं मोक्ष्यसे कर्मबन्धनैः।
संन्यासयोगयुक्तात्मा विमुक्तो मामुपैष्यसि॥ २८॥

*śubhāśubhaphalairevaṁ*
*mokṣyase karmabandhanaiḥ*
*sannyāsayogayuktātmā*
*vimukto māmupaiṣyasi*

(28) Thus, you will remain free from the bonds of actions, yielding auspicious and inauspicious results. With the mind ever united in the Self with the Yoga of renunciation, you will be liberated and come to Me.

समोऽहं सर्वभूतेषु न मे द्वेष्योऽस्ति न प्रियः ।
ये भजन्ति तु मां भक्त्या मयि ते तेषु चाप्यहम् ॥ २९ ॥

*samo'haṁ sarvabhūteṣu*
*na me dveṣyo'sti na priyaḥ*
*ye bhajanti tu māṁ bhaktyā*
*mayi te teṣu cāpyaham*

(29) I am alike to all beings; to Me there is none hateful or dear, but those who worship Me with devotion are in Me and I am also in them.

अपि चेत्सुदुराचारो भजते मामनन्यभाक् ।
साधुरेव स मन्तव्यः सम्यग्व्यवसितो हि सः ॥ ३० ॥

*api cetsu durācāro*
*bhajate mām ananyabhāk*

*sādhureva sa mantavyaḥ*
*samyag vyavasito hi saḥ*

(30) Even if the most wicked person worships Me with undivided devotion, he too should be regarded a saint, for he has taken a right resolve.

क्षिप्रं भवति धर्मात्मा शश्वच्छान्तिं निगच्छति।
कौन्तेय प्रति जानीहि न मे भक्तः प्रणश्यति॥ ३१॥

*kṣipraṁ bhavati dharmātmā*
*śaśvacchāntiṁ nigacchati*
*kaunteya pratijānīhi*
*na me bhaktaḥ praṇaśyati*

(31) Soon he becomes virtuous (righteous) and secures lasting peace, O'Kaunteya, know for sure, My devotee does not perish.

मां हि पार्थ व्यपाश्रित्य येऽपि स्युः पापयोनयः।
स्त्रियो वैश्यास्तथा शूद्रास्तेऽपि यान्ति परां गतिम्॥ ३२॥

*māṁ hi pārtha vyapāśritya*
*ye'pi syuḥ pāpayonayaḥ*
*striyo vaiśyās tathā śūdras-*
*te'pi yānti parām gatim*

(32) Seeking refuge in Me O'

Partha, even those who are born of the wombs of sin—as well as the women, merchants and *sudras,* they all attain the Supreme state.

**किं पुनर्ब्राह्मणाः पुण्या भक्ता राजर्षयस्तथा।**
**अनित्यमसुखं लोकमिमं प्राप्य भजस्व माम्॥ ३३॥**

*kiṁ punarbrāhmaṇāḥ puṇyā*
*bhaktā rājarṣayas tathā*
*anityam asukhaṁ lokam*
*imaṁ prāpya bhajasva mām*

(33) How much more then the holy brahmins and the devoted royal sages; therefore, having come to this transitory, sorrowful world, devote yourself in worship to Me.

**मन्मना भव मद्भक्तो मद्याजी मां नमस्कुरु।**
**मामेवैष्यसि युक्त्वैवमात्मानं मत्परायणः॥ ३४॥**

*manmanā bhava madbhakto*
*madyājī māṁ namaskuru*
*māmevaiṣyasi yuktvaivam-*
*ātmānaṁ matparāyaṇaḥ*

(34) Fix your mind on Me, be devoted to Me, adore Me, salute Me in reverence; thus being united in Yoga

with Me and taking Me as your ultimate goal, surely you will come to Me.

ॐ तत्सदिति श्रीमद्भगवद्गीतासूपनिषत्सु ब्रह्मविद्यायां योगशास्त्रे श्रीकृष्णार्जुनसंवादे राजविद्याराजगुह्य-योगो नाम नवमोऽध्यायः ॥ ९ ॥

***Aum tatsaditi Srīmadbhagawadgeeta supanisatsu brahmavidyayam yogasastre Srīkṛṣṇarjunasamvade Rajavidya-rajaguhyayogo nama navamodhyayah***

**'AUM TAT SAT'**—Thus, in the Upanishad of the glorious Bhagawad Geeta, the science of the Brahman (Absolute) the scripture of yoga, the dialogue between Srī Kṛṣṇa and Arjuna—thus, ends the chapter nine entitled *"Rajavidya-Rajaghuyayoga"*

इति श्रीमद्भगवद्गीतासु नवमोऽध्यायः ॥ ९ ॥

# *Chapter Ten*

# VIBHUTIYOGA

## THE YOGA OF THE DIVINE MANIFESTATIONS

श्रीभगवानुवाच

भूय एव महाबाहो शृणु मे परमं वचः ।
यत्तेऽहं प्रीयमाणाय वक्ष्यामि हितकाम्यया ॥ १ ॥

*bhūya eva mahābāho*
*śṛṇu me paramaṁ vacaḥ*
*yatte'haṁ prīyamāṇāya*
*vakṣyāmi hitakāmyayā*

**The Blessed Lord said :**

(1) Once again, O' mighty armed, listen to My Supreme word, since you are very dear to Me, I will speak to you for your welfare.

न मे विदुः सुरगणाः प्रभवं न महर्षयः ।
अहमादिर्हि देवानां महर्षीणां च सर्वशः ॥ २ ॥

*na me viduḥ suragaṇāḥ*
*prabhavaṁ na maharṣayaḥ*
*aham ādir hi devānaṁ*
*maharṣīṇāṁ ca sarvaśaḥ*

(2) Neither the gods, nor the great seers, know about My origin. I am the prime cause of all the gods as well as of the great seers in every way (in all respects).

यो मामजमनादिं च वेत्ति लोकमहेश्वरम्।
असम्मूढः स मर्त्येषु सर्वपापैः प्रमुच्यते॥ ३॥

*yo māmajamanādiṁ ca*
*vetti lokamaheśvaram*
*asammūḍhaḥ sa martyeṣu*
*sarvapāpaiḥ pramucyate*

(3) He who knows Me as unborn, beginningless and as the Supreme Lord of the universe; he is undeluded among the mortals and is liberated from all sins.

बुद्धिर्ज्ञानमसम्मोहः क्षमा सत्यं दमः शमः।
सुखं दुःखं भवोऽभावो भयं चाभयमेव च॥ ४॥

*buddhirjñānamasammohaḥ*
*kṣamā satyaṁ damaḥ śamaḥ*
*sukhaṁ duḥkhaṁ bhavo'bhāvo*
*bhayaṁ cābhayameva ca*

**अहिंसा समता तुष्टिस्तपो दानं यशोऽयशः ।**
**भवन्ति भावा भूतानां मत्त एव पृथग्विधाः ॥ ५ ॥**

*ahinsā samatā tuṣṭis-*
*tapo dānaṁ yaśo'yaśaḥ*
*bhavanti bhāvā bhūtānāṁ*
*matta eva pṛthagvidhāḥ*

(4, 5) Intellect, wisdom, undeludedness, forgiveness, truthfulness, self-restraint, self-control, pleasure and pain, being and non-being, fear and fearlessness, non-violence, equanimity, contentment, austerity, charity honour and ignomy—all these various qualities of the beings originate from Me alone.

**महर्षयः सप्त पूर्वे चत्वारो मनवस्तथा ।**
**मद्भावा मानसा जाता येषां लोक इमाः प्रजाः ॥ ६ ॥**

*maharṣayaḥ sapta pūrve*
*catvāro manāvas tathā*

*madbhāvā mānasā jātā*

*yeṣāṁ loka imāḥ prajāḥ*

(6) The seven great sages, and the more ancient Sanaka etc, and the Manus are possessed of powers like Me and born of My mind; all these creatures in the world have descended from them.

एतां विभूतिं योगं च मम यो वेत्ति तत्त्वतः ।

सोऽविकम्पेन योगेन युज्यते नात्र संशयः ॥ ७ ॥

*etāṁ vibhūtiṁ yogaṁ ca*

*mama yo vetti tattvataḥ*

*so'vikampena yogena*

*yujyate nātra saṅśayaḥ*

(7) He who knows this divine glory and the yogic power of Mine in essence, becomes established in unshakable yogic communion, there is no doubt about it.

अहं सर्वस्य प्रभवो मत्तः सर्वं प्रवर्तते ।

इति मत्वा भजन्ते मां बुधा भावसमन्विताः ॥ ८ ॥

*ahaṁ sarvasya prabhavo*

*mattaḥ sarvaṁ pravartate*

*iti matvā bhajante māṁ*
*budhā bhāvasamanvitāḥ*

(8) I am the source of all, from Me everything proceeds; understanding thus, the men of wisdom worship Me, endowed with devotion.

मच्चित्ता मद्गतप्राणा बोधयन्तः परस्परम्।
कथयन्तश्च मां नित्यं तुष्यन्ति च रमन्ति च॥ ९॥

*maccittā madgataprāṇā*
*bodhayantaḥ parasparam*
*kathayantaśca māṁ nityaṁ*
*tuṣyanti ca ramanti ca*

(9) With their mind absorbed in Me, and their life centred on Me, enlightening each other, always speaking of Me, they ever remain contented and delighted.

तेषां सततयुक्तानां भजतां प्रीतिपूर्वकम्।
ददामि बुद्धियोगं तं येन मामुपयान्ति ते॥ १०॥

*teṣāṁ satatayuktānāṁ*
*bhajatāṁ prītipūrvakam*
*dadāmi buddhiyogaṁ taṁ*
*yena māmupayānti te*

(10) To those who are ever united in devotion, and worship Me with love, I grant that Yoga of integral wisdom by which they attain Me.

तेषामेवानुकम्पार्थमहमज्ञानजं तमः।
नाशयाम्यात्मभावस्थो ज्ञानदीपेन भास्वता॥ ११॥

*teṣāmevānukampārtham-*
*ahamajñānajaṁ tamaḥ*
*nāśayāmyātmabhāvastho*
*jñānadīpena bhāsvatā*

(11) For them, out of mere compassion I dwell in their hearts (self) and destroy the ignorance-born darkness by the luminous lamp of wisdom.

अर्जुन उवाच

परं ब्रह्म परं धाम पवित्रं परमं भवान्।
पुरुषं शाश्वतं दिव्यमादिदेवमजं विभुम्॥ १२॥

*paraṁ brahma paraṁ dhāma*
*pavitraṁ paramaṁ bhavān*
*puruṣaṁ śāśvataṁ divyam-*
*ādidevamajaṁ vibhum*

**Arjuna said :**

(12) Thou are the Supreme Brahman, the Supreme abode, the Supreme purifier, the primordial Divine Purusha, the Primal God, unborn and the omnipresent.

**आहुस्त्वामृषयः सर्वे देवर्षिर्नारदस्तथा।**
**असितो देवलो व्यासः स्वयं चैव ब्रवीषि मे॥ १३॥**

*āhus tvām ṛṣayaḥ sarve*
*devarṣir nāradastathā*
*asito devalo vyāsaḥ*
*svayam caiva bravīṣi me*

(13) All the sages have thus declared of You, as also the celestial sage Narada, so also Asita, Devala and Vyasa, and even You—Yourself are telling this to me.

**सर्वमेतदृतं मन्ये यन्मां वदसि केशव।**
**न हि ते भगवन्व्यक्तिं विदुर्देवा न दानवाः॥ १४॥**

*sarvametad ṛtaṁ manye*
*yanmāṁ vadasi keśava*
*na hi te bhagavanvyaktiṁ*
*vidur devā na dānavāḥ*

(14) I believe all this to be true which You are telling me O' Kesava, neither the gods nor the demons O' Blessed Lord, know your manifestation.

स्वयमेवात्मनात्मानं वेत्थ त्वं पुरुषोत्तम।
भूतभावन भूतेश देवदेव जगत्पते॥ १५॥

*svayamevātmanātmanaṁ*
*vettha tvaṁ puruṣottama*
*bhūtabhāvana bhūteśa*
*devadeva jagatpate*

(15) You alone know Yourself, by Yourself, O' Supreme person, O' source and Lord of beings, O' God of gods, O' master of the universe.

वक्तुमर्हस्यशेषेण दिव्या ह्यात्मविभूतयः।
याभिर्विभूतिभिर्लोकानिमांस्त्वं व्याप्य तिष्ठसि॥ १६॥

*vaktumarhasyaśeṣeṇa*
*divyā hyātmavibhūtayaḥ*
*yābhir vibhūtibhir lokān-*
*imāṅs tvaṁ vyāpya tiṣṭhasi*

(16) Therefore, You alone without reserve, can describe in full

Your Divine manifestations, by which attributes and glories, You remain pervading in these worlds.

कथं विद्यामहं योगिंस्त्वां सदा परिचिन्तयन्।
केषु केषु च भावेषु चिन्त्योऽसि भगवन्मया॥ १७॥

*katham̐ vidyāmaham̐ yogin̐s-*
*tvām̐ sadā paricintayan*
*keṣu-keṣu ca bhāveṣu*
*cintyo'si bhagavan mayā*

(17) How may I know You, O' Master of Yoga, while constantly meditating upon You; in what particular form, O' blessed Lord, You are to be meditated upon by me?

विस्तरेणात्मनो योगं विभूतिं च जनार्दन।
भूयः कथय तृप्तिर्हि श‍ृण्वतो नास्ति मेऽमृतम्॥ १८॥

*vistareṇātmano yagam̐*
*vibhūtim̐ ca janārdana*
*bhūyaḥ kathaya tṛptirhi*
*śṛṇvato nāsti me'mṛtam*

(18) Tell me again in full detail, Your power of yoga and Your divine manifestations O' Janardana

(O'Kṛṣṇa); for I am not yet satisfied by hearing Your nectar-like words.

श्रीभगवानुवाच

हन्त ते कथयिष्यामि दिव्या ह्यात्मविभूतयः ।
प्राधान्यतः कुरुश्रेष्ठ नास्त्यन्तो विस्तरस्य मे ॥ १९ ॥

*hanta te kathayiṣyāmi*
*divyā hyātmavibhūtayaḥ*
*prādhānyataḥ kuruśreṣtha*
*nāstyanto vistarasya me*

**The Blessed Lord said :**

(19) Yes, I must tell you My Divine manifestations but only the specific ones, O' best of the Kurus, for there is no limit to My magnitude.

अहमात्मा गुडाकेश सर्वभूताशयस्थितः ।
अहमादिश्च मध्यं च भूतानामन्त एव च ॥ २० ॥

*aham ātmā guḍākeśa*
*sarvabhūtāśayasthitaḥ*
*ahamādiśca madhyaṁ ca*
*bhūtānāmanta eva ca*

(20) I am the indwelling-soul, O'Gudakesha, (Arjuna) seated in the

hearts of all beings, I am the beginning, the middle, as well as the end of all beings.

आदित्यानामहं विष्णुर्ज्योतिषां रविरंशुमान्।
मरीचिर्मरुतामस्मि नक्षत्राणामहं शशी ॥ २१ ॥

*ādityānaṁ ahaṁ viṣṇur*
*jyotiṣāṁ raviraṅśumān*
*marīcir marutāmasmi*
*nakṣatrāṇāmahaṁ śaśī*

(21) Among the Adityas, I am Vishnu, among the luminaries, the radiant Sun, I am Marichi among the Maruts, and the Moon among the stars.

वेदानां सामवेदोऽस्मि देवानामस्मि वासवः।
इन्द्रियाणां मनश्चास्मि भूतानामस्मि चेतना ॥ २२ ॥

*vedānāṁ sāmavedo'smi*
*devānāmasmi vasavaḥ*
*indriyāṇāṁ manaś cāsmi*
*bhūtānāmasmi cetanā*

(22) Of the *Vedas,* I am the *Samaveda;* I am Vasva (Indra), among

the gods; among the senses I am the mind; and of the living beings, I am the consciousness.

रुद्राणां शंकरश्चास्मि वित्तेशो यक्षरक्षसाम्।
वसूनां पावकश्चास्मि मेरुः शिखरिणामहम्॥ २३॥

*rudrāṇāṁ śaṅkaraś cā'smi*
*vitteśo yakṣarakṣasām*
*vasūnāṁ pāvakaścāsmi*
*meruḥ śikhariṇāmaham*

(23) Among the Rudras, I am Sankara, among the Yakshas and Rakshasa (demons), I am Kubera. Among the Vasus I am the god of fire and of the mountains, I am the Meru.

पुरोधसां च मुख्यं मां विद्धि पार्थ बृहस्पतिम्।
सेनानीनामहं स्कन्दः सरसामस्मि सागरः॥ २४॥

*purodhasāṁ ca mukhyaṁ māṁ*
*viddhi pārtha bṛhaspatim*
*senānīnāmahaṁ skandaḥ*
*sarasāmasmi sāgaraḥ*

(24) Among the priests, know Me to be their chief, the Brihaspati,

O'Partha. Among the army generals, I am Skanda (Kartikeya) and of the reservoirs of water, I am the ocean.

महर्षीणां भृगुरहं गिरामस्म्येकमक्षरम्।
यज्ञानां जपयज्ञोऽस्मि स्थावराणां हिमालयः॥ २५॥

*maharṣīṇāṁ bhṛguraham*
*girāmasmyekamakṣaram*
*yajñānāṁ japayajño'smi*
*sthāvarāṇāṁ himālayaḥ*

(25) Among the great seers, I am Bhrigu; of the words, I am the monosyllable 'AUM'; of yajñas, I am the *Jaap-yajña* (silent repetition of the Lord's name) and among the immovables, the Himalaya.

अश्वत्थः सर्ववृक्षाणां देवर्षीणां च नारदः।
गन्धर्वाणां चित्ररथः सिद्धानां कपिलो मुनिः॥ २६॥

*aśvatthaḥ sarvavṛkṣāṇāṁ*
*devarṣīṇāṁ ca nāradaḥ*
*gandharvāṇāṁ citrarathaḥ*
*siddhānāṁ kapilo muniḥ*

(26) Among all the trees, I am the

Asvattha, among the celestial sages I am Narada, Chitraratha among the gandharvas and among the perfected sages, I am the sage Kapila.

**उच्चैःश्रवसमश्वानां विद्धि माममृतोद्भवम्।**
**ऐरावतं गजेन्द्राणां नराणां च नराधिपम्॥ २७॥**

*uccaiḥśravasamaśvānāṁ*
*viddhi māṁ amṛtodbhavam*
*airāvataṁ gajendrāṇāṁ*
*narāṇāṁ ca narādhipam*

(27) Among the horses know Me to be the nectar-born celestial horse Ucchaisrava, The Airavata among the lordly elephants and among men the King.

**आयुधानामहं वज्रं धेनूनामस्मि कामधुक्।**
**प्रजनश्चास्मि कन्दर्पः सर्पाणामस्मि वासुकिः॥ २८॥**

*āyudhānāmahaṁ vajraṁ*
*dhenūnām asmi kāmadhuk*
*prajanaścāsmi kandarpaḥ*
*sarpāṇāmasmi vāsukiḥ*

(28) Of weapons I am the

thunderbolt, among cows, I am the celestial wish-yielding cow (Kamadhenu); of the progenitors, I am the God of Love, of the Serpents, I am Vasuki.

अनन्तश्चास्मि नागानां वरुणो यादसामहम्।
पितॄणामर्यमा चास्मि यमः संयमतामहम्॥ २९॥

*anantaścāsmi nāgānāṁ*
*varuṇo yādasāmaham*
*pitṝṇāmaryamā cāsmi*
*yamaḥ saṁyamatāmaham*

(29) I am Ananta among the snakes and among the aquatic creatures and water gods, I am the Varuna. Among the ancestors, I am the Aryaman and I am Yama among the governors.

प्रह्लादश्चास्मि दैत्यानां कालः कलयतामहम्।
मृगाणां च मृगेन्द्रोऽहं वैनतेयश्च पक्षिणाम्॥ ३०॥

*prahlādaścāsmi daityānaṁ*
*kālaḥ kalayatāmaham*
*mṛgāṇāṁ ca mṛgendro'haṁ*
*vainateyaśca pakṣiṇām*

(30) I am Prahlada among the demons; among the reckoners I am Time, among the beasts I am the Lion, and Garuda among the birds.

पवनः पवतामस्मि रामः शस्त्रभृतामहम्।
झषाणां मकरश्चास्मि स्त्रोतसामस्मि जाह्नवी॥ ३१॥

*pavanaḥ pavatāmasmi*
*rāmaḥ śastrabhṛtāmaham*
*jhaṣāṇāṁ makaraścāsmi*
*srotasāmasmi jāhnavī*

(31) I am the wind among the purifiers (the speeders), among the wielders of weapons, I am Rama; among the fishes I am alligator and among the rivers I am the holy Ganga.

सर्गाणामादिरन्तश्च मध्यं चैवाहमर्जुन।
अध्यात्मविद्या विद्यानां वादः प्रवदतामहम्॥ ३२॥

*sargāṇāmādirantaś ca*
*madhyaṁ caivāhamarjuna*
*adhyātmavidyā vidyānāṁ*
*vādaḥ pravadatāmaham*

(32) Among creations, I am the

beginning, the middle, and the end O' Arjuna. Among sciences, I am the science of the Self and the *Vadah* (logic) of those who debate.

अक्षराणामकारोऽस्मि द्वन्द्वः सामासिकस्य च।
अहमेवाक्षयः कालो धाताहं विश्वतोमुखः॥ ३३॥

*akṣarāṇāmakāro'smi*
*dvandvaḥ sāmāsikasya ca*
*ahamevākṣayaḥ kālo*
*dhātāhaṁ viśvatomukhaḥ*

(33) Of letters I am 'A', of word-compounds, I am the dual, I am verily the imperishable Time; I am the sustainer, facing in all directions.

मृत्युः सर्वहरश्चाहमुद्भवश्च भविष्यताम्।
कीर्तिः श्रीर्वाक्च नारीणां स्मृतिर्मेधा धृतिः क्षमा॥ ३४॥

*mṛtyuḥ sarvaharaś cāham-*
*udbhavaś ca bhaviṣyatām*
*kīrtiḥ śrīr vāk ca nārīṇāṁ*
*smṛtir medhā dhṛtiḥ kṣamā*

(34) I am the all devouring death and the source of things yet to come.

Among the feminine virtues I am glory, fortune, speech, memory, wisdom, steadfastness, firmness and forgiveness.

बृहत्साम तथा साम्नां गायत्री छन्दसामहम्।

मासानां मार्गशीर्षोऽहमृतूनां कुसुमाकरः॥ ३५॥

*bṛhatsāma tathā sāmnāṁ*

*gāyatrī chandasāmaham*

*māsānāṁ mārgaśīrṣo'ham-*

*ṛtūnāṁ kusumākaraḥ*

(35) Of the hymns, I am the *Brihatsaman,* among the Vedic metres I am the *Gayatri.* Among the months I am Margashirsha, and of seasons the spring.

द्यूतं छलयतामस्मि तेजस्तेजस्विनामहम्।

जयोऽस्मि व्यवसायोऽस्मि सत्त्वं सत्त्ववतामहम्॥ ३६॥

*dyūtaṁ chalayatāmasmi*

*tejaste jasvināmaham*

*jayo'smi vyavasāyo'smi*

*sattvaṁ sattvavatāmaham*

(36) Of the deceitful, I am the

gambling; I am the glory of the glorious and the victory of the victorious. I am determination and the goodness of the good.

वृष्णीनां वासुदेवोऽस्मि पाण्डवानां धनञ्जयः ।
मुनीनामप्यहं व्यासः कवीनामुशना कविः ॥ ३७ ॥

*vṛṣṇīnām vāsudevo'smi*
*pāṇḍavānāṁ dhanañjayaḥ*
*munīnāmapyahaṁ vyāsaḥ*
*kavīnāmuśanā kaviḥ*

(37) Among the Vrishnis I am Vasudeva; among the Pandavas I am Dhananjaya (Arjuna), I am Vyasa among the sages and among the poets I am Shukracharya.

दण्डो दमयतामस्मि नीतिरस्मि जिगीषताम् ।
मौनं चैवास्मि गुह्यानां ज्ञानं ज्ञानवतामहम् ॥ ३८ ॥

*daṇḍo damayatāmasmi*
*nītirasmi jigīṣatām*
*maunaṁ caivāsmi guhyānāṁ*
*jñānaṁ jñānavatāmaham*

(38) I am the principle of

punishment, of those who punish. I am statesmanship of those who seek victory. Among the secrets I am silence and wisdom of the wise.

यच्चापि सर्वभूतानां बीजं तदहमर्जुन।
न तदस्ति विना यत्स्यान्मया भूतं चराचरम्॥ ३९॥

*yaccāpi sarvabhūtānāṁ*
*bījaṁ tad ahamarjuna*
*na tadasti vinā yat syān*
*mayā bhūtaṁ carācaraṁ*

(39) I am seed of all living beings O' Arjuna. There is no being animate or inanimate that can exist without Me.

नान्तोऽस्ति मम दिव्यानां विभूतीनां परन्तप।
एष तूद्देशतः प्रोक्तो विभूतेर्विस्तरो मया॥ ४०॥

*nānto'sti mama divyānāṁ*
*vibhūtīnāṁ parantapa*
*eṣa tū'ddeśataḥ prokto*
*vibhūter vistaro mayā*

(40) There is no end of My Divine attributes O' Arjuna. This is only a

brief description given by Me of the particulars of My infinite glories.

यद्यद्विभूतिमत्सत्त्वं श्रीमदूर्जितमेव वा।
तत्तदेवावगच्छ त्वं मम तेजोंऽशसम्भवम्॥ ४१ ॥

*yad-yad vibhūtimat sattvaṁ*
*śrīmadūrjitameva vā*
*tat-tad evāvagaccha tvaṁ*
*mama tejoṁśasambhavam*

(41) Every such thing as is glorious, prosperous, powerful, know that to be a manifestation of the fragment of My divine splendour.

अथवा बहुनैतेन किं ज्ञातेन तवार्जुन।
विष्टभ्याहमिदं कृत्स्नमेकांशेन स्थितो जगत्॥ ४२ ॥

*athavā bahunaitena*
*kiṁ jñātena tavārjuna*
*viṣṭabhyāhamidaṁ kṛtsnam-*
*ekāṅśena sthito jagat*

(42) What is the need of your knowing all these in detail O' Arjuna. I exist supporting the whole universe, with the single fragment of Myself.

ॐ तत्सदिति श्रीमद्भगवद्गीतासूपनिषत्सु ब्रह्मविद्यायां
योगशास्त्रे श्रीकृष्णार्जुनसंवादे विभूतियोगो
नाम दशमोऽध्यायः ॥ १० ॥

***Aum tatsaditi Srīmadbhagawadgeetasupanisatsu brahmavidyayam yogasastre Srīkṛṣṇarjunasamvade vibhutiyogo nama dasamodhyayah***

**'AUM TAT SAT'**—Thus, in the Upanishad of the glorious Bhagawad Geeta, the science of the Brahman (Absolute) the scripture of yoga, the dialogue between Srī Kṛṣṇa and Arjuna—thus, ends the chapter ten entitled *"Vibhuti-Yoga"*.

इति श्रीमद्भगवद्गीतासु दशमोऽध्यायः ॥ १० ॥

## *Chapter Eleven*

# VISVARUPADARSANAYOGA

# THE YOGA OF THE VISION OF THE UNIVERSAL FORM

अर्जुन उवाच

मदनुग्रहाय परमं गुह्यमध्यात्मसञ्ज्ञितम्।
यत्त्वयोक्तं वचस्तेन मोहोऽयं विगतो मम ॥ १ ॥

*madanugrahāya paramaṁ*
*guhyamadhyātmasañjñitam*
*yattvayo'ktaṁ vacastena*
*moho'yaṁ vigato mama*

**Arjuna said :**

(1) By the most profound words of spiritual wisdom which You have spoken out of Your compassion for me, my delusion has been dispelled.

भवाप्ययौ हि भूतानां श्रुतौ विस्तरशो मया।
त्वत्तः कमलपत्राक्ष माहात्म्यमपि चाव्ययम्॥ २ ॥

*bhavāpyayau hi bhūtānāṁ*
*śrutau vistaraśo mayā*
*tvattaḥ kamalapatrākṣa*
*māhātmyamapi cāvyayam*

(2) The origin and dissolution of beings have been heard by me in full detail from Thee, O' Lotus-eyed Lord, and also your immortal glory O' Supreme Lord.

**एवमेतद् यथात्थ त्वमात्मानं परमेश्वर।**
**द्रष्टुमिच्छामि ते रूपमैश्वरं पुरुषोत्तम॥ ३॥**

*evametad yathāttha tvam-*
*ātmānaṁ parameśvara*
*draṣṭumicchāmi te rūpam*
*aiśvaraṁ puruṣottama*

(3) You are precisely what you have declared Yourself to be O' Supreme Lord, but I have a desire to see Your Divine form, O' Purushottama (Supreme Purusha).

**मन्यसे यदि तच्छक्यं मया द्रष्टुमिति प्रभो।**
**योगेश्वर ततो मे त्वं दर्शयात्मानमव्ययम्॥ ४॥**

*manyase yadi tacchakyam*
*mayā draṣṭumiti prabho*

*yogeśvara tato me tvaṁ*
*darśayātmānamavyayam*

(4) O'Lord, if you think that it can be seen by me, then, O'Lord of the Yoga, reveal to me Your imperishable form.

श्रीभगवानुवाच

पश्य मे पार्थ रूपाणि शतशोऽथ सहस्रशः।
नानाविधानि दिव्यानि नानावर्णाकृतीनि च॥५॥

*paśye me pārtha rūpāṇi*
*śataśo'tha sahasraśaḥ*
*nānāvidhāni divyāni*
*nānāvarṇākṛtīni ca*

**The Blessed Lord said :**

(5) Behold My forms O'Partha by hundreds and thousands, multifarious and divine, of many colours and shapes.

पश्यादित्यान्वसून्रुद्रानश्विनौ मरुतस्तथा।
बहून्यदृष्टपूर्वाणि पश्याश्चर्याणि भारत॥६॥

*paśyādityān vasūn rudrān*
*aśvinau marutastathā*

*bahūny adṛṣṭapūrvāṇi*
*paśyāścāryāṇi bhārata*

(6) Behold the Adityas, the Vasus, the Rudras, the Asvins, and also the Maruts. Behold many more wonders, never seen before, O' Bharta (Arjuna).

इहैकस्थं जगत्कृत्स्नं पश्याद्य सचराचरम्।
मम देहे गुडाकेश यच्चान्यद् द्रष्टुमिच्छसि ॥ ७ ॥

*ihaikastham̐ jagat kṛtsnam̐*
*paśyādya sacarācaram*
*mama dehe guḍākeśa*
*yaccānyad draṣṭumicchasi*

(7) Now behold within this body of Mine, the whole universe centred in One—the moving and the unmoving, O'Arjuna, and whatever else you desire to see.

न तु मां शक्यसे द्रष्टुमनेनैव स्वचक्षुषा।
दिव्यं ददामि ते चक्षुः पश्य मे योगमैश्वरम् ॥ ८ ॥

*na tu mām̐ śakyase draṣṭum-*
*anenaiva svacakṣuṣā*

*divyaṁ dadāmi te cakṣuḥ*
*paśya me yogamaiśvaram*

(8) But surely, you cannot see Me with these eyes of yours; therefore, I must bless you with divine vision. Behold My divine power of yoga.

संजय उवाच

एवमुक्त्वा ततो राजन्महायोगेश्वरो हरिः ।
दर्शयामास पार्थाय परमं रूपमैश्वरम् ॥ ९ ॥

*evamuktvā tato rājan*
*mahāyogeśvaro hariḥ*
*darśayāmāsa pārthāya*
*paramaṁ rūpamaiśvaram*

**Sanjaya said :**

(9) After saying this, O' King, the great Lord of Yoga, Hari (Srī Kṛṣṇa) revealed to Arjuna His supreme Divine form.

अनेकवक्त्रनयनमनेकाद्भुतदर्शनम् ।
अनेकदिव्याभरणं दिव्यानेकोद्यतायुधम् ॥ १० ॥

*anekavaktranayanam-*
*anekādbhutadarśanam*

*anekadivyābharaṇaṁ*
*divyānekodyatāyudham*

दिव्यमाल्याम्बरधरं दिव्यगन्धानुलेपनम्।
सर्वाश्चर्यमयं देवमनन्तं विश्वतोमुखम्॥ ११॥

*divyamālyāmbaradharaṁ*
*divyagandhānulepanam*
*sarvāścaryamayaṁ devam-*
*anantaṁ viśvatomukham*

(10, 11) Possessing many mouths and eyes, presenting many wonderful sights, with numerous celestial ornaments and with numerous divine uplifted weapons. Wearing heavenly garlands and garments, anointed all over with divine sandal-pastes; totally marvellous, resplendent, boundless and facing in all directions.

दिवि सूर्यसहस्रस्य भवेद्युगपदुत्थिता।
यदि भाः सदृशी सा स्याद्भासस्तस्य महात्मनः॥ १२॥

*divi sūryasahasrasya*
*bhaved yugapadutthitā*
*yadi bhāḥ sadṛśī sā syad*
*bhāsas tasya mahātmanaḥ*

(12) If the effulgence of a thousand suns were to blaze forth all at once in the sky, that might resemble the effulgence of that mighty Being.

तत्रैकस्थं जगत्कृत्स्नं प्रविभक्तमनेकधा।
अपश्यद्देवदेवस्य शरीरे पाण्डवस्तदा॥ १३॥

*tatraikastharn jagatkṛtsnaṁ*
*pravibhaktamanekadhā*
*apaśyad devadevasya*
*śarīre pāṇḍavas tadā*

(13) There, resting at one place in the body of the God of gods, Arjuna then saw the whole universe with its manifold divisions.

ततः स विस्मयाविष्टो हृष्टरोमा धनञ्जयः।
प्रणम्य शिरसा देवं कृताञ्जलिरभाषत॥ १४॥

*tataḥ sa vismayāviṣṭo*
*hṛṣṭaromā dhanañjayaḥ*
*praṇamya śirasā devaṁ*
*kṛtāñjlirabhāṣata*

(14) Then Arjuna overwhelmed with amazement, his hair standing on

end, reverentially bowed down his head before the Lord and spoke with folded hands.

अर्जुन उवाच

पश्यामि देवांस्तव देव देहे,
सर्वांस्तथा भूतविशेषसंघान्।
ब्रह्माणमीशं कमलासनस्थ-
मृषींश्च सर्वानुरगांश्च दिव्यान्॥ १५॥

*paśyāmi devāns tava deva dehe*
*sarvāṅs tathā bhūtaviśeṣasaṅghān*
*brahmāṇamīśaṁ kamalāsanastha-*
*mṛṣīṅś ca sarvān uragānś ca divyān*

**Arjuna said :**

(15) O'Lord, I see all the gods in Your body, and also the various multitude of beings; Brahma the Lord seated on His lotus-throne, Shiva and all the other sages and the celestial serpents.

अनेकबाहूदरवक्त्रनेत्रम्,
पश्यामि त्वां सर्वतोऽनन्तरूपम्।
नान्तं न मध्यं न पुनस्तवादिं,
पश्यामि विश्वेश्वर विश्वरूप॥ १६॥

*anekabāhūdaravaktranetraṁ*

*paśyāmi tvāṁ sarvato'nantarūpam*

*nāntaṁ na madhyaṁ na punastavādiṁ*

*paśyāmi viśveśvara viśvarūpa*

(16) I see Your infinite form on all sides with numerous arms, stomachs, mouths and eyes. I see neither Your end, nor the middle nor the beginning. O' Lord of the universe, O' cosmic form.

किरीटिनं गदिनं चक्रिणं च,

तेजोराशिं सर्वतो दीप्तिमन्तम्।

पश्यामि त्वां दुर्निरीक्ष्यं समन्ताद्-

दीप्तानलार्कद्युतिमप्रमेयम्॥ १७॥

*kirīṭinaṁ gadinaṁ cakriṇaṁ ca*

*tejorāśiṁ sarvato dīptimantam*

*paśyāmi tvāṁ durnirīkṣyaṁ samantād*

*dīptānalārkadyutimaprameyam*

(17) I see You with the crown, mace and discus—a mass of radiance shining everywhere; having a brilliance like that of a blazing fire and sun; dazzling and immeasurable on all

sides.

त्वमक्षरं परमं वेदितव्यं,

त्वमस्य विश्वस्य परं निधानम्।

त्वमव्ययः शाश्वतधर्मगोप्ता,

सनातनस्त्वं पुरुषो मतो मे ॥ १८ ॥

*tvamakṣaraṁ paramaṁ veditavyaṁ*

*tvamaśya viśvasya paraṁ nidhānam*

*tvamavyayaḥ śāśvatadharmagoptā*

*sanātanas tvaṁ puruṣo mato me*

(18) You are the imperishable, the Supreme being, worthy to be known. You are the ultimate resort of the universe, you are the eternal guardian of the primeval Dharma (Righteousness). You are indeed the primeval Purusha, so I believe.

अनादिमध्यान्तमनन्तवीर्य-

मनन्तबाहुं शशिसूर्यनेत्रम्।

पश्यामि त्वां दीप्तहुताशवक्त्रम्,

स्वतेजसा विश्वमिदं तपन्तम्॥ १९ ॥

*anādimadhyāntamanantavīrya-*

*manantabāhuṁ śaśisūryanetram*

*paśyāmi tvāṁ dīptahutāśavaktram*

*śvatejasā viśvamidaṁ tapantam*

(19) I see You without beginning, middle or end, of infinite power—with innumerable arms and with the moon and the sun as your eyes. The blazing fire, Your mouth—scorching the universe with your radiance.

द्यावापृथिव्योरिदमन्तरं हि,

व्याप्तं त्वयैकेन दिशश्च सर्वाः ।

दृष्ट्वाद्भुतं रूपमुग्रं तवेदं,

लोकत्रयं प्रव्यथितं महात्मन् ॥ २० ॥

*dyāvāpṛthivyoridamantaraṁ hi*

*vyāptaṁ tvayaikena diśaśca sarvāḥ*

*dṛṣṭvādbhutaṁ rūpamugraṁ tavedaṁ*

*lokatrayaṁ pravyathitaṁ mahātman*

(20) The space between heaven and earth and in all the quarters is indeed pervaded by You alone. Seeing this most miraculous and dreadful form of Yours, the three worlds are trembling with fear, O' Supreme-soul.

अमी हि त्वां सुरसंघा विशन्ति,
केचिद्भीताः प्राञ्जलयो गृणन्ति।
स्वस्तीत्युक्त्वा महर्षिसिद्धसंघाः,
स्तुवन्ति त्वां स्तुतिभिः पुष्कलाभिः ॥ २१ ॥

*amī hi tvāṁ surasaṁghā viśanti*
*kecid bhītaḥ prāñjalayo gṛṇanti*
*svastītyuktvā maharṣisiddhasaṅghāḥ*
*stuvanti tvāṁ stutibhiḥ puṣkalābhiḥ*

(21) The hosts of gods are entering in You; some in fear with palms joined together are chanting your glories. The multitudes of sages and perfected ones are saying "May it be well" and adore Thee with special hymns of devotional praises.

रुद्रादित्या वसवो ये च साध्या,
विश्वेऽश्विनौ मरुतश्चोष्मपाश्च।
गन्धर्वयक्षासुरसिद्धसंघा,
वीक्षन्ते त्वां विस्मिताश्चैव सर्वे ॥ २२ ॥

*rudrādityā vasavo ye ca sādhyā*
*viśve'śvinau marutaś coṣmapāś ca*
*gandharvayakṣāsursiddhasaṅghā*
*vīkṣante tvāṁ vismitāś caiva sarve*

(22) The Rudras, Adityas, Vasus, the Sadhyas, Viswas, the Aswins, the Maruts, the manes, the host of Gandharvas, Yakshas, Asuras, and the perfected ones, they are all looking at You in deep amazement.

रूपं महत्ते बहुवक्त्रनेत्रं,
महाबाहो बहुबाहूरुपादम्।
बहूदरं बहुदंष्ट्राकरालं,
दृष्ट्वा लोकाः प्रव्यथितास्तथाहम्॥ २३॥

*rūpaṁ mahatte bahuvaktranetraṁ*
*mahābāho bahubāhūrupādam*
*bahūdaraṁ bahudaṅṣṭrākarālaṁ*
*dṛṣṭvā lokāḥ pravyathitāstathāham*

(23) Having seen Thy immeasurable form with numerous mouths, and eyes, O'Kṛṣṇa, with myriad arms and thighs, feet, bellies and fearful teeth, the entire world is in panic, and so am I.

नभःस्पृशं दीप्तमनेकवर्णं,
व्यात्ताननं दीप्तविशालनेत्रम्।
दृष्ट्वा हि त्वां प्रव्यथितान्तरात्मा,
धृतिं न विन्दामि शमं च विष्णो॥ २४॥

*nabhaḥspṛśaṁ dīptamanekavarṇaṁ*
*vyāttānanaṁ dīptaviśālanetram*
*dṛṣṭvā hi tvāṁ pravyathitāntarātmā*
*dhṛtiṁ na vindāmi śamaṁ ca viṣṇo*

(24) When I see Thee touching the sky, blazing with numerous colours, with your mouth wide open and the large shining eyes, my heart trembles with fear and I find neither courage nor peace, O' Lord Vishnu.

दंष्ट्राकरालानि च ते मुखानि,
दृष्ट्वैव कालानलसन्निभानि।
दिशो न जाने न लभे च शर्म,
प्रसीद देवेश जगन्निवास॥ २५॥

*daṁṣṭrākarālāni ca te mukhāni*
*dṛṣṭvaiva kālānalasannibhāni*
*diśo na jāne na labhe ca śarma*
*prasīda deveśa jagannivāsa*

(25) Having seen your mouth with fearful teeth, resembling the blazing fire of the cosmic dissolution, I have lost the sense of direction and inner peace. Be gracious O' Lord of

the Gods and the abode of the universe.

अमी च त्वां धृतराष्ट्रस्य पुत्राः,
सर्वे सहैवावनिपालसंघैः ।
भीष्मो द्रोणः सूतपुत्रस्तथासौ,
सहास्मदीयैरपि योधमुख्यैः ॥ २६ ॥

*amī ca tvāṁ dhṛtarāṣṭrasya putrāḥ*
*sarve sahaivāvanipālasaṅghaiḥ*
*bhīṣmo droṇaḥ sūtaputrastathāsau*
*sahāsmadīyairapi yodhamukhyaiḥ*

वक्त्राणि ते त्वरमाणा विशन्ति,
दंष्ट्राकरालानि भयानकानि ।
केचिद्विलग्ना दशनान्तरेषु,
संदृश्यन्ते चूर्णितैरुत्तमाङ्गैः ॥ २७ ॥

*vaktrāṇi te tvaramāṇā viśanti*
*daṅṣṭrākarālāni bhayānakāni*
*kecidvilagnā daśanāntareṣu*
*saṁdṛśyante cūrṇitairuttamāṅgaiḥ*

(26, 27) All the sons of Dhritarastra with the crowds of other kings, Bhishma, Drona, Karna and with the chief warriors of our side as well, are rushing into your mouths, which is so fearful to look at. Some can be seen sticking in the gaps between the teeth with their heads crushed completely.

यथा नदीनां बहवोऽम्बुवेगाः,
समुद्रमेवाभिमुखा द्रवन्ति।
तथा तवामी नरलोकवीरा,
विशन्ति वक्त्राण्यभिविज्वलन्ति ॥ २८ ॥

*yathā nadīnāṁ bahavo'mbuvegāḥ*
*samudramevā'bhimukhā dravanti*
*tathā tavāmī naralokavīrā*
*viśanti vaktrāṇyabhivijvalanti*

(28) As the diverse torrents of rivers rush towards the ocean, similarly these warriors of the mortal world are rushing into Your blazing mouths.

यथा प्रदीप्तं ज्वलनं पतङ्गा,
विशन्ति नाशाय समृद्धवेगाः।
तथैव नाशाय विशन्ति लोकास्-
तवापि वक्त्राणि समृद्धवेगाः ॥ २९ ॥

*yathā pradīptaṁ jvalanaṁ pataṅgā*
*viśanti nāśāya samṛaddhavegāḥ*
*tathaiva nāśāya viśanti lokās*
*tavāpi vaktrāṇi samṛddhavegāḥ*

(29) As the moths rush into the blazing fire for their own destruction, so also these creatures are hurriedly rushing into Your mouth for their destruction.

लेलिह्यसे ग्रसमानः समन्ताल्-
लोकान्समग्रान्वदनैर्ज्वलद्भिः ।
तेजोभिरापूर्य जगत्समग्रं,
भासस्तवोग्राः प्रतपन्ति विष्णो ॥ ३० ॥

*lelihyase grasamānaḥ samantāl-*
*lokān samagrān vadanair jvaladbhiḥ*
*tejobhirāpūrya jagat samagraṁ*
*bhāsasta vogrāḥ pratapanti viṣṇo*

(30) Devouring all the worlds on every side with Thy flaming mouths, Your fiery rays are filling the whole world with your effulgence O' Lord Vishnu.

आख्याहि मे को भवानुग्ररूपो,
नमोऽस्तु ते देववर प्रसीद।
विज्ञातुमिच्छामि भवन्तमाद्यं,
न हि प्रजानामि तव प्रवृत्तिम्॥ ३१॥

*ākhyāhi me ko bhavānugrarūpo*
*namo'stu te devavara prasīda*
*vijñātumicchāmi bhavantamādyaṁ*
*na hi prajānāmi tava pravṛttim*

(31) Tell me who You are in this dreadful form? I bow down to You, O' Supreme Divinity. Be gracious—I want to know You, O'Primal one in reality, for I fail to comprehend Your purpose (intent).

श्रीभगवानुवाच

कालोऽस्मि लोकक्षयकृत् प्रवृद्धो,
लोकान्समाहर्तुमिह प्रवृत्तः।
ऋतेऽपि त्वां न भविष्यन्ति सर्वे,
येऽवस्थिताः प्रत्यनीकेषु योधाः॥ ३२॥

*kālo'smi lokakṣayakṛt pravṛddho*
*lokān samāhartumiha pravṛttaḥ*

*ṛte'pi tvāṁ na bhaviṣyanti sarve*

*ye'vasthitāḥ pratyanīkeṣu yodhāḥ*

**The Blessed Lord said :**

(32) I am the Time, the mighty world-destroyer; here engaged in the extermination of the worlds. Even without you all these warriors arrayed in hostile battle will cease to be.

तस्मात्त्वमुत्तिष्ठ यशो लभस्व,

जित्वा शत्रून् भुङ्क्ष्व राज्यं समृद्धम्।

मयैवैते निहताः पूर्वमेव,

निमित्तमात्रं भव सव्यसाचिन्॥ ३३ ॥

*tasmāt tvamuttiṣṭha yaśo labhasva*

*jitvā śatrūn bhuṅkṣva rājyaṁ samṛddham*

*mayaivaite nihatāḥ pūrvameva*

*nimittamātraṁ bhava savyasācin*

(33) Therefore, you stand up, and win the glory. Conquer the enemies and enjoy the unrivalled empire. They have been already killed by Me; you be merely an instrument O' Arjuna.

द्रोणं च भीष्मं च जयद्रथं च,

कर्णं तथान्यानपि योधवीरान्।

**मया हतांस्त्वं जहि मा व्यथिष्ठा,**

**युध्यस्व जेतासि रणे सपत्नान्॥ ३४॥**

*droṇaṁ ca bhīṣmaṁ ca jayadrathaṁ ca*
*karṇaṁ tathānyānapi yodhavīrān*
*mayā hatāṅstvaṁ jahi mā vyathiṣṭhā*
*yudhyasva jetāsi raṇe sapatnān*

(34) Drona, Bhishma, Jayadrath, Karna and other brave warriors—these have been already killed by Me. Do not be distressed with fear. Fight, you will surely conquer the enemies in the battle.

**संजय उवाच**

**एतच्छ्रुत्वा वचनं केशवस्य,**

**कृताञ्जलिर्वेपमानः किरीटी।**

**नमस्कृत्वा भूय एवाह कृष्णं,**

**सगद्गदं भीतभीतः प्रणम्य॥ ३५॥**

*etacchrutvā vacanaṁ keśavasya*
*kṛtāñjalir vepamānaḥ kirīṭī*
*namaskṛtvā bhūya evāha kṛṣṇaṁ*
*sagadgadaṁ bhītabhītaḥ praṇamya*

**Sanjaya said :**

(35) Having heard these words of Srī Kṛṣṇa, Arjuna with his both hands joined together in respect, trembling and prostrating, once again addressed to Lord Kṛṣṇa in a chocked voice overwhelmed with fear and reverence.

अर्जुन उवाच

स्थाने हृषीकेश तव प्रकीर्त्या,
जगत् प्रहृष्यत्यनुरज्यते च।
रक्षांसि भीतानि दिशो द्रवन्ति,
सर्वे नमस्यन्ति च सिद्धसंघाः ॥ ३६ ॥

*sthāne hṛṣīkeśa tava prakīrtyā*
*jagat prahṛṣyaty anurajyate ca*
*rakṣāṅsi bhītāni diśo dravanti*
*sarve namasyanti ca siddhasaṅghāḥ*

**Arjuna said :**

(36) O'Kṛṣṇa, right it is that the universe rejoices and is filled with love while glorifying Thee. The terrified demons flee in all directions and all the perfected ones bow to you.

कस्माच्च ते न नमेरन्महात्मन्,

गरीयसे ब्रह्मणोऽप्यादिकर्त्रे।

अनन्त देवेश जगन्निवास,

त्वमक्षरं सदसत्तत्परं यत्॥ ३७॥

*kasmācca te na nameran mahātman*

*garīyase brahmaṇo'pyādikartre*

*ananta deveśa jagannivāsa*

*tvam akṣaraṁ sadasat tat paraṁ yat*

(37) And why should they not salute you O' great Supreme-soul. Thou are the greatest, even greater than Brahma, the original creator. O' Infinite Being, O' God of the gods. Thou are the imperishable, the being, the non-being and that which is beyond both.

त्वमादिदेवः पुरुषः पुराणस्–

त्वमस्य विश्वस्य परं निधानम्।

वेत्तासि वेद्यं च परं च धाम

त्वया ततं विश्वमनन्तरूप॥ ३८॥

*tvamādidevaḥ puruṣaḥ purāṇas-*

*tvamasya viśvasya paraṁ nidhānam*

*vettā'si vedyaṁ ca paraṁ ca dhāma*

*tvayā tataṁ viśvam anantarūpa*

(38) You are the Primal God, the most ancient Purusha and the ultimate resort of the universe. You are the knower, the knowable and the Supreme abode. The universe is pervaded by you, O'Lord of infinite forms.

वायुर्यमोऽग्निर्वरुणः शशाङ्कः,

प्रजापतिस्त्वं प्रपितामहश्च ।

नमो नमस्तेऽस्तु सहस्रकृत्वः,

पुनश्च भूयोऽपि नमो नमस्ते ॥ ३९ ॥

*vāyur yamo'gnir varuṇaḥ śaśāṅkaḥ*

*prajāpatis tvaṁ prapitāmahaśca*

*namo namaste'stu sahasrakṛtvaḥ*

*punaśca bhūyo'pi namo namaste*

(39) You are the windgod, the god of death, the god of fire and the god of water, the moongod. You are the creator, the Father of Brahma and the great-grandsire of all. Salutations to You a thousand times; salutations, repeated salutations to You once

again.

नमः पुरस्तादथ पृष्ठतस्ते,

नमोऽस्तु ते सर्वत एव सर्व।

अनन्तवीर्यामितविक्रमस्त्वं,

सर्वं समाप्नोषि ततोऽसि सर्वः ॥ ४० ॥

*namaḥ purastād atha pṛṣṭhtaste*

*namo'stu te sarvata eva sarva*

*anantavīryāmitvikramas tvaṁ*

*sarvaṁ samāpnoṣi tato'si sarvaḥ*

(40) Salutation to Thee in front and from behind, I salute You from all sides, O' infinite in might and infinite in prowess You encompass all, therefore You are all.

सखेति मत्वा प्रसभं यदुक्तं,

हे कृष्ण हे यादव हे सखेति।

अजानता महिमानं तवेदं,

मया प्रमादात् प्रणयेन वापि ॥ ४१ ॥

*sakheti matvā prasabhaṁ yaduktaṁ*

*he kṛṣṇa he yādava he sakheti*

*ajānatā mahimānaṁ tavedaṁ*

*mayā pramādāt praṇayena vāpi*

यच्चावहासार्थमसत्कृतोऽसि,
विहारशय्यासनभोजनेषु।
एकोऽथवाप्यच्युत तत्समक्षं,
तत्क्षामये त्वामहमप्रमेयम् ॥ ४२ ॥

*yaccāvahāsārtham asatkṛto'si*
*vihārśayyāsanabhojaneṣu*
*eko'thavā'pyacyuta tatsamakṣaṁ*
*tatkṣāmaye tvāmahamaprameyam*

(41, 42) Regarding Thee as a friend, I have carelessly addressed You, O' Kṛṣṇa, O' Yadava, O' friend and so on, not knowing Your greatness and magnificence. It has been merely out of my ignorance or affection that You have been slighted by me in jest, while playing, resting or at mealtime, either alone or in the company of others, O'Kṛṣṇa, please forgive me, O' incomprehensible one.

पितासि लोकस्य चराचरस्य,
त्वमस्य पूज्यश्च गुरुर्गरीयान्।
न त्वत्समोऽस्त्यभ्यधिकः कुतोऽन्यो,
लोकत्रयेऽप्यप्रतिमप्रभाव ॥ ४३ ॥

*pitāsi lokasya carācarasya*
*tvamasya pūjyaś ca gururgarīyān*
*na tvatsamo'sty abhyadhikaḥ kuto'nyo*
*lokatraye'pyapratimaprabhāva*

(43) You are the Father of the world, moving and unmoving. You are the most venerable teacher (Guru) and highly adorable. There is no one equal to You in all the three worlds; how can there be any one greater than You. O' Lord of unequalled power.

**तस्मात् प्रणम्य प्रणिधाय कायं,**
**प्रसादये त्वामहमीशमीड्यम्।**
**पितेव पुत्रस्य सखेव सख्युः,**
**प्रियः प्रियायार्हसि देव सोढुम्॥ ४४॥**

*tasmāt praṇamya praṇidhāya kāyaṁ*
*prasādaye tvāmahamīśamīḍyam*
*piteva putrasya sakheva sakhyuḥ*
*priyaḥ priyāyārhasi deva soḍhum*

(44) Therefore I prostrate before You and request for Your grace O' Lord. As a father forgives his son, a

friend to his friend, a lover to his beloved; even so shouldst Thou forgive me, O' Lord.

अदृष्टपूर्वं हृषितोऽस्मि दृष्ट्वा,

भयेन च प्रव्यथितं मनो मे।

तदेव मे दर्शय देव रूपं,

प्रसीद देवेश जगन्निवास ॥ ४५ ॥

*adṛṣṭapūrvaṁ hṛṣito'smi dṛṣṭvā*

*bhayena ca pravyathitaṁ mano me*

*tad eva me darśaya deva rūpaṁ*

*prasīda deveśa jagannivāsa*

(45) Having seen what was never seen before—I am delighted, but my mind is distressed with fear. Reveal to me, O'God, that other form of Yours. Be gracious, O' Lord of the gods, and abode of the universe.

किरीटिनं गदिनं चक्रहस्त-

मिच्छामि त्वां द्रष्टुमहं तथैव।

तेनैव रूपेण चतुर्भुजेन,

सहस्त्रबाहो भव विश्वमूर्ते ॥ ४६ ॥

*kirīṭinaṁ gadinaṁ cakrahastam*

*icchāmi tvāṁ draṣṭumahaṁ tathaiva*

*tenaiva rūpeṇa caturbhujena*

*sahasrabāho bhava viśvamūrte*

(46) I desire to see You as before, with Your crown, holding a mace and a discus in your hand. Please resume again that four-armed form, O' thousand-armed, universal Being.

श्रीभगवानुवाच

मया प्रसन्नेन तवार्जुनेदं,

रूपं परं दर्शितमात्मयोगात्।

तेजोमयं विश्वमनन्तमाद्यं,

यन्मे त्वदन्येन न दृष्टपूर्वम्॥ ४७॥

*mayā prasannena tavā'rjune'daṁ*

*rūpaṁ paraṁ darśitam ātmayogāt*

*tejomayaṁ viśvamanantamādyaṁ*

*yanme tvadanyena na dṛṣṭapūrvam*

**The Blessed lord said :**

(47) O'Arjuna, being pleased with you I have revealed to you through My

power of Yoga, this Supreme, effulgent, infinite, primeval cosmic form of Mine; which no one else has seen before.

न वेदयज्ञाध्ययनैर्न दानैर्–
न च क्रियाभिर्न तपोभिरुग्रैः ।
एवंरूपः शक्य अहं नृलोके,
द्रष्टुं त्वदन्येन कुरुप्रवीर ॥ ४८ ॥

*na vedayajñādhyayanairna dānair*
*na ca kriyābhir na tapobhirugraiḥ*
*evaṁrūpaḥ śakya ahaṁ nṛloke*
*draṣṭuṁ tvadanyena kurupravīra*

(48) Neither by the study of *Vedas* and yajña, nor by charity, nor by rituals and neither by severe penances, can I be seen in this form in the world of men by any one else except you, O' hero of the Kurus.

मा ते व्यथा मा च विमूढभावो,
दृष्ट्वा रूपं घोरमीदृङ् ममेदम् ।
व्यपेतभीः प्रीतमनाः पुनस्त्वं,
तदेव मे रूपमिदं प्रपश्य ॥ ४९ ॥

*mā te vyathā mā ca vimūḍhabhāvo*
*dṛṣtvā rūpaṁ ghoramīdṛṅ mamedam*
*vyapetabhīḥ prītamanāḥ punas tvaṁ*
*tad eva me rūpamidaṁ prapaśya.*

(49) Do not be afraid, nor bewildered, on seeing such an awesome form of Mine. Shedding all your fears and with a gladdened heart, behold once again the other familiar form of Mine.

संजय उवाच

इत्यर्जुनं वासुदेवस्तथोक्त्वा,
स्वकं रूपं दर्शयामास भूयः ।
आश्वासयामास च भीतमेनं,
भूत्वा पुनः सौम्यवपुर्महात्मा ।। ५० ।।

*ityarjunaṁ vāsudevas tathoktvā*
*svakaṁ rūpaṁ darśayāmāsa bhūyaḥ*
*āśvāsayāmāsa ca bhītamenaṁ*
*bhūtvā punaḥ saumyavapur mahātmā*

**Sanjaya said :**

(50) Having thus spoken to

Arjuna, Lord Vasudeva showed to him again His own form. Assuming His gentle appearance, the exalted one (Srī Kṛṣṇa) comforted and consoled the terrified Arjuna.

अर्जुन उवाच

दृष्ट्वेदं मानुषं रूपं तव सौम्यं जनार्दन।
इदानीमस्मि संवृत्तः सचेताः प्रकृतिं गतः ॥५१॥

*dṛṣṭvedaṁ mānuṣaṁ rūpaṁ*
*tava saumyaṁ janārdana*
*idānīmasmi saṁvṛttaḥ*
*sacetāḥ prakṛtiṁ gataḥ*

**Arjuna said :**

(51) Having seen this human form of yours which is graciously peaceful O' Kṛṣṇa, now I have regained my composure and am restored to my own natural self again.

श्रीभगवानुवाच

सुदुर्दर्शमिदं रूपं दृष्टवानसि यन्मम।
देवा अप्यस्य रूपस्य नित्यं दर्शनकांक्षिणः ॥५२॥

*sudurdarśamidaṁ rūpaṁ*
*dṛṣṭavānasi yan mama*
*devā apyasya rūpasya*
*nityaṁ darśanakāṅkṣiṣaḥ*

**The Blessed Lord said :**

(52) It is indeed very difficult to see this form of Mine which you have just seen. Even the gods are always desirous to behold this form.

नाहं वेदैर्न तपसा न दानेन न चेज्यया।
शक्य एवंविधो द्रष्टुं दृष्टवानसि मां यथा॥५३॥

*nāhaṁ vedairna tapasā*
*na dānena na cejyayā*
*śakya evaṁvidho draṣṭuṁ*
*draṣṭavān asi māṁ yathā*

(53) Neither by the study of the *Vedas,* nor by penances and charities, nor by rituals, can I be seen in this form as you have seen Me.

भक्त्या त्वनन्यया शक्य अहमेवंविधोऽर्जुन।
ज्ञातुं द्रष्टुं च तत्त्वेन प्रवेष्टुं च परन्तप॥५४॥

*bhaktyā tvananyayā śakya*
*ahamevaṁvidho'rjuna*

*jñātuṁ draṣṭuṁ ca tattvena*
*praveṣṭuṁ ca parantapa*

(54) But only by undivided devotion, however, O' Arjuna, I can be seen in this form, be known in essence and also perceived and experienced.

**मत्कर्मकृन्मत्परमो मद्भक्तः सङ्गवर्जितः ।**
**निर्वैरः सर्वभूतेषु यः स मामेति पाण्डव ॥ ५५ ॥**

*matkarmakṛn matparamo*
*madbhaktaḥ saṅgavarjitaḥ*
*nirvairaḥ sarvabhūteṣu*
*yaḥ sa māmeti pāṇḍava*

(55) He who performs all his actions for Me, considers me as his Supreme goal, and is totally devoted to Me, who is non-attached and free from malice towards all beings, surely comes to Me, O' Arjuna.

**ॐ तत्सदिति श्रीमद्भगवद्गीतासूपनिषत्सु ब्रह्मविद्यायां योगशास्त्रे श्रीकृष्णार्जुनसंवादे विश्वरूपदर्शनयोगो नाम एकादशोऽध्यायः ॥ ११ ॥**

***'Aum' tatsaditi***
***Srīmadbhagawadgeeta supanisatsu brahmavidyayam yogasastre Srīkṛṣṇarjunasamvade visvarupadarsanayogo nama eikadasodhyayah***

**'AUM TAT SAT'**—Thus, in the Upanishad of the glorious Bhagawad Geeta, the science of the Brahman (Absolute) the scripture of yoga, the dialogue between Srī Kṛṣṇa and Arjuna—thus, ends the chapter eleven entitled *"Visvarupadarsanayoga"*.

इति श्रीमद्भगवद्गीतासु एकादशोऽध्यायः ॥ ११ ॥

## *Chapter Twelve*

# BHAKTIYOGA

## THE YOGA OF DEVOTION

अर्जुन उवाच

एवं सततयुक्ता ये भक्तास्त्वां पर्युपासते।
ये चाप्यक्षरमव्यक्तं तेषां के योगवित्तमाः ॥ १ ॥

*evaṁ satatayuktā ye*
*bhaktāstvāṁ paryupāsate*
*ye cāpyakṣaramavyaktaṁ*
*teṣāṁ ke yogavittamāḥ*

**Arjuna said :**

(1) Those devotees who are ever steadfast and thus worship Thee, and those who worship the imperishable and unmanifested, which of these are better versed in Yoga?

श्रीभगवानुवाच

मय्यावेश्य मनो ये मां नित्ययुक्ता उपासते।
श्रद्धया परयोपेतास्ते मे युक्ततमा मताः ॥ २ ॥

*mayyāveśya mano ye māṁ*
*nityayuktā upāsate*
*śraddhayā parayo'petās*
*te me yuktatamā matāḥ*

**The Blessed Lord said :**

(2) Those who concentrate their mind on Me, stay united with Me in contemplation; those are steadfast and worship Me with supreme faith—I consider them to be the best in Yoga.

ये त्वक्षरमनिर्देश्यमव्यक्तं पर्युपासते।
सर्वत्रगमचिन्त्यं च कूटस्थमचलं ध्रुवम्॥ ३॥

*ye tvakṣharam anirdeśya-*
*mavyaktaṁ paryupāsate*
*sarvatragamacintyaṁ ca*
*kūṭasthamacalaṁ dhruvam*

सन्नियम्येन्द्रियग्रामं सर्वत्र समबुद्धयः।
ते प्राप्नुवन्ति मामेव सर्वभूतहिते रताः॥ ४॥

*saṁniyamyendriyagrāmaṁ*
*sarvatra samabuddhayaḥ*
*te prāpnuvanti māmeva*
*sarvabhūtahite ratāḥ*

(3, 4) But those who are devoted to the imperishable, the indefinable, the unmanifest, the omnipresent, the unthinkable, the immovable and the eternal; having restrained all their senses in totality, with equanimity of mind, also reach Me, while intent on the welfare of all beings.

क्लेशोऽधिकतरस्तेषामव्यक्तासक्तचेतसाम्।
अव्यक्ता हि गतिर्दुःखं देहवद्भिरवाप्यते॥ ५॥

*kleśo'dhikataras teṣām-*
*avyaktāsaktacetasām*
*avyaktā hi gatir duḥkhaṁ*
*dehvadbhiravāpyate*

(5) There are greater obstacles for those whose minds are set on the unmanifest; for the goal—the unmanifested is very difficult to attain by the embodied beings.

ये तु सर्वाणि कर्माणि मयि संन्यस्य मत्पराः।
अनन्येनैव योगेन मां ध्यायन्त उपासते॥ ६॥

*ye tu sarvāṇi karmāṇi*
*mayi sannyasya matparāḥ*

*ananyenaiva yogena*
*māṁ dhyāyanta upāsate*

तेषामहं समुद्धर्ता मृत्युसंसारसागरात्।
भवामि नचिरात्पार्थ मय्यावेशितचेतसाम्॥ ७॥

*teṣāmahaṁ samuddhartā*
*mṛtyusaṁsārasāgrāt*
*bhavāmi nacirāt pārtha*
*mayyāveśitacetasām*

(6, 7) But those who worship Me, surrendering all their actions to Me, regarding Me as their supreme goal, meditate on Me with undivided devotion—whose minds are totally absorbed in Me, I become their saviour and liberate them from the ocean of death-bound existence, Oh! Arjuna.

मय्येव मन आधत्स्व मयि बुद्धिं निवेशय।
निवसिष्यसि मय्येव अत ऊर्ध्वं न संशयः॥ ८॥

*mayyeva mana ādhatsva*
*mayi buddhiṁ niveśaya*
*nivasiṣyasi mayyeva*
*ata ūrdhvaṁ na saṅśayaḥ*

(8) Settle your mind in Me alone, let your intellect dwell in Me, then you will live in Me alone, there is no doubt about this.

**अथ चित्तं समाधातुं न शक्नोषि मयि स्थिरम्।**

**अभ्यासयोगेन ततो मामिच्छाप्तुं धनञ्जय॥ ९॥**

*atha cittaṁ samādhātuṁ*

*na śaknoṣi mayi sthiram*

*abhyāsayogena tato*

*māmicchāptuṁ dhanañjaya*

(9) If, however, you are not able to fix your mind steadily on Me, then through the Yoga of constant practice seek to attain Me, Oh! Arjuna.

**अभ्यासेऽप्यसमर्थोऽसि मत्कर्मपरमो भव।**

**मदर्थमपि कर्माणि कुर्वन्सिद्धिमवाप्स्यसि॥ १०॥**

*abhyāse'pyasamartho'si*

*matkarmaparamo bhava*

*madarthamapi karmāṇi*

*kurvan siddhimavāpsyasi*

(10) If you are not capable of such practice, be thou intent on doing

work for My sake, even by performing actions for My sake you will attain perfection.

अथैतदप्यशक्तोऽसि कर्तुं मद्योगमाश्रितः।

सर्वकर्मफलत्यागं ततः कुरु यतात्मवान्॥ ११॥

*athaitadapyaśakto'si*

*kartuṁ madyogamāśritaḥ*

*sarvakarmaphalatyāgaṁ*

*tataḥ kuru yatātmavān*

(11) If you are unable to do even this, then take refuge in My yogic unity and renounce the fruit of all actions, being self-controlled.

श्रेयो हि ज्ञानमभ्यासाज्ज्ञानाद्ध्यानं विशिष्यते।

ध्यानात्कर्मफलत्यागस्त्यागाच्छान्तिरनन्तरम्॥ १२॥

*śreyo hi jñānamabhyāsā-*

*jjñānād dhyānaṁ viśiṣyate*

*dhyānāt karmaphalatyāgas*

*tyāgācchāntiranantaram*

(12) Better indeed is knowledge than practice, (without proper insight) better than knowledge is meditation,

superior to meditation is renunciation of the fruits of actions—from renunciation one attains peace immediately.

अद्वेष्टा सर्वभूतानां मैत्रः करुण एव च।
निर्ममो निरहङ्कारः समदुःखसुखः क्षमी ॥ १३ ॥

*adveṣṭā sarvabhūtānāṁ*
*maitraḥ karuṇa eva ca*
*nirmamo nirahaṅkāraḥ*
*samduḥkhasukhaḥ kṣamī*

सन्तुष्टः सततं योगी यतात्मा दृढनिश्चयः।
मय्यर्पितमनोबुद्धिर्यो मद्भक्तः स मे प्रियः ॥ १४ ॥

*santuṣṭaḥ satataṁ yogī*
*yatātmā dṛḍhaniścayaḥ*
*mayyarpitamanobuddhir*
*yo madbhaktaḥ sa me priyaḥ*

(13, 14) He who is free from hatred towards all creatures, friendly and compassionate, who is free from the feeling of mineness and egoism, balanced in pain and pleasure, forgiving, always contented, steadfast in Yoga, self-controlled and very determined, with his mind and intellect dedicated to Me—that devotee of Mine is very dear to Me.

यस्मान्नोद्विजते लोको लोकान्नोद्विजते च यः।
हर्षामर्षभयोद्वेगैर्मुक्तो यः स च मे प्रियः॥ १५॥

*yasmān nodvijate loko*
*lokān nodvijate ca yaḥ*
*harṣāmarṣabhayodvegair*
*mukto yaḥ sa ca me priyaḥ*

(15) He by whom the world is not agitated and who cannot be agitated by the world; who is free from exhilaration, resentment, fear and anxiety—he is dear to Me.

अनपेक्षः शुचिर्दक्ष उदासीनो गतव्यथः।
सर्वारम्भपरित्यागी यो मद्भक्तः स मे प्रियः॥ १६॥

*anapekṣah śucir dakṣa*
*udāsīno gatavyathaḥ*
*sarvārambhaparityāgī*
*yo madbhaktaḥ sa me priyaḥ*

(16) He who is free from desires, pure, dexterous, and mature, who is free from disappointments and totally

detached from all commencements, that devotee of Mine is very dear to Me.

योो न हृष्यति न द्वेष्टि न शोचति न काङ्क्षति।
शुभाशुभपरित्यागी भक्तिमान्यः स मे प्रियः॥ १७॥

*yo na hṛṣyati na dveṣṭi*
*na śocati na kāṅkṣati*
*śubhāśubhaparityāgī*
*bhaktimānyāḥ sa me priyaḥ.*

(17) He who neither exhilarates nor hates, neither grieves nor craves, who is the renouncer of both auspicious and inauspicious, and also endowed with devotion—he is dear to Me.

समः शत्रौ च मित्रे च तथा मानापमानयोः।
शीतोष्णसुखदुःखेषु समः सङ्गविवर्जितः॥ १८॥

*samaḥ śatrau ca mitre ca*
*tathā mānāpamānayoḥ*
*śītoṣṇasukhaduḥkheṣu*
*samaḥ saṅgavivarjitaḥ*

(18) Who is alike to a foe and a

friend and also the same in honour and dishonour, cold and heat, pleasure and pain, who is poised and detached.

तुल्यनिन्दास्तुतिर्मौनी सन्तुष्टो येन केनचित्।
अनिकेतः स्थिरमतिर्भक्तिमान्मे प्रियो नरः ॥ १९ ॥

*tulyanindāstutir maunī*
*santuṣṭo yena kenacit*
*aniketaḥ sthiramatir*
*bhaktimān me priyo naraḥ*

(19) Who remains balanced in criticism and praise and holds control over speech, who is contented with anything that comes and not attached to his place of dwelling; who is firm in mind and fully devoted—that man is dear to Me.

ये तु धर्म्यामृतमिदं यथोक्तं पर्युपासते।
श्रद्दधाना मत्परमा भक्तास्तेऽतीव मे प्रियाः ॥ २० ॥

*ye tu dharmyāmṛtamidaṁ*
*yathoktaṁ paryupāsate*
*śraddadhānā matparamā*
*bhaktās te'tīva me priyāḥ*

(20) Those who follow this

immortal Dharma as declared above, endowed with faith, who regard Me as their supreme goal, those devotees are exceedingly dear to Me.

ॐ तत्सदिति श्रीमद्भगवद्गीतासूपनिषत्सु ब्रह्मविद्यायां
योगशास्त्रे श्रीकृष्णार्जुनसंवादे भक्तियोगो
नाम द्वादशोऽध्यायः ॥ १२ ॥

***'Aum' tatsaditi***
***Srīmadbhagawadgeeta supanisatsu***
***brahmavidyayam yogasastre***
***Srīkṛṣṇarjunasamvade***
***bhaktiyogo nama dvadasodhyayah***

**'AUM TAT SAT'**—Thus, in the Upanishad of the glorious Bhagawad Geeta, the science of the Brahman (Absolute) the scripture of yoga, the dialogue between Srī Kṛṣṇa and Arjuna—thus, ends the chapter twelve entitled *"Bhaktiyoga"*.

इति श्रीमद्भगवद्गीतासु द्वादशोऽध्यायः ॥ १२ ॥

## *Chapter Thirteen*

# KṢETRAKṢETRAJÑA VIBHĀGAYOGA

## THE YOGA OF THE KNOWLEDGE OF THE FIELD AND THE KNOWER OF THE FIELD

श्रीभगवानुवाच

इदं शरीरं कौन्तेय क्षेत्रमित्यभिधीयते।

एतद्यो वेत्ति तं प्राहुः क्षेत्रज्ञ इति तद्विदः ॥ १ ॥

*idaṁ śarīraṁ kaunteya*

*kṣetramityabhidhīyate*

*etad yo vetti taṁ prāhuḥ*

*kṣetrajña iti tadvidaḥ*

**The Blessed Lord said :**

(1) This body O' Arjuna is called the field and he, who knows this, is called the knower of the field by the Sages.

क्षेत्रज्ञं चापि मां विद्धि सर्वक्षेत्रेषु भारत।
क्षेत्रक्षेत्रज्ञयोर्ज्ञानं यत्तज्ज्ञानं मतं मम॥ २॥

*kṣetrajñaṁ cāpi māṁ viddhi*
*sarvakṣetreṣu bhārata*
*kṣetrakṣetrajñayor jñānaṁ*
*yat tajjñānaṁ mataṁ mama*

(2) Know Me as the knower of the field in all fields, O' Arjuna. The knowledge of the field and the knower of the field is considered to be the true knowledge by Me.

तत्क्षेत्रं यच्च यादृक्च यद्विकारि यतश्च यत्।
स च यो यत्प्रभावश्च तत्समासेन मे शृणु॥ ३॥

*tat kṣetraṁ yācca yādṛk ca*
*yadvikāri yataśca yat*
*sa ca yo yatprabhāvaś ca*
*tat samāsena me śṛṇu*

(3) That field, what it is like, and what are its modifications and whence it is, also who is the knower of the field and what are his powers—hear all that from Me in brief.

ऋषिभिर्बहुधा गीतं छन्दोभिर्विविधैः पृथक्।
ब्रह्मसूत्रपदैश्चैव हेतुमद्भिर्विनिश्चितैः ॥ ४ ॥

*ṛsibhirbahudhā gītaṁ*
*chandobhir vividhaiḥ pṛthak*
*brahmasūtrapadaiś caiva*
*hetumadbhir viniścitaiḥ*

(4) The sages have sung about this very distinctively in Vedic hymns with multifold descriptions and also in the conclusive and reasoned text of the *Brahma-sutras.*

महाभूतान्यहङ्कारो बुद्धिरव्यक्तमेव च।
इन्द्रियाणि दशैकं च पञ्च चेन्द्रियगोचराः ॥ ५ ॥

*mahābhūtānyahaṅkāro*
*buddhiravyaktameva ca*
*indriyāṇi daśaikaṁ ca*
*pañca cendriyagocarāḥ*

इच्छा द्वेषः सुखं दुःखं संघातश्चेतना धृतिः।
एतत्क्षेत्रं समासेन सविकारमुदाहृतम् ॥ ६ ॥

*icchā dveṣaḥ sukhaṁ duḥkhaṁ*
*saṁghātaś cetanā dhṛtiḥ*

*etat kṣetraṁ samāsena*
*savikāramudāhṛtam*

(5, 6) The great elements, the ego, intellect, unmanifested primordial Nature, the ten senses, alongwith mind and five objects of senses. Desire, aversion, pleasure and pain, body, consciousness, fortitude—this is the field with its modifications described briefly.

अमानित्वमदम्भित्वमहिंसा क्षान्तिरार्जवम्।
आचार्योपासनं शौचं स्थैर्यमात्मविनिग्रहः॥ ७॥

*amānitvam adambhitvam-*
*ahiṁsā kṣāntirārjavam*
*ācāryopāsanaṁ śaucaṁ*
*sthairyamātmavinigrahaḥ*

इन्द्रियार्थेषु वैराग्यमनहङ्कार एव च।
जन्ममृत्युजराव्याधिदुःखदोषानुदर्शनम्॥ ८॥

*indriyārtheṣu vairāgyam-*
*anahaṅkāra eva ca*
*janmamṛtyujarāvyadhi-*
*duḥkhadoṣānudarśanam*

(7, 8) Absence of vanity, unpretentiousness, non-violence, forbearance, uprightness, service to the teacher, purity, steadfastness and self-control. Dispassion towards the objects of the senses, absence of egoism, perception of misery and evil, inherent in birth, death old age and disease.

असक्तिरनभिष्वङ्गः पुत्रदारगृहादिषु।
नित्यं च समचित्तत्वमिष्टानिष्टोपपत्तिषु॥ ९॥

*asaktiranabhiṣvaṅgaḥ*
*putradāragṛhādiṣu*
*nityam ca samacittatvam*
*iṣṭāniṣṭopapattiṣu*

मयि चानन्ययोगेन भक्तिरव्यभिचारिणी।
विविक्तदेशसेवित्वमरतिर्जनसंसदि ॥ १०॥

*mayi cānanyayogena*
*bhaktiravyabhicāriṇī*
*viviktadeśasevitvam-*
*aratir janasaṅsadi*

(9, 10) Non-attachment and the attitude of non-possessiveness towards son, wife, home and others. Perennial equal-mindedness on the attainment of all desirable and the undesirable. An undivided devotion for Me through Yoga of contemplation. Resort to solitary places and avoidance from the mass of people.

अध्यात्मज्ञाननित्यत्वं तत्त्वज्ञानार्थदर्शनम्।
एतज्ज्ञानमिति प्रोक्तमज्ञानं यदतोऽन्यथा॥ ११॥

*adhyātmajñānanityatvaṁ*
*tattvajñānārthadarśanam*
*etajjñānamiti proktam-*
*ajñānaṁ yadato'nyathā*

(11) Steadfastness in the knowledge of the Self, clear perception of the aim of true knowledge—All this is declared to be the knowledge and whatever opposed to this is called ignorance.

ज्ञेयं यत्तत् प्रवक्ष्यामि यज्ज्ञात्वामृतमश्नुते।
अनादिमत्परं ब्रह्म न सत्तन्नासदुच्यते॥ १२॥

*jñeyaṁ yat tat pravakṣyāmi*
*yaj jñātvāmṛtamaśnute*

*anādimat paraṁ brahma*
*na sat tannāsad ucyate*

(12) I shall tell you that which has to be known, and by knowing which one attains immortality; the beginningless Supreme Brahman, which is called neither existent *(sat)* nor non-existent *(asat)*.

सर्वतः पाणिपादं तत्सर्वतोऽक्षिशिरोमुखम्।
सर्वतः श्रुतिमल्लोके सर्वमावृत्य तिष्ठति॥ १३॥

*sarvataḥ pāṇipādaṁ tat*
*sarvato'kṣiśiromukham*
*sarvataḥśrutimalloke*
*sarvamāvṛtya tiṣṭhati*

(13) With hands and feet everywhere, with eyes, heads and face on all sides, with ears everywhere He pervades in the worlds enveloping everything.

सर्वेन्द्रियगुणाभासं सर्वेन्द्रियविवर्जितम्।
असक्तं सर्वभृच्चैव निर्गुणं गुणभोक्तृ च॥ १४॥

*sarvendriyaguṇābhāsaṁ*
*sarvendriyavivarjitam*

*asaktaṁ sarvabhṛccaiva*
*nirguṇaṁ guṇabhoktṛ ca*

(14) Perceived through the functions of senses, yet devoid of all senses; unattached yet sustaining all; transcends the qualities of nature yet their experiencer.

बहिरन्तश्च भूतानामचरं चरमेव च।
सूक्ष्मत्वात्तदविज्ञेयं दूरस्थं चान्तिके च तत्॥ १५॥

*bahirantaś ca bhūtānām-*
*acaraṁ carameva ca*
*sūkṣmatvāt tad avijñeyaṁ*
*dūrasthaṁ cāntike ca tat*

(15) Exists without and within all beings, the unmoving and also the moving. Extremely subtle and incomprehensible; very far away and yet so near is That.

अविभक्तं च भूतेषु विभक्तमिव च स्थितम्।
भूतभर्तृ च तज्ज्ञेयं ग्रसिष्णु प्रभविष्णु च॥ १६॥

*avibhaktaṁ ca bhūteṣu*
*vibhaktamiva ca sthitam*

*bhūtabhartṛ ca tajjñeyaṁ*

*grasiṣṇu prabhaviṣṇu ca*

(16) The 'One' which is undivided yet exists as if divided in all beings; known as the sustainer of all beings, and also the devourer and the creator.

ज्योतिषामपि तज्ज्योतिस्तमसः परमुच्यते।

ज्ञानं ज्ञेयं ज्ञानगम्यं हृदि सर्वस्य विष्ठितम्॥ १७॥

*jyotiṣāmapi tajjyotis*

*tamasaḥ param ucyate*

*jñānaṁ jñeyaṁ jñānagamyaṁ*

*hṛdi sarvasya viṣṭhitam*

(17) That, the Light of all lights, is said to be beyond darkness: The knowledge, the object of knowledge, as well as the goal of knowledge is seated in the hearts of all.

इति क्षेत्रं तथा ज्ञानं ज्ञेयं चोक्तं समासतः।

मद्भक्त एतद्विज्ञाय मद्भावायोपपद्यते॥ १८॥

*iti kṣetraṁ tathā jñānaṁ*

*jñeyaṁ coktaṁ samāsataḥ*

*madbhakta etad vijñāya*

*madbhāvāyopapadyate*

(18) Thus the field, the knowledge and the knowable have been illustrated briefly. My devotee who understands all this, he enters into My being.

प्रकृतिं पुरुषं चैव विद्ध्यनादी उभावपि।
विकारांश्च गुणांश्चैव विद्धि प्रकृतिसम्भवान्॥ १९॥

*prakṛtiṁ puruṣaṁ caiva*

*viddhyanādī ubhāvapi*

*vikārānś ca guṇānś caiva*

*viddhi prakṛtisambhavān*

(19) Know that the Prakriti (Nature) and Purusha (Spirit) are both beginningless; and also understand, that all modifications and the qualities are born of Nature.

कार्यकरणकर्तृत्वे हेतुः प्रकृतिरुच्यते।
पुरुषः सुखदुःखानां भोक्तृत्वे हेतुरुच्यते॥ २०॥

*kārya karaṇa kartṛtve*

*hetuḥ prakṛtirucyate*

*puruṣaḥ sukhaduḥkhānāṁ*
*bhoktṛtve heturucyate*

(20) The Primordial Nature is considered to be the cause of effect, instrument and agent; while the embodied-soul is said to be the cause in regard to the experience of pleasure and pain.

**पुरुषः प्रकृतिस्थो हि भुंक्ते प्रकृतिजान्गुणान्।**
**कारणं गुणसङ्गोऽस्य सदसद्योनिजन्मसु॥ २१॥**

*puruṣaḥ prakṛtistho hi*
*bhuṅkte prakṛtijān guṇān*
*kāraṇaṁ guṇasaṅgo'sya*
*sadasadyo nijanmasu*

(21) The soul while settled in identification with Nature experiences the qualities born of nature; it is the attachment to these qualities that becomes the cause of birth in good and evil wombs.

**उपद्रष्टानुमन्ता च भर्ता भोक्ता महेश्वरः।**
**परमात्मेति चाप्युक्तो देहेऽस्मिन्पुरुषः परः॥ २२॥**

*upadraṣṭānumantā ca*
*bhartā bhoktā maheśvaraḥ*

*paramātmeti cāpyukto*
*dehe'smin puruṣaḥ paraḥ*

(22) The Supreme spirit while dwelling in this body is also called the spectator, the counsellor, the sustainer, the experiencer, the great Lord and the Supreme-Self.

य एवं वेत्ति पुरुषं प्रकृतिं च गुणैः सह।
सर्वथा वर्तमानोऽपि न स भूयोऽभिजायते॥ २३॥

*ya evaṁ vetti puruṣaṁ*
*prakṛtiṁ ca guṇaiḥ saha*
*sarvathā vartamāno'pi*
*na sa bhūyo'bhijāyate*

(23) He who thus knows the Purusha (soul) as well as the Prakriti (Nature) with the qualities (attributes); even though engaged in all respects, he is not born again.

ध्यानेनात्मनि पश्यन्ति केचिदात्मानमात्मना।
अन्ये सांख्येन योगेन कर्मयोगेन चापरे॥ २४॥

*dhyānenātmani paśyanti*
*kecid ātmānamātmanā*
*anye sāṅkhyena yogena*
*karmayogena cāpare*

(24) Some, by meditation, perceive the Self, in the self, by the self; others by the Yoga of knowledge, and still others by the Yoga of action.

अन्ये त्वेवमजानन्तः श्रुत्वान्येभ्य उपासते।
तेऽपि चातितरन्त्येव मृत्युं श्रुतिपरायणाः॥ २५॥

*anye tvevamajānantaḥ*
*śrutvānyebhya upāsate*
*te'pi cātitarantyeva*
*mṛtyuṁ śrutiparāyaṇaḥ*

(25) Others, not knowing thus; worship as they have heard from others; they too cross beyond death, by being devoted to whatever they hear respectfully.

यावत्सञ्जायते किंचित्सत्त्वं स्थावरजङ्गमम्।
क्षेत्रक्षेत्रज्ञसंयोगात्तद्विद्धि भरतर्षभ॥ २६॥

*yāvat sañjāyate kiñcit*
*sattvaṁ sthāvarajaṅgamam*
*kṣetrakṣetrajñasaṁyogāt*
*tad viddhi bharatarṣabha*

(26) Whatever being is born,

moving or unmoving, know that it is through the union of the field and the knower of the field, O'. best of the Bharatas.

समं सर्वेषु भूतेषु तिष्ठन्तं परमेश्वरम्।
विनश्यत्स्वविनश्यन्तं यः पश्यति स पश्यति॥ २७॥

*samaṁ sarveṣu bhūteṣu*
*tiṣṭhantaṁ parameśvaram*
*vinaśyatsvavinaśyantaṁ*
*yaḥ paśyati sa pasyati*

(27) He who beholds the Supreme Lord existing equally in all beings, as the imperishable within the perishable, he truly sees.

समं पश्यन्हि सर्वत्र समवस्थितमीश्वरम्।
न हिनस्त्यात्मनात्मानं ततो याति परां गतिम्॥ २८॥

*samaṁ paśyan hi sarvatra*
*samavasthitamīśvaram*
*na hinstyātmanātmānaṁ*
*tato yāti parāṁ gatim*

(28) Who sees the Supreme Lord present, equally everywhere, he does not destroy the Self by the self;

therefore, he attains the Supreme goal.

प्रकृत्यैव च कर्माणि क्रियमाणानि सर्वशः।
यः पश्यति तथात्मानमकर्तारं स पश्यति॥ २९॥

*prakṛtyaiva ca karmāṇi*
*kriyamāṇāni sarvaśaḥ*
*yaḥ paśyati tathātmānam-*
*akartāraṁ sa paśyati*

(29) He who sees, that all the actions are being performed by Prakriti (Nature) and the Self is not the doer, he truly sees.

यदा भूतपृथग्भावमेकस्थमनुपश्यति।
तत एव च विस्तारं ब्रह्म सम्पद्यते तदा॥ ३०॥

*yadā bhūtapṛthagbhāvam-*
*ekasthamanupaśyati*
*tata eva ca vistāraṁ*
*brahma saṁpadyate tadā*

(30) When he sees, that the whole variety of beings are centred in 'One' and their expansion is from that 'One' alone, then he attains Brahman.

अनादित्वान्निर्गुणत्वात्परमात्मायमव्ययः।
शरीरस्थोऽपि कौन्तेय न करोति न लिप्यते॥ ३१ ॥

*anāditvānnirguṇatvāt*
*paramātmāyamavyayaḥ*
*śarīrastho'pi kaunteya*
*na karoti na lipyate*

(31) Beginningless, and beyond the qualities of Nature, the Supreme-Self is imperishable. Although existing in the body O' Arjuna, neither acts nor is attached.

यथा सर्वगतं सौक्ष्म्यादाकाशं नोपलिप्यते।
सर्वत्रावस्थितो देहे तथात्मा नोपलिप्यते॥ ३२ ॥

*yathā sarvagataṁ saukṣmyād*
*ākāśaṁ nopalipyate*
*sarvatrāvasthito dehe*
*tathātmā nopalipyate*

(32) As the all-pervading ether is not tainted, because of its subtlety, even so the Self, although dwelling everywhere in the body, is not tainted.

यथा प्रकाशयत्येकः कृत्स्नं लोकमिमं रविः।
क्षेत्रं क्षेत्री तथा कृत्स्नं प्रकाशयति भारत॥ ३३ ॥

*yathā prakaśayatyekaḥ*

*kṛtsnaṁ lokamimaṁ raviḥ*

*kṣetraṁ kṣetrī tathā kṛtsnaṁ*

*prakāśayati bhārata*

(33) As the one sun illuminates the whole universe, so also the Lord of the field illuminates the entire field, O' Arjuna.

क्षेत्रक्षेत्रज्ञयोरेवमन्तरं ज्ञानचक्षुषा।
भूतप्रकृतिमोक्षं च ये विदुर्यान्ति ते परम्॥ ३४॥

*kṣetrakṣetrajñayorevam-*

*antaraṁ jñānacakṣuṣā*

*bhūtaprakṛtimokṣaṁ ca*

*ye vidur yānti te param*

(34) Those, who perceive the distinction between the field and the knower of the field with the eye of wisdom; and the deliverance of beings from *Prakriti* (Nature), they attain the Supreme.

ॐ तत्सदिति श्रीमद्भगवद्गीतासूपनिषत्सु ब्रह्मविद्यायां योगशास्त्रे श्रीकृष्णार्जुनसंवादे क्षेत्रक्षेत्रज्ञविभागयोगो नाम त्रयोदशोऽध्यायः॥ १३॥

***'Aum' tatsaditi***
***Srīmadbhagawadgeeta supanisatsu***
***brahmavidyayam yogasastre***
***Srīkṛṣṇarjunasamvade***
***ksetraksetrajñavibhagayogo nama***
***trayodasodhyayah***

'AUM TAT SAT'—Thus, in the Upanishad of the glorious Bhagawad Geeta, the science of the Brahman (Absolute) the scripture of yoga, the dialogue between Srī Kṛṣṇa and Arjuna—thus, ends the chapter thirteen entitled *"Ksetraksetrajña-vibhagayoga"*.

**इति श्रीमद्भगवद्गीतासु त्रयोदशोऽध्यायः ॥ १३ ॥**

## Chapter Fourteen

# GUNATRIYA VIBHAGAYOGA

## THE YOGA OF THE DIVISION OF THE THREE GUNAS

श्रीभगवानुवाच

परं भूयः प्रवक्ष्यामि ज्ञानानां ज्ञानमुत्तमम्।
यज्ज्ञात्वा मुनयः सर्वे परां सिद्धिमितो गताः॥ १॥

*paraṁ bhūyaḥ pravakṣyāmi*
*jñānānāṁ jñānamuttamam*
*yajjñātvā munayaḥ sarve*
*parāṁ siddhim ito gatāḥ*

**The Blessed Lord said :**

(1) I shall teach you again the supreme knowledge, the highly reverend knowledge; by knowing which, all the sages have attained the supreme perfection, being liberated from the world.

इदं ज्ञानमुपाश्रित्य मम साधर्म्यमागताः।
सर्गेऽपि नोपजायन्ते प्रलये न व्यथन्ति च॥ २॥

*idaṁ jñānamupāśritya*
*mama sādharmyamāgatāḥ*
*sarge'pi nopajāyante*
*pralaye na vyathanti ca*

(2) Those who have taken refuge in this knowledge, have attained unity with Me. They are not born at the time of creation, nor are they disturbed at the time of dissolution.

मम योनिर्महद् ब्रह्म तस्मिन्गर्भं दधाम्यहम्।
सम्भवः सर्वभूतानां ततो भवति भारत॥ ३॥

*mama yonir mahad brahma*
*tasmin garbhaṁ dadhāmyaham*
*sambhavaḥ sarvabhūtānāṁ*
*tato bhavati bhārata*

(3) The great Brahma (primordial nature) is My womb; in that, I place the seed, from that, is the birth of all beings O'Arjuna.

सर्वयोनिषु कौन्तेय मूर्तयः सम्भवन्ति याः।
तासां ब्रह्म महद्योनिरहं बीजप्रदः पिता॥ ४॥

*sarvayoniṣu kaunteya*
*mūrtayaḥ sambhavanti yāḥ*
*tāsāṁ brahma mahad yonir-*
*ahaṁ bījapradaḥ pitā*

(4) Of all the bodies, those take birth from different wombs, O' Arjuna—the great Brahma (Mother nature) is their womb and I am the seed giving Father.

**सत्त्वं रजस्तम इति गुणाः प्रकृतिसम्भवाः।**
**निबध्नन्ति महाबाहो देहे देहिनमव्ययम्॥ ५॥**

*sattvaṁ rajas tama iti*
*guṇāḥ prakṛtisambhavāḥ*
*nibadhnanti mahābāho*
*dehe dehinamavyayam*

(5) *Sattva* (purity), *Rajas* (passion) and *Tamas* (dullness)—these qualities born of Nature O' Arjuna, bind the imperishable spirit to the body.

**तत्र सत्त्वं निर्मलत्वात् प्रकाशकमनामयम्।**
**सुखसङ्गेन बध्नाति ज्ञानसङ्गेन चानघ॥ ६॥**

*tatra sattvaṁ nirmalatvāt*
*prakāśakamanāmayam*
*sukhasaṅgena badhnāti*
*jñānasaṅgena cānagha*

(6) Of these *Sattva* (purity) being immaculate, luminous and healthy binds by attachment to happiness and by attachment to knowledge, O' Arjuna.

रजो रागात्मकं विद्धि तृष्णासङ्गसमुद्भवम्।
तन्निबध्नाति कौन्तेय कर्मसङ्गेन देहिनम्॥ ७॥

*rajo rāgātmakaṁ viddhi*
*tṛṣṇāsaṅgasamudbhavam*
*tannibadhnāti kaunteya*
*karmasaṅgena dehinam*

(7) Know thou, *Rajas* to be of the nature of passion, which is the source of thirst and attachment; it binds O'Kaunteya, the embodied-self through attachment to action.

तमस्त्वज्ञानजं विद्धि मोहनं सर्वदेहिनाम्।
प्रमादालस्यनिद्राभिस्तन्निबध्नाति भारत॥ ८॥

*tamastvajñānajaṁ viddhi*
*mohanaṁ sarvadehinām*
*pramādālasyanidrābhis*
*tannibadhnāti bhārata*

(8) Know, *Tamas* to be born of ignorance, it deludes the embodied beings and binds through negligence, indolence and sleep O' Arjuna.

सत्त्वं सुखे सञ्जयति रजः कर्मणि भारत।
ज्ञानमावृत्य तु तमः प्रमादे सञ्जयत्युत॥ ९॥

*sattvaṁ sukhe sañjayati*
*rajaḥ karmaṇi bhārata*
*jñānamāvṛtya tu tamaḥ*
*pramāde sañjayatyuta*

(9) The mode of *Sattva* binds one with attachment to happiness, *Rajas* attaches one with obsession to work O'Arjuna, while *Tamas* veiling the knowledge attaches one to heedlessness and laziness.

रजस्तमश्चाभिभूय सत्त्वं भवति भारत।
रजः सत्त्वं तमश्चैव तमः सत्त्वं रजस्तथा॥ १०॥

*rajas tamaś cābhibhūya*
*sattvaṁ bhavati bhārata*
*rajaḥ sattvaṁ tamaś caiva*
*tamaḥ sattvaṁ rajastathā*

(10) *Sattva* prevails having overpowered *Rajas* and *Tamas,* O'Arjuna. *Rajas* prevails having overpowered *Sattva* and *Tamas* and likewise *Tamas* manifests overpowering *Sattva* and *Rajas.*

सर्वद्वारेषु देहेऽस्मिन्प्रकाश उपजायते।
ज्ञानं यदा तदा विद्याद्विवृद्धं सत्त्वमित्युत॥ ११ ॥

*sarvadvāreṣu dehe'smin*
*prakāśa upajāyate*
*jñānaṁ yadā tadā vidyād*
*vivṛddhaṁ sattvamityuta*

(11) When through every gate of the body, the light of wisdom shines forth, then it may be understood that *Sattva* is predominant.

लोभः प्रवृत्तिरारम्भः कर्मणामशमः स्पृहा।
रजस्येतानि जायन्ते विवृद्धे भरतर्षभ॥ १२ ॥

*lobhaḥ pravṛttirārambhaḥ*
*karmaṇāmaśamaḥ spṛhā*
*rajasyetāni jāyante*
*vivṛddhe bharatarṣabha*

(12) Covetousness, activity, enterprise, restlessness and craving—these arise when *Rajas* is predominant, O' Arjuna.

अप्रकाशोऽप्रवृत्तिश्च प्रमादो मोह एव च।
तमस्येतानि जायन्ते विवृद्धे कुरुनन्दन॥ १३॥

*aprakāśo'pravṛttiś ca*
*pramādo moha eva ca*
*tamasyetāni jāyante*
*vivṛddhe kurunandana*

(13) Darkness, lack of effort, negligence and mere delusion—these arise when *Tamas* is predominant, O' Arjuna

यदा सत्त्वे प्रवृद्धे तु प्रलयं याति देहभृत्।
तदोत्तमविदां लोकानमलान्प्रतिपद्यते॥ १४॥

*yadā sattve pravṛddhe tu*
*pralayaṁ yāti dehabhṛt*

*tadottamavidāṁ lokān-*

*amalān pratipdyate*

(14) When the embodied-self meets death, while *Sattva* is predominant, then he attains to the pure world of the knowers of the highest.

रजसि प्रलयं गत्वा कर्मसङ्गिषु जायते।

तथा प्रलीनस्तमसि मूढयोनिषु जायते॥ १५॥

*rajasi pralayaṁ gatvā*

*karmasaṅgiṣu jāyate*

*tathā pralīnas tamasi*

*mūḍhayoniṣu jāyate*

(15) When the individual dies with the predominance of *Rajas,* he is born among those who are attached to action. Meeting death in *Tamas,* he is born in the wombs of the deluded.

कर्मणः सुकृतस्याहुः सात्त्विकं निर्मलं फलम्।

रजसस्तु फलं दुःखमज्ञानं तमसः फलम्॥ १६॥

*karmaṇaḥ sukṛtasyāhuḥ*

*sāttvikaṁ nirmalaṁ phalam*

*rajasas tu phalaṁ duḥkham-*

*ajñānaṁ tamasaḥ phalam*

(16) The fruit of good action is *Sattvic* and pure; while the fruit of *Rajas* is pain and sorrow—ignorance is the fruit of *Tamas.*

सत्त्वात्सञ्जायते ज्ञानं रजसो लोभ एव च।

प्रमादमोहौ तमसो भवतोऽज्ञानमेव च॥ १७॥

*sattvāt sañjāyate jñānaṁ*

*rajaso lobha eva ca*

*pramādamohau tamaso*

*bhavato'jñānameva ca*

(17) *Sattva* promotes knowledge and *Rajas* promotes greed, while heedlessness and delusion arise from *Tamas* and also the ignorance.

ऊर्ध्वं गच्छन्ति सत्त्वस्था मध्ये तिष्ठन्ति राजसाः।

जघन्यगुणवृत्तिस्था अधो गच्छन्ति तामसाः॥ १८॥

*ūrdhvaṁ gacchanti sattvasthā*

*madhye tiṣṭhanti rājasāḥ*

*jaghanyaguṇavṛttisthā*

*adho gacchanti tāmasāḥ*

(18) Those who are settled in *Sattva* go upward. The *Rajasic* dwell in the middle and the *Tamasic* remaining under the influence of the lowest qualities go downward.

नान्यं गुणेभ्यः कर्तारं यदा द्रष्टानुपश्यति।
गुणेभ्यश्च परं वेत्ति मद्भावं सोऽधिगच्छति॥ १९॥

*nānyaṁ guṇebhyaḥ kartāraṁ*
*yadā draṣṭānupaśyati*
*guṇebhyaś ca paraṁ vetti*
*madbhāvaṁ so'dhigacchati*

(19) When the seer beholds no agent other than the qualities of nature, and perceives the transcendent beyond the qualities, he attains to My being.

गुणानेतानतीत्य त्रीन्देही देहसमुद्भवान्।
जन्ममृत्युजरादुःखैर्विमुक्तोऽमृतमश्नुते॥ २०॥

*guṇān etānatītya trīn*
*dehī dehasamudbhavān*
*janmamṛtyujarāduḥkhair*
*vimukto'mṛtamaśnute*

(20) When the embodied-self

transcends the three Gunas, out of which the body is evolved, then he is released from birth, death, old age and misery; he attains immortality.

अर्जुन उवाच

कैर्लिङ्गैस्त्रीन्गुणानेतानतीतो भवति प्रभो।
किमाचारः कथं चैतांस्त्रीन्गुणानतिवर्तते॥ २१॥

*kair liṅgais trīn guṇānetān-*
*atīto bhavati prabho*
*kimācāraḥ kathaṁ caitāṅs*
*trīn gunānativartate*

**Arjuna said :**

(21) What are the hallmarks of the man, who has transcended the three Gunas, O'Lord? What is his conduct, and how does he transcend the three Gunas (qualities)?

श्रीभगवानुवाच

प्रकाशं च प्रवृत्तिं च मोहमेव च पाण्डव।
न द्वेष्टि सम्प्रवृत्तानि न निवृत्तानि कांक्षति॥ २२॥

*prakāśaṁ ca pravṛttiṁ ca*
*mohameva ca pāṇḍava*

*na dveṣṭi sampravṛttāni*
*na nivṛttāni kāṅkṣati*

**The Blessed Lord said :**

(22) When there is enlightenment, activity and delusion in life O'Arjuna, he does not dislike them; nor does he long for them when they are absent.

उदासीनवदासीनो गुणैर्यो न विचाल्यते।
गुणा वर्तन्त इत्येव योऽवतिष्ठति नेङ्गते॥ २३॥

*udāsīnavadāsīno*
*guṇair yo na vicālyate*
*guṇā vartanta ityeva*
*yo'vatiṣṭhati neṅgate*

(23) He, who remains unconcerned and does not feel disturbed by these qualities; he acts merely as a witness. He understands that only the Gunas are in operation, so he remains firm and established in the Self.

समदुःखसुखः स्वस्थः समलोष्टाश्मकाञ्चनः।
तुल्यप्रियाप्रियो धीरस्तुल्यनिन्दात्मसंस्तुतिः॥ २४॥

*samaduḥkhasukhaḥ svasthaḥ*
*samaloṣṭāśmakāñcanaḥ*

*tulyapriyāpriyo dhīras*
*tulyanindātmasaṅstutiḥ*

(24) He, who is balanced in pain and pleasure and remains centred in the Self; who looks upon a clod, a stone, and a piece of gold as of equal worth, who remains balanced amidst the pleasant and the unpleasant, who is steadfast and regards both blame and praise of himself as equal.

मानापमानयोस्तुल्यस्तुल्यो मित्रारिपक्षयोः।
सर्वारम्भपरित्यागी गुणातीतः स उच्यते॥ २५॥

*mānāpamānayostulyas*
*tulyo mitrāripakṣayoḥ*
*sarvārambhaparityāgī*
*guṇātītaḥ sa ucyate*

(25) Who maintains his balance in honour and dishonour, who is equal to a friend and foe, who is detached in all undertakings—he is said to have transcended the Gunas (qualities).

मां च योऽव्यभिचारेण भक्तियोगेन सेवते।
स गुणान्समतीत्यैतान्ब्रह्मभूयाय कल्पते॥ २६॥

*mām ca yo'vyabhicāreṇa*
*bhaktiyogena sevate*
*sa guṇān samatītyaitān*
*brahmabhūyāya kalpate*

(26) Who serves Me with an undeviated Yoga of devotion, he rises above the Gunas and becomes fit, to be one with Brahman.

ब्रह्मणो हि प्रतिष्ठाहममृतस्याव्ययस्य च।
शाश्वतस्य च धर्मस्य सुखस्यैकान्तिकस्य च॥ २७॥

*brahmaṇo hi pratiṣṭhāham*
*amṛtasyāvyayasya ca*
*śāśvatasya ca dharmasya*
*sukhasyaikāntikasya ca*

(27) For, I am the abode of Brahman, the immortal and the imperishable, of the primordial eternal Dharma and of Absolute Bliss.

ॐ तत्सदिति श्रीमद्भगवद्गीतासूपनिषत्सु ब्रह्मविद्यायां योगशास्त्रे श्रीकृष्णार्जुनसंवादे गुणत्रयविभागयोगो नाम चतुर्दशोऽध्यायः॥ १४॥

***'Aum' tatsaditi***
***Srīmadbhagawadgeetasupanisatsu***
***brahmavidyayam yogasastre***
***Srīkrṣṇarjunasamvade***
***gunatriyavibhagayogo nama***
***caturdasodhyayah***

**'AUM TAT SAT'**—Thus, in the Upanishad of the glorious Bhagawad Geeta, the science of the Brahman (Absolute) the scripture of yoga, the dialogue between Srī Krṣṇa and Arjuna—thus, ends the chapter fourteen entitled *"Gunatriya-vibhagayoga"*.

इति श्रीमद्भगवद्गीतासु चतुर्दशोऽध्यायः ॥ १४ ॥

## *Chapter Fifteen*

# PURUSHOTTAMAYOGA

## THE YOGA OF THE SUPREME PERSON

श्रीभगवानुवाच

ऊर्ध्वमूलमधःशाखमश्वत्थं प्राहुरव्ययम्।
छन्दांसि यस्य पर्णानि यस्तं वेद स वेदवित्॥ १ ॥

*ūrdhvamūlamadhaḥśākham*
*aśvatthaṁ prāhuravyayam*
*chandānsi yasya parṇāni*
*yas taṁ veda sa vedavit*

**The Blessed Lord said :**

(1) Having its roots above and branches below, the *asvattha*, tree is known to be indestructible. Its leaves are the Vedic hymns (metres); he who knows it, is the knower of the Vedas.

अधश्चोर्ध्वं प्रसृतास्तस्य शाखा,
गुणप्रवृद्धा विषयप्रवालाः।

अधश्च मूलान्यनुसन्ततानि,

कर्मानुबन्धीनि मनुष्यलोके ॥ २ ॥

*adhaścordhvaṁ prasṛtās tasya śākhā*

*guṇapravṛddhā viṣayapravālāḥ*

*adhaś ca mūlānyanusantatāni*

*karmānubandhīni manuṣyaloke*

(2) Its branches extend below and above, nourished by the Gunas. The objects of the senses are the shoots and its rootings are stretched forth—below in the world of men, resulting in the bondage of actions.

न रूपमस्येह तथोपलभ्यते,

नान्तो न चादिर्न च सम्प्रतिष्ठा।

अश्वत्थमेनं सुविरूढमूल-

मसङ्गशस्त्रेण दृढेन छित्त्वा ॥ ३ ॥

*na rūpamasyeha tathopalabhyate*

*nānto na cādirna ca sampratiṣthā*

*aśvatthamenaṁ suvirūḍhamūlam*

*asaṅgaśastreṇa dṛḍhena chittvā*

(3) Its real form is not thus perceived here, neither its end, nor its

origin, nor its foundation; having cut off this deep-rooted tree with the strong axe of non-attachment.

ततः पदं तत्परिमार्गितव्यं,
यस्मिन्गता न निवर्तन्ति भूयः ।
तमेव चाद्यं पुरुषं प्रपद्ये,
यतः प्रवृत्तिः प्रसृता पुराणी ॥ ४ ॥

*tataḥ padaṁ tat parimārgitavyaṁ*
*yasmin gatā na nivartanti bhūyaḥ*
*tameva cādyaṁ puruṣaṁ prapadye*
*yataḥ pravṛttiḥ prasṛtā purāṇī*

(4) Then, that highest goal should be pursued, whither having reached no one returns again. Saying "I seek refuge in the primordial Purusha, from whom has streamed forth this ancient current of the world".

निर्मानमोहा जितसङ्गदोषा,
अध्यात्मनित्या विनिवृत्तकामाः ।
द्वन्द्वैर्विमुक्ताः सुखदुःखसंज्ञैर्-
गच्छन्त्यमूढाः पदमव्ययं तत् ॥ ५ ॥

*nirmānamohā jitasaṅgadoṣā*
*adhyātmanityā vinivṛttakāmāḥ*

*dvandvairvimuktāḥ sukhaduḥkhasaṅjñair*
*gacchantyamūḍhāḥ padamavyayaṁ tat*

(5) Free from egoism and delusion, victorious over the evils of attachment, perennially absorbed in the study of the Self; totally free from desires and the pairs of opposites such as pleasure and pain, the undeluded reach the eternal state.

न तद्भासयते सूर्यो न शशाङ्को न पावकः।
यद् गत्वा न निवर्तन्ते तद्धाम परमं मम॥ ६॥

*na tad bhāsayate sūryo*
*na śaśāṅko na pāvakaḥ*
*yad gatvā na nivartante*
*tad dhāma paramaṁ mama*

(6) Neither the sun, nor the moon, nor the fire illuminates that; having reached there, they do not return that is My Supreme Abode.

ममैवांशो जीवलोके जीवभूतः सनातनः।
मनःषष्ठानीन्द्रियाणि प्रकृतिस्थानि कर्षति॥ ७॥

*mamaivāṅśo jīvaloke*
*jīvabhūtaḥ sanātanaḥ*

*manaḥṣaṣṭhānīndriyāṇi*
*prakṛtisthāni karṣati*

(7) An eternal fragment of Myself, having become the embodied-soul in the world of living; draws to itself the senses with the mind as the sixth, which rests in Prakriti (Nature).

शरीरं यदवाप्नोति यच्चाप्युत्क्रामतीश्वरः।
गृहीत्वैतानि संयाति वायुर्गन्धानिवाशयात्॥ ८ ॥

*śarīraṁ yad avāpnoti*
*yaccāpyutkrāmatīśvaraḥ*
*gṛhītvaitāni saṁyāti*
*vāyur gandhānivaśayāt*

(8) When the soul (as embodied-soul) takes up a body and also when he leaves it, he takes along these (the mind and senses) and goes as the wind carries the perfumes from their seats.

श्रोत्रं चक्षुः स्पर्शनं च रसनं घ्राणमेव च।
अधिष्ठाय मनश्चायं विषयानुपसेवते॥ ९ ॥

*śrotraṁ cakṣuḥ sparśanaṁ ca*
*rasanaṁ ghrāṇameva ca*

*adhiṣṭhāya manaścāyaṁ*

*viṣayānupasevate*

(9) Presiding over the ears, the eyes, the touch, taste and smell as well as the mind; the embodied-soul enjoys the object of the senses.

उत्क्रामन्तं स्थितं वापि भुञ्जानं वा गुणान्वितम्।

विमूढा नानुपश्यन्ति पश्यन्ति ज्ञानचक्षुषः ॥१०॥

*utkrāmantaṁ sthitaṁ vāpi*

*bhuñjānaṁ vā guṇānvitam*

*vimūḍhā nānupaśyanti*

*paśyanti jñānacakṣuṣaḥ*

(10) The deluded do not perceive the indwelling-soul, while departing from or dwelling in the body and experiencing the objects of the senses in contact with the modes; but they who possess the eye of wisdom truly see.

यतन्तो योगिनश्चैनं पश्यन्त्यात्मन्यवस्थितम्।

यतन्तोऽप्यकृतात्मानो नैनं पश्यन्त्यचेतसः ॥११॥

*yatanto yoginaś cainaṁ*

*paśyantyātmanyavasthitam*

*yatanto'pyakṛtātmāno*

*nainaṁ paśyanty acetasaḥ*

(11) The striving yogins do perceive the indwelling-soul, established in the Self but the ignorant those have not purified their hearts; even though endeavouring, do not perceive the indweller.

यदादित्यगतं तेजो जगद्भासयतेऽखिलम्।

यच्चन्द्रमसि यच्चाग्नौ तत्तेजो विद्धि मामकम्॥ १२॥

*yadādityagataṁ tejo*

*jagad bhāsayate'khilam*

*yaccandramasi yaccāgnau*

*tat tejo viddhi māmakam*

(12) The light of the sun which illumines the whole universe, that which is also in the moon and fire—know that light to be My splendour.

गामाविश्य च भूतानि धारयाम्यहमोजसा।

पुष्णामि चौषधीः सर्वाः सोमो भूत्वा रसात्मकः॥ १३॥

*gāmāviśya ca bhūtāni*

*dhārayāmyaham ojasā*

*puṣṇāmi cauṣadhīḥ sarvāḥ*

*somo bhūtvā rasātmakaḥ*

(13) Penetrating the earth I support all beings with my vital energy and nourish all the herbs by becoming the sapful soma (moon).

अहं वैश्वानरो भूत्वा प्राणिनां देहमाश्रितः।

प्राणापानसमायुक्तः पचाम्यन्नं चतुर्विधम्॥ १४॥

*ahaṁ vaiśvānaro bhūtvā*

*prāṇināṁ deham āśritaḥ*

*prāṇāpānasamāyuktaḥ*

*pacāmyannaṁ caturvidham*

(14) I am the universal fire (vaishvanara) dwelling in the body of all living beings; and joined with the rhythm of inhalation and exhalation I digest the four kinds of food.

सर्वस्य चाहं हृदि संनिविष्टो,

मत्तः स्मृतिर्ज्ञानमपोहनं च।

वेदैश्च सर्वैरहमेव वेद्यो,

वेदान्तकृद्वेदविदेव चाहम्॥ १५॥

*sarvasya cāhaṁ hṛdi sanniviṣṭo*

*mattaḥ smṛtir jñānamapohanaṁ ca*

*vedaiś ca sarvairahameva vedyo*

*vedāntakṛd vedavideva cāham*

(15) I am seated in the hearts of all. I am the source of memory, wisdom and ratiocinative faculty. I am subject to be known through all the *Vedas:* I am the author of Vedanta, as well as the knower of the *Vedas.*

द्वाविमौ पुरुषौ लोके क्षरश्चाक्षर एव च।

क्षरः सर्वाणि भूतानि कूटस्थोऽक्षर उच्यते॥ १६ ॥

*dvāvimau puruṣau loke*

*kṣaraś cākṣara eva ca*

*kṣaraḥ sarvāṇi bhūtāni*

*kūṭastho'kṣara ucyate*

(16) There are two kinds of purushas in this world, the perishable and the imperishable. All beings are perishable—The unchanging (the soul) is called the imperishable.

उत्तमः पुरुषस्त्वन्यः परमात्मेत्युदाहृतः।

यो लोकत्रयमाविश्य बिभर्त्यव्यय ईश्वरः॥ १७॥

*uttamaḥ puruṣas tvanyaḥ*

*paramātmetyudāhṛtaḥ*

*yo lokatrayamāviśya*
*bibhartyavyaya īśvaraḥ*

(17) The Supreme Purusha is yet other than these—called the highest Self; the indestructible Lord. Who enters the three worlds, upholds and sustains them.

**यस्मात्क्षरमतीतोऽहमक्षरादपि चोत्तमः।**
**अतोऽस्मि लोके वेदे च प्रथितः पुरुषोत्तमः॥ १८॥**

*yaśmāt kṣaramatīto'ham-*
*akṣarādapi cottamaḥ*
*ato'smi loke vede ca*
*prathitaḥ puruṣottamaḥ*

(18) Since I transcend the perishable and am even higher than the imperishable; therefore in this world as well as in *Vedas,* I am declared to be the Supreme Purusha.

**यो मामेवमसम्मूढो जानाति पुरुषोत्तमम्।**
**स सर्वविद्भजति मां सर्वभावेन भारत॥ १९॥**

*yo māmevamasammūḍho*
*jānāti puruṣotttamaṁ*
*sa sarvavid bhājati māṁ*
*sarvabhāvena bhārata*

(19) The undeluded one, who knows Me thus, as the Supreme Purusha, is the knower of all. He worships Me with his whole being (whole heartedly) O' Arjuna.

इति गुह्यतमं शास्त्रमिदमुक्तं मयानघ।
एतद्बुद्ध्वा बुद्धिमान्स्यात्कृतकृत्यश्च भारत॥ २०॥

*iti guhyatamaṁ śāstram-*
*idamuktaṁ mayānagha*
*etad buddhvā buddhimān syāt*
*kṛtakṛtyaś ca bhārata*

(20) Thus, this most profound teaching has been imparted by Me, O'sinless one; by understanding this, one becomes self-enlightened and his goal in life is accomplished, O'Arjuna.

ॐ तत्सदिति श्रीमद्भगवद्गीतासूपनिषत्सु ब्रह्मविद्यायां
योगशास्त्रे श्रीकृष्णार्जुनसंवादे पुरुषोत्तमयोगो
नाम पञ्चदशोऽध्यायः॥ १५॥

***'Aum' tatsaditi***
***Srīmadbhagawadgeetasupanisatsu***

***brahmavidyayam yogasastre***
***Srīkṛṣṇarjunasamvade***
***purusottamayogo nama***
***pancadasodhyayah***

**'AUM TAT SAT'**—Thus, in the Upanishad of the glorious Bhagawad Geeta, the science of the Brahman (Absolute) the scripture of yoga, the dialogue between Srī Kṛṣṇa and Arjuna—thus, ends the chapter fifteen entitled *"Purusottamayoga"*.

इति श्रीमद्भगवद्गीतासु पञ्चदशोऽध्यायः ॥ १५ ॥

## *Chapter Sixteen*

# THE DEVASURSAMPATTI VIBHAGYOGA

## THE YOGA OF THE DISTINCTION BETWEEN THE DIVINE AND THE DEMONIACAL ENDOWMENTS

श्रीभगवानुवाच

अभयं सत्त्वसंशुद्धिर्ज्ञानयोगव्यवस्थितिः ।
दानं दमश्च यज्ञश्च स्वाध्यायस्तप आर्जवम् ॥ १ ॥

*abhayaṁ sattvasaṅśuddhir*
*jñānayogavyavasthitiḥ*
*dānaṁ damaśca yajñaś ca*
*svādhyāyas tapa ārjavam*

**The Blessed Lord said :**

(1) Fearlessness, purity of heart, steadfastness in Yoga of knowledge, charity, self-control, performance of yajña, study of the scriptures, austerity and straightforwardness.

अहिंसा सत्यमक्रोधस्त्यागः शान्तिरपैशुनम्।
दया भूतेष्वलोलुप्त्वं मार्दवं ह्रीरचापलम्॥ २॥

*ahimsā satyamakrodhas*
*tyāgaḥ śāntirapaiśunaṁ*
*dayā bhūteṣvaloluptvaṁ*
*mārdavaṁ hrīracāpalaṁ*

(2) Non-violence, truthfulness, absence of anger, renunciation, peacefulness, aversion to fault finding, compassion towards all beings, non-covetousness, gentleness, modesty and absence of fickleness.

तेजः क्षमा धृतिः शौचमद्रोहो नातिमानिता।
भवन्ति सम्पदं दैवीमभिजातस्य भारत॥ ३॥

*tejaḥ kṣamā dhṛtiḥ śaucam-*
*adroho nātimanitā*
*bhavanti sampadaṁ daivīm-*
*abhijātasya bhārata*

(3) Brilliance, forgiveness, fortitude, purity, absence of hatred, absence of arrogance—These are the marks of the one who is endowed with divine nature, O'Arjuna.

दम्भो दर्पोऽभिमानश्च क्रोधः पारुष्यमेव च।
अज्ञानं चाभिजातस्य पार्थ सम्पदमासुरीम्॥४॥

*dambho darpoabhimānaś ca*
*krodhaḥ pāruṣyameva ca*
*ajñānaṁ cābhijātasya*
*pārtha saṁpadamāsurīṁ*

(4) Hypocrisy, arrogance, self-conceit, anger, rudeness and ignorance are the characteristics of the one who is endowed with demoniac nature O'Arjuna.

दैवी सम्पद्विमोक्षाय निबन्धायासुरी मता।
मा शुचः सम्पदं दैवीमभिजातोऽसि पाण्डव॥५॥

*daivī saṁpad vimokṣāya*
*nibandhāyāsurī matā*
*mā śucaḥ saṁpadaṁ daivīm-*
*abhijāto'si pāṇḍava*

(5) The divine nature is conducive to emancipation and the demoniac to bondage. Grieve not, O'Arjuna, thou art born with divine endowments.

द्वौ भूतसर्गौ लोकेऽस्मिन्दैव आसुर एव च।
दैवो विस्तरशः प्रोक्त आसुरं पार्थ मे शृणु॥ ६॥

*dvau bhūtasargau loke'smin-*
*daiva āsura eva ca*
*daivo vistaraśaḥ prokta*
*āsuraṁ pārtha me śṛṇu*

(6) There are two types of beings in the world : The divine and the demoniac. The divine has been explained in detail, now hear about the demoniac from Me, O' Arjuna.

प्रवृत्तिं च निवृत्तिं च जना न विदुरासुराः।
न शौचं नापि चाचारो न सत्यं तेषु विद्यते॥ ७॥

*pravṛttiṁ ca nivṛttiṁ ca*
*janā na vidurāsurāḥ*
*na śaucaṁ nāpi cācāro*
*na satyaṁ teṣu vidyate*

(7) The demoniac people do not know what to do and what to refrain from; neither purity nor good conduct, nor truth is found in them.

असत्यमप्रतिष्ठं ते जगदाहुरनीश्वरम्।
अपरस्परसम्भूतं किमन्यत्कामहैतुकम्॥ ८॥

*asatyam apratiṣṭhaṁ te*
*jagadāhuranīśvaraṁ*
*aparasparasambhūtaṁ*
*kimanyat kāmahaitukaṁ.*

(8) They say, that the world is without truth, without any foundation and without a God; brought about only by the mutual union with the desire for its cause.

एतां दृष्टिमवष्टभ्य नष्टात्मानोऽल्पबुद्धयः।
प्रभवन्त्युग्रकर्माणः क्षयाय जगतोऽहिताः॥ ९॥

*etāṁ dṛṣṭimavaṣṭabhya*
*naṣṭātmāno'lpabuddhayaḥ*
*prabhavantyugrakarmāṇaḥ*
*kṣayāya jagato'hitāḥ*

(9) Holding fast to this view, these ruined beings of meagre understanding and cruel deeds; come forth as the enemies of the world, for its destruction.

काममाश्रित्य दुष्पूरं दम्भमानमदान्विताः।
मोहाद् गृहीत्वासद्ग्राहान्प्रवर्तन्तेऽशुचिव्रताः॥ १०॥

*kāmaṁ āśritya duṣpūraṁ*
*dambhamānamadānvitāḥ*
*mohād gṛhītvāsadgrāhān*
*pravartante'śucivratāḥ*

(10) Filled with insatiable desires, motivated by hypocrisy, vanity and arrogance; they hold false values through delusion and work with impure resolves.

**चिन्तामपरिमेयां च प्रलयान्तामुपाश्रिताः।**
**कामोपभोगपरमा एतावदिति निश्चिताः॥११॥**

*cintāmaparimeyāṁ ca*
*pralayāntāmupāśritāḥ*
*kāmopabhogaparamā*
*etāvaditi niścitāḥ*

(11) Obsessed with innumerable anxieties, those end only with their death, they regard the enjoyment of sensuous pleasures as their highest goal of life and are fully convinced that, that is all.

**आशापाशशतैर्बद्धाः कामक्रोधपरायणाः।**
**ईहन्ते कामभोगार्थमन्यायेनार्थसञ्चयान्॥१२॥**

*āśāpāśaśatairbaddhāḥ*
*kāmakrodhaparāyaṇāḥ*
*īhante kāmabhogārtham-*
*anyāyenārthasañcayān*

(12) Bound by hundreds of fetters of expectations, given over to lust and anger; they strive to collect wealth by illegal means for the gratification of their desires.

इदमद्य मया लब्धमिमं प्राप्स्ये मनोरथम्।
इदमस्तीदमपि मे भविष्यति पुनर्धनम्॥ १३ ॥

*idamadya mayā labdham-*
*imaṁ prāpsye manoratham*
*idam astīdamapi me*
*bhaviṣyati punardhanam*

(13) This has been secured by me today and that desire I must fulfil soon. This wealth is mine, and that wealth will also be mine in future.

असौ मया हतः शत्रुर्हनिष्ये चापरानपि।
ईश्वरोऽहमहं भोगी सिद्धोऽहं बलवान्सुखी॥ १४ ॥

*asau mayā hataḥ śatrur*
*haniṣye cāparānapi*

*iśvaroahmahaṁ bhogī*

*siddho'haṁ balovan sukhi*

(14) This enemy has been destroyed by me and others too I will finish soon. I am the master and the enjoyer. I am successful, powerful and very prosperous.

आढ्योऽभिजनवानस्मि,

कोऽन्योऽस्ति सदृशो मया।

यक्ष्ये दास्यामि मोदिष्य,

इत्यज्ञानविमोहिताः ॥ १५ ॥

*āḍhyo'bhijanavānasmi*

*ko'nyo'sti sadṛśo mayā*

*yakṣye dāsyāmi modiṣya*

*ityajñānavimohitāḥ*

(15) I am wealthy and born in a noble family. Who else is equal to me? I perform sacrifices, give charity and rejoice; thus they are deluded by ignorance.

अनेकचित्तविभ्रान्ता मोहजालसमावृताः।

प्रसक्ताः कामभोगेषु पतन्ति नरकेऽशुचौ ॥ १६ ॥

*anekacittavibhrāntā*
*mohajālasamāvṛtāḥ*
*prasaktāḥ kāmabhogeṣu*
*patanti narake'śucau*

(16) Bewildered by many fantasies, entangled in the snare of delusion, addicted to the sensual enjoyments, they fall into the foul hell.

आत्मसम्भाविताः स्तब्धा धनमानमदान्विताः ।
यजन्ते नामयज्ञैस्ते दम्भेनाविधिपूर्वकम् ॥ १७ ॥

*ātmasambhāvitāḥ stabdhā*
*dhanamānamadānvitāḥ*
*yajante nāmayajñais te*
*dambhenāvidhipūrvakam*

(17) Self-conceited, stubborn, intoxicated with arrogance of wealth, they perform sacrifices which are only for name, with ostentation and with disregard to the scriptural ordinance.

अहङ्कारं बलं दर्पं कामं क्रोधं च संश्रिताः ।
मामात्मपरदेहेषु प्रद्विषन्तोऽभ्यसूयकाः ॥ १८ ॥

*ahaṅkāraṁ balaṁ darpaṁ*

*kāmaṁ krodhaṁ ca saṅśritāḥ*

*māmātmaparadeheṣu*

*pradviṣanto'bhyasūyakāḥ*

(18) Possessed of egoism, power, arrogance, lust and anger, these malicious people despise Me, in their own bodies and in those of others.

तानहं द्विषतः क्रूरान्संसारेषु नराधमान्।

क्षिपाम्यजस्रमशुभानासुरीष्वेव योनिषु॥ १९॥

*tān ahaṁ dviṣataḥ krūrān*

*saṅsāreṣu narādhamān*

*kṣipāmyajasramaśubhān*

*āsurīṣveva yoniṣu*

(19) These cruel haters, the most degraded among men in the world; I hurl these evildoers repeatedly into the wombs of demons only.

आसुरीं योनिमापन्ना मूढा जन्मनि जन्मनि।

मामप्राप्यैव कौन्तेय ततो यान्त्यधमां गतिम्॥ २०॥

*āsurīṁ yonimāpannā*

*mūḍhā janmani-janmani*

*māmaprāpyaiva kaunteya*
*tato yāntyadhamāṁ gatim*

(20) Fallen into the wombs of demons, these deluded beings from birth to birth do not attain Me O'Kaunteya. They fall further into the lower state than that.

**त्रिविधं नरकस्येदं द्वारं नाशनमात्मनः।**
**कामः क्रोधस्तथा लोभस्तस्मादेतत्त्रयं त्यजेत्॥ २१॥**

*trividhaṁ narakasyedaṁ*
*dvāraṁ nāśanamātmanaḥ*
*kāmaḥ krodhas tathā lobhas*
*tasmādetat trayaṁ tyajet*

(21) This is the triple gate of hell, that leads to the destruction of the embodied-self—'Lust, anger and greed'. Therefore, one must abandon these three.

**एतैर्विमुक्तः कौन्तेय तमोद्वारैस्त्रिभिर्नरः।**
**आचरत्यात्मनः श्रेयस्ततो याति परां गतिम्॥ २२॥**

*etair vimuktaḥ kaunteya*
*tamodvārais tribhir naraḥ*
*ācarātyatmanaḥ śreyas*
*tato yāti parāṁ gatim*

(22) The man who is released from these three gates of darkness O'Arjuna, he practises, what is good for him and thus goes to the highest state.

यः शास्त्रविधिमुत्सृज्य वर्तते कामकारतः।
न स सिद्धिमवाप्नोति न सुखं न परां गतिम्॥ २३॥

*yaḥ śāstravidhimutsṛjya*
*vartate kāmakārataḥ*
*na sa siddhimavāpnoti*
*na sukhaṁ na parāṁ gatim*

(23) He who abandons the ordinances of the scriptures and acts merely under the impulse of his desire, he does not attain either perfection, or happiness or the Supreme Goal.

तस्माच्छास्त्रं प्रमाणं ते कार्याकार्यव्यवस्थितौ।
ज्ञात्वा शास्त्रविधानोक्तं कर्म कर्तुमिहार्हसि॥ २४॥

*tasmācchāstraṁ pramāṇaṁ te*
*kāryākāryavyavasthitau*
*jñātvā śāstravidhānoktaṁ*
*karma kartumihārhasi*

(24) Therefore, let the scripture

be thy authority, in deciding what ought to be done and what should not to be done; having known what is declared in the ordinance of the scriptures, you should perform your work.

ॐ तत्सदिति श्रीमद्भगवद्गीतासूपनिषत्सु ब्रह्मविद्यायां
योगशास्त्रे श्रीकृष्णार्जुनसंवादे दैवासुरसम्पत्ति-
विभागयोगो नाम षोडशोऽध्यायः ॥ १६ ॥

***'Aum' tatsaditi***
***Srīmadbhagawadgeeta supanisatsu***
***brahmavidyayam yogasastre***
***Srīkṛṣṇarjunasamvade***
***daivasurasampattivibhagayogo***
***nama sodasodhyayah***

**'AUM TAT SAT'**—Thus, in the Upanishad of the glorious Bhagawad Geeta, the science of the Brahman (Absolute) the scripture of yoga, the dialogue between Srī Kṛṣṇa and Arjuna—thus, ends the chapter sixteen entitled *"Daivasurasampatti-vibhagayoga"*.

इति श्रीमद्भगवद्गीतासु षोडशोऽध्यायः ॥ १६ ॥

# *Chapter Seventeen*

# ŚRADDHĀTRIYA VIBHAGYOGA

## THE YOGA OF THE THREEFOLD DIVISION OF THE FAITH

अर्जुन उवाच

ये शास्त्रविधिमुत्सृज्य यजन्ते श्रद्धयान्विताः।
तेषां निष्ठा तु का कृष्ण सत्त्वमाहो रजस्तमः ॥ १ ॥

*ye śāstravidhimutsrjya*
*yajante śraddhayānvitāḥ*
*teṣāṁ niṣthā tu kā kṛṣṇa*
*sattvamāho rajas tamaḥ*

**Arjuna said :**

(1) Those who, neglecting the ordinances of the scriptures, perform yajña (worship) with faith, what is their status O'Kṛṣṇa? Is it *sattva, ṛajas* or *tamas*?

श्रीभगवानुवाच

त्रिविधा भवति श्रद्धा देहिनां सा स्वभावजा।
सात्त्विकी राजसी चैव तामसी चेति तां शृणु ॥ २ ॥

*trividhā bhavati śraddhā*
*dehināṁ sā svabhāvajā*
*sāttvikī rājasī caiva*
*tāmasī ceti tāṁ śṛṇu*

**The Blessed Lord said :**

(2) The faith of the embodied beings is of three kinds, born of their innate disposition—the *sattvic* (pure) the *rajasic* (passionate) and the *tamasic* (ignorant). Thus thou hear of it.

सत्त्वानुरूपा सर्वस्य श्रद्धा भवति भारत।
श्रद्धामयोऽयं पुरुषो यो यच्छ्रद्धः स एव सः ॥ ३ ॥

*sattvānurūpā sarvasya*
*śraddhā bhavati bhārata*
*śraddhāmayo'yaṁ puruṣo*
*yo yacchraddhaḥ sa eva saḥ*

(3) The faith of each person is in accordance with his innate nature O'Arjuna. Man is made of his faith; as a man's faith is, so is he.

यजन्ते सात्त्विका देवान्यक्षरक्षांसि राजसाः।
प्रेतान्भूतगणांश्चान्ये यजन्ते तामसा जनाः ॥ ४ ॥

*yajante sāttvikā devān*
*yakṣarakṣāṅsi rājasāḥ*
*pretān bhūtagaṇānścānye*
*yajante tāmasā janāḥ*

(4) The *sattvic* (pure) men worship the gods; the *rajasic* (passionate) worship the Yakshas and Rakshasas; while others—the *tamasic* (deluded) men worship the ghosts and spirits.

अशास्त्रविहितं घोरं तप्यन्ते ये तपो जनाः।
दम्भाहङ्कारसंयुक्ताः कामरागबलान्विताः॥ ५॥

*aśāstravihitaṁ ghoraṁ*
*tapyante ye tapo-janāḥ*
*dambhāhaṅkārsaṁyuktāḥ*
*kāmarāgabalānvitāḥ*

(5) Those men, who practise fierce austerities which are not enjoined by the scriptures, being given to hypocrisy and arrogance, impelled by the force of lust and attachment.

कर्षयन्तः शरीरस्थं भूतग्राममचेतसः।
मां चैवान्तःशरीरस्थं तान्विद्ध्यासुरनिश्चयान्॥ ६॥

*karṣayantaḥ śarīrasthaṁ*
*bhūtagrāmamacetasaḥ*
*māṁ caivā'ntaḥśarīrasthaṁ*
*tān viddhyāsuraniścayān*

(6) Senselessly torturing all the elements in the body they also hurt Me, who dwells within the body—know them to be of demoniacal resolves.

आहारस्त्वपि सर्वस्य त्रिविधो भवति प्रियः।
यज्ञस्तपस्तथा दानं तेषां भेदमिमं शृणु॥७॥

*āhārastvapi sarvasya*
*trividho bhavati priyaḥ*
*yajñastapas tathā dānaṁ*
*teṣāṁ bhedamimaṁ śṛṇu*

(7) The food, which is liked by everyone, is of three kinds, so is the *yajña,* austerity and charity. Hear thou the distinction of these.

आयुः सत्त्वबलारोग्य-
सुखप्रीतिविवर्धनाः।
रस्याः स्निग्धाः स्थिरा हृद्या
आहाराः सात्त्विकप्रियाः॥८॥

*āyuḥ sattvabalārogya-*
*sukhaprītivivardhanāḥ*
*rasyāḥ snigdhāḥ sthirā hṛdyā*
*āhārāḥ sāttvikapriyāḥ*

(8) The foods which promote longevity, purity, strength, health, happiness and cheerfulness, which are tasty, oleaginous, substantial and agreeable are liked by the *sattvic* (pure) people.

कट्वम्ललवणात्युष्णतीक्ष्णरूक्षविदाहिनः।
आहारा राजसस्येष्टा दुःखशोकामयप्रदाः॥९॥

*kaṭvamlalavaṇātyuṣṇa-*
*tīkṣṇarūkṣavidāhinaḥ*
*āhārā rājasasyeṣṭā*
*duḥkhaśokāmayapradāḥ*

(9) The foods which are bitter, sour, saline, excessively hot, pungent, dry and burning are liked by *rajasic;* which cause discomfort, pain and disease.

यातयामं गतरसं पूति पर्युषितं च यत्।
उच्छिष्टमपि चामेध्यं भोजनं तामसप्रियम्॥१०॥

*yātayāmaṁ gatarasaṁ*
*pūti paryuṣitaṁ ca yat*
*ucchiṣṭamapi cāmedhyaṁ*
*bhojanaṁ tāmasapriyam*

(10) That which is stale, insipid, putrid, discarded and impure is the food liked by the *tamasic*.

अफलाकांक्षिभिर्यज्ञो विधिदृष्टो य इज्यते।
यष्टव्यमेवेति मनः समाधाय स सात्त्विकः॥ ११॥

*aphalākāṅkṣibhir yajño*
*vidhidṛsto ya ijyate*
*yaṣṭavyameveti manaḥ*
*samādhāya sa sāttvikaḥ*

(11) The *yajña* which is performed selflessly, enjoined by the scriptural ordinance and merely out of the feeling of duty is *sattvic* (pure).

अभिसन्धाय तु फलं दम्भार्थमपि चैव यत्।
इज्यते भरतश्रेष्ठ तं यज्ञं विद्धि राजसम्॥ १२॥

*abhisandhāya tu phalaṁ*
*dambhārthamapi caiva yat*
*ijyate bharataśreṣtha*
*taṁ yajñaṁ viddhi rājasam*

(12) The *yajña* which is performed, keeping in view its reward and also for the sake of mere display, O'Arjuna, know that to be *rajasic* (passionate).

**विधिहीनमसृष्टान्नं मन्त्रहीनमदक्षिणम्।**
**श्रद्धाविरहितं यज्ञं तामसं परिचक्षते॥ १३॥**

*vidhihīnamasṛṣṭānnaṁ*
*mantrahīnamadakṣiṇam*
*śraddhāvirahitaṁ yajñaṁ*
*tāmasaṁ paricakṣate*

(13) That which is contrary to the scriptural injunctions and performed without the distribution of food, without chanting the holy hymns, giving gifts and sincere devotion, that *yajña* is said to be *tamasic*.

**देवद्विजगुरुप्राज्ञपूजनं शौचमार्जवम्।**
**ब्रह्मचर्यमहिंसा च शारीरं तप उच्यते॥ १४॥**

*devadvijagurupṛājña-*
*pūjanaṁ śaucamārjavam*
*brahmacaryam ahinsā ca*
*śārīraṁ tapa ucyate*

(16) Serenity of mind, gentleness, silence, self-control and total honesty of thoughts—this is called the austerity of the mind.

श्रद्धया परया तप्तं तपस्तत्त्रिविधं नरैः।
अफलाकांक्षिभिर्युक्तैः सात्त्विकं परिचक्षते॥ १७॥

*śraddhayā parayā taptaṁ*
*tapas tat trividhaṁ naraiḥ*
*aphalākāṅkṣibhir yuktaiḥ*
*sāttvikaṁ paricakṣate*

(17) This threefold austerity, practised with utmost faith by men of steadfast wisdom, without the expectation of a reward, is said to be *sattvic*.

सत्कारमानपूजार्थं तपो दम्भेन चैव यत्।
क्रियते तदिह प्रोक्तं राजसं चलमध्रुवम्॥ १८॥

*satkāramānapūjārthaṁ*
*tapo dambhena caiva yat*
*kriyate tadiha proktaṁ*
*rājasaṁ calamadhruvam*

(18) The penance which is practised in order to gain respect,

recognition, honour, and with hypocrisy—is said to be *rajasic.* It is unstable and transient.

मूढग्राहेणात्मनो यत्पीडया क्रियते तपः।
परस्योत्सादनार्थं वा तत्तामसमुदाहृतम्॥ १९॥

*mūḍhagrāheṇātmano yat*
*pīḍayā kriyate tapaḥ*
*parasyotsādanārthaṁ vā*
*tat tāmasamudāhṛtam*

(19) The austerity which is practised with deluded understanding and with self-torture or the purpose of causing harm to others, is declared to be *tamasic.*

दातव्यमिति यद्दानं दीयतेऽनुपकारिणे।
देशे काले च पात्रे च तद्दानं सात्त्विकं स्मृतम्॥ २०॥

*dātavyamiti yad dānaṁ*
*dīyate'nupakāriṇe*
*deśe kāle ca pātre ca*
*tad dānaṁ sāttvikaṁ smṛtam*

(20) Charity which is given with a sense of duty to the one from whom nothing is expected in return, and also

at the right place and time to a deserving person—that charity has been pronounced as *sattvic.*

यत्तु प्रत्युपकारार्थं फलमुद्दिश्य वा पुनः।
दीयते च परिक्लिष्टं तद्दानं राजसं स्मृतम्॥ २१॥

*yat tu pratyupakārārthaṁ*
*phalamuddiśya vā punaḥ*
*dīyate ca parikliṣṭaṁ*
*tad dānaṁ rājasaṁ smṛtam*

(21) The gift, which is given with the hope of receiving a favour in return or with the expectation of a reward and also given reluctantly, is considered to be *rajasic.*

अदेशकाले यद्दानमपात्रेभ्यश्च दीयते।
असत्कृतमवज्ञातं तत्तामसमुदाहृतम्॥ २२॥

*adeśakāle yad dānam*
*apātrebhyaś ca dīyate*
*asatkṛtamavajñātaṁ*
*tat tāmasamudāhṛtam*

(22) The charity that is given at an inappropriate place and time, to an

unworthy recipient with disrespect and contempt is declared to be *tamasic.*

ॐ तत्सदिति निर्देशो ब्रह्मणस्त्रिविधः स्मृतः।
ब्राह्मणास्तेन वेदाश्च यज्ञाश्च विहिताः पुरा॥ २३॥

*oṁ tatsaditi nirdeśo*
*brahmaṇas trividhaḥ smṛtaḥ*
*brāhmaṇās tena vedāś ca*
*yajñāś ca vihitāḥ purā*

(23) 'Aum Tat Sat'—this has been declared to be the threefold designation of the Brahman; by that, the *Vedas,* the *Brahmanas* and sacrifices were created in the ancient past.

तस्मादोमित्युदाहृत्य यज्ञदानतपःक्रियाः।
प्रवर्तन्ते विधानोक्ताः सततं ब्रह्मवादिनाम्॥ २४॥

*tasmādomityudāhṛtya*
*yajñadanatapaḥkriyāḥ*
*pravartante vidhānoktāḥ*
*satatam brahmavādinām*

(24) Therefore with the utterance of the holy syllable "AUM" the acts

of *yajña*, charity and austerity are commenced; as enjoined in the scriptures by the expounders of the *Brahman*.

**तदित्यनभिसन्धाय फलं यज्ञतपःक्रियाः।**
**दानक्रियाश्च विविधाः क्रियन्ते मोक्षकांक्षिभिः॥ २५॥**

*tadityanabhisandhāya*
*phalaṁ yajñatapaḥkriyāḥ*
*dānakriyāś ca vividhāḥ*
*kriyante mokṣakāṅkṣibhiḥ*

(25) With the utterance of the word *Tat*, without aiming at the fruit; the various acts of *yajña* (sacrifice) austerity and charity are performed by the seekers of liberation.

**सद्भावे साधुभावे च सदित्येतत् प्रयुज्यते।**
**प्रशस्ते कर्मणि तथा सच्छब्दः पार्थ युज्यते॥ २६॥**

*sadbhāve sādhubhāve ca*
*sadityetat prayujyate*
*praśaste karmaṇi tathā*
*sacchabdaḥ pārtha yujyate*

(26) The word *Sat* is used, to express Realty and that which is

good. Similarly O'Arjuna, the word *Sat* is used in the sense of an auspicious act.

यज्ञे तपसि दाने च स्थितिः सदिति चोच्यते।
कर्म चैव तदर्थीयं सदित्येवाभिधीयते॥ २७॥

*yajñe tapasi dāne ca*
*sthitiḥ saditi cocyate*
*karma caiva tadarthīyaṁ*
*sadity evābhidhīyate*

(27) Steadfastness in *yajña* (selfless action) asceticism and charity is also called *Sat;* and also the action which is in connection with these, is called *Sat.*

अश्रद्धया हुतं दत्तं तपस्तप्तं कृतं च यत्।
असदित्युच्यते पार्थ न च तत् प्रेत्य नो इह॥ २८॥

*aśraddhayā hutaṁ dattaṁ*
*tapas taptaṁ kṛtaṁ ca yat*
*asadityucyate pārtha*
*na ca tat pretya no iha*

(28) Whatever is offered in *yajña,* given as charity, practised as austerity and whatever rite is observed without

faith (sincere devotion), is called *asat* O'Arjuna. It bears nothing, neither here nor hereafter.

ॐ तत्सदिति श्रीमद्भगवद्गीतासूपनिषत्सु ब्रह्मविद्यायां योगशास्त्रे श्रीकृष्णार्जुनसंवादे श्रद्धात्रयविभागयोगो नाम सप्तदशोऽध्यायः ॥ १७ ॥

***'Aum' tatsaditi***
***Srīmadbhagawadgeeta supanisatsu***
***brahmavidyayam yogasastre***
***Srīkṛṣṇarjunasamvade***
***sraddhatriyavibhagayogo nama***
***saptadasodhyayah***

**'AUM TAT SAT'**—Thus, in the Upanishad of the glorious Bhagawad Geeta, the science of the Brahman (Absolute) the scripture of yoga, the dialogue between Srī Kṛṣṇa and Arjuna—thus, ends the chapter seventeen entitled *"Sraddhatriya-vibhagayoga"*.

इति श्रीमद्भगवद्गीतासु सप्तदशोऽध्यायः ॥ १७ ॥

# Chapter Eighteen

# MOKSASANNYASAYOGA

## THE YOGA OF LIBERATION THROUGH RENUNCIATION

अर्जुन उवाच

संन्यासस्य महाबाहो तत्त्वमिच्छामि वेदितुम्।
त्यागस्य च हृषीकेश पृथक्केशिनिषूदन॥ १॥

*sannyāsasya mahābāho*
*tattvamicchāmi veditum*
*tyāgasya ca hṛṣīkeśa*
*pṛthak keśiniṣūdana*

**Arjuna Said :**

(1) I desire to know in detail the truth about renunciation *(sannyasa)* and also about relinquishment separately, O' Hrishikesa (Srī Kṛṣṇa).

श्रीभगवानुवाच

काम्यानां कर्मणां न्यासं संन्यासं कवयो विदुः।
सर्वकर्मफलत्यागं प्राहुस्त्यागं विचक्षणाः॥ २॥

*kāmyānāṁ karmaṇāṁ nyāsaṁ*
*sannyāsaṁ kavayo viduḥ*
*sarvakarmaphalatyāgaṁ*
*prāhuṣ tyāgaṁ vicakṣaṇāḥ*

**The Blessed Lord said :**

(2) The sages understand *sannyasa* to be the renunciation of all actions prompted by desire; the learned declare the abandonment of the fruits of all actions to be the *tyaga* (relinquishment).

त्याज्यं दोषवदित्येके कर्म प्राहुर्मनीषिणः।
यज्ञदानतपः कर्म न त्याज्यमिति चापरे ॥ ३ ॥

*tyājyaṁ doṣavadityeke*
*karma prāhur manīṣinaḥ*
*yajñadānatapaḥ karma*
*na tyājyamiti cāpare*

(3) Some sages declare that actions should be abandoned as an evil, while others say that the act of *yajña* (sacrifice), charity and austerity should not be relinquished.

निश्चयं शृणु मे तत्र त्यागे भरतसत्तम।
त्यागो हि पुरुषव्याघ्र त्रिविधः सम्प्रकीर्तितः ॥ ४ ॥

(14) Worship of the gods, learned men, teachers and men of wisdom; cleanliness, straightforwardness, celibacy and non-violence—are called the austerities of the body.

अनुद्वेगकरं वाक्यं सत्यं प्रियहितं च यत्।
स्वाध्यायाभ्यसनं चैव वाङ्मयं तप उच्यते॥ १५ ॥

*anudvegakaraṁ vākyaṁ*
*satyaṁ priyahitaṁ ca yat*
*svādhyāyābhyasanaṁ caiva*
*vāṅmayaṁ tapa ucyate*

(15) The austerity of speech is considered to be the utterance of the words, which do not cause annoyance and are truthful, pleasant and beneficial; also the regular study of *Vedas;* and recitation of the Divine name.

मनःप्रसादः सौम्यत्वं मौनमात्मविनिग्रहः।
भावसंशुद्धिरित्येतत्तपो मानसमुच्यते॥ १६ ॥

*manaḥprasādaḥ saumyatvaṁ*
*maunamātmavinigrahaḥ*
*bhāvasaṁśuddhirityetat*
*tapo mānasamucyate*

*niścayaṁ śṛṇu me tatra*
*tyāge bharatasattama*
*tyāgo hi puruṣavyāghra*
*trividhaḥ samprakirtitaḥ*

(4) Listen from Me the final truth about the relinquishment, O'best of the Bharatas (Arjuna). The abandonment, O'best among men, has been declared to be of three kinds.

यज्ञदानतपः कर्म न त्याज्यं कार्यमेव तत्।
यज्ञो दानं तपश्चैव पावनानि मनीषिणाम्॥ ५॥

*yajñadānatapaḥ karma*
*na tyājyaṁ kāryameva tat*
*yajño dānaṁ tapaś caiva*
*pāvanāni manīṣiṇām*

(5) *Yajña* (sacrifice), charity and austerity are not to be abandoned; these should be performed, for the acts of *yajña,* charity and austerity are the purifiers of the wise.

एतान्यपि तु कर्माणि सङ्गं त्यक्त्वा फलानि च।
कर्तव्यानीति मे पार्थ निश्चितं मतमुत्तमम्॥ ६॥

*etānyapi tu karmāṇi*

*saṅgaṁ tyaktvā phalāni ca*

*kartavyānīti me pārtha*

*niścitaṁ matamuttamam*

(6) Even these actions should be performed abandoning all attachments and desire for fruits. O'Arjuna, this is for certain my decisive opinion.

**नियतस्य तु संन्यासः कर्मणो नोपपद्यते।**

**मोहात्तस्य परित्यागस्तामसः परिकीर्तितः॥ ७॥**

*niyatasya tu sannyāsaḥ*

*karmaṇo nopapadyate*

*mohāttasya parityāgas*

*tāmasaḥ parikīrtitaḥ*

(7) The renunciation of an obligatory act is not proper; its abandonment through delusion is considered to be *tamasic.*

**दुःखमित्येव यत्कर्म कायक्लेशभयात्त्यजेत्।**

**स कृत्वा राजसं त्यागं नैव त्यागफलं लभेत्॥ ८॥**

*duḥkhamityeva yat karma*

*kāyakleśabhayāt tyajet*

*sa kṛtvā rājasaṁ tyāgaṁ*
*naiva tyāgaphalaṁ labhet*

(8) He, who renounces his action, because it is painful or from the fear of physical suffering, his act of renunciation is considered to be *rajasic.* He does not attain the merit of relinquishment.

कार्यमित्येव यत्कर्म नियतं क्रियतेऽर्जुन।
सङ्गं त्यक्त्वा फलं चैव स त्यागः सात्त्विको मतः ॥ ९ ॥

*kāryamityeva yat karma*
*niyataṁ kriyate'rjuna*
*saṅgaṁ tyaktvā phalaṁ caiva*
*sa tyāgaḥ sāttviko mataḥ*

(9) He, who performs the obligatory actions, simply because it ought to be done; by abandoning attachment and also the desire for the fruit—that relinquishment is regarded to be *sattvic.*

न द्वेष्ट्यकुशलं कर्म कुशले नानुषज्जते।
त्यागी सत्त्वसमाविष्टो मेधावी छिन्नसंशयः ॥ १० ॥

*na dveṣṭyakuśalaṁ karma*
*kuśale nānuṣajjate*

*tyāgī sattvasamāviṣṭo*
*medhāvī chinnasaṅśayaḥ*

(10) The wise man of renunciation is the one who is imbued with the purity of *sattva,* whose doubts are dispelled, who does not hate the disagreeable work nor is attached to the agreeable one.

न हि देहभृता शक्यं त्यक्तुं कर्माण्यशेषतः।
यस्तु कर्मफलत्यागी स त्यागीत्यभिधीयते॥ ११॥

*na hi dehabhṛtā śakyaṁ*
*tyaktuṁ karmāṇyaśeṣataḥ*
*yastu karmaphalatyāgī*
*sa tyāgītyabhidhīyate*

(11) Verily, it is not possible for an embodied being to renounce actions altogether. He, who abandons the fruits of actions—he is said to be the renouncer.

अनिष्टमिष्टं मिश्रं च त्रिविधं कर्मणः फलम्।
भवत्यत्यागिनां प्रेत्य न तु संन्यासिनां क्वचित्॥ १२॥

*aniṣṭamiṣṭaṁ miśraṁ ca*
*trividhaṁ karmaṇaḥ phalam*

*bhavatyatyāgināṁ pretya*
*na tu sannyāsināṁ kvacit*

(12) Disagreeable, agreeable and mixed—threefold is the fruit of action, accruing after death, to those who have not relinquished—but there is none whatsoever for those who have renounced.

**पञ्चैतानि महाबाहो कारणानि निबोध मे।**
**सांख्ये कृतान्ते प्रोक्तानि सिद्धये सर्वकर्मणाम्॥ १३॥**

*pañcaitāni mahābāho*
*kāraṇāni nibodha me*
*sāṅkhye kṛtānte proktāni*
*siddhaye sarvakarmaṇām*

(13) Learn from Me, O'mighty armed (Arjuna), these five causes as declared in the *Samkhya* philosophy for the accomplishment of all actions.

**अधिष्ठानं तथा कर्ता करणं च पृथग्विधम्।**
**विविधाश्च पृथक्चेष्टा दैवं चैवात्र पञ्चमम्॥ १४॥**

*adhiṣṭhānaṁ tathā kartā*
*karaṇaṁ ca pṛthagvidham*
*vividhāś ca pṛthakceṣṭā*
*daivaṁ caivātra pañcamam*

(14) The seat of action (body) and likewise the doer, the instruments of various sorts (sense organs and mind) many kinds of efforts and providence (destiny) being the fifth.

शरीरवाङ्मनोभिर्यत्कर्म प्रारभते नरः।
न्याय्यं वा विपरीतं वा पञ्चैते तस्य हेतवः ॥ १५ ॥

*śarīravāṅgmanobhir yat*
*karma prārabhate naraḥ*
*nyāyyaṁ vā viparītaṁ vā*
*pañcaite tasya hetavaḥ*

(15) Whatever action a man performs with his body, speech and mind—whether it is right or wrong, these five are its causes.

तत्रैवं सति कर्तारमात्मानं केवलं तु यः।
पश्यत्यकृतबुद्धित्वान्न स पश्यति दुर्मतिः ॥ १६ ॥

*tatraivaṁ sati kartāram-*
*ātmānaṁ kevalaṁ tu yaḥ*
*paśyatyakṛtabuddhitvān*
*na sa paśyati durmatiḥ*

(16) Now, such being the case, the man of impure intellect, who on

account of his perverse understanding looks upon himself as the sole agent, he does not see (truly).

**यस्य नाहंकृतो भावो बुद्धिर्यस्य न लिप्यते।**

**हत्वापि स इमाँल्लोकान्न हन्ति न निबध्यते॥ १७॥**

*yasya nāhaṅkṛto bhāvo*

*buddhiryasya na lipyate*

*hatvāpi sa imāṁllokān*

*na hanti na nibadhyate*

(17) He, who is free from the egoistic notion of 'I-ness'; and whose mind is not tainted—even though he kills these people, he neither slays nor is he bound.

**ज्ञानं ज्ञेयं परिज्ञाता त्रिविधा कर्मचोदना।**

**करणं कर्म कर्तेति त्रिविधः कर्मसंग्रहः॥ १८॥**

*jñānaṁ jñeyaṁ parijñātā*

*trividhā karmacodanā*

*karaṇaṁ karma karteti*

*trividhaḥ karmasaṅgrahaḥ*

(18) Knowledge, the object of knowledge, and the knower, form the threefold impulse to action; the

instrument, the action and the agent form the threefold basis of action.

ज्ञानं कर्म च कर्ता च त्रिधैव गुणभेदतः।
प्रोच्यते गुणसंख्याने यथावच्छृणु तान्यपि॥ १९॥

*jñānaṁ karma ca kartā ca*
*tridhaiva guṇabhedataḥ*
*procyate guṇasaṅkhyāne*
*yathāvacchṛṇu tānyapi*

(19) The knowledge, action and the actor are also declared to be threefold, in the science of the gunas, according to the distinction of the gunas. Listen about them also as they are.

सर्वभूतेषु येनैकं भावमव्ययमीक्षते।
अविभक्तं विभक्तेषु तज्ज्ञानं विद्धि सात्त्विकम्॥ २०॥

*sarvabhūteṣu yenaikaṁ*
*bhāvamavyayamīkṣate*
*avibhaktaṁ vibhakteṣu*
*tajjñanaṁ viddhi sāttvikam*

(20) The knowledge by which one perceives in all beings the 'One' imperishable existence as undivided

in the divided—know that knowledge to be *sattvic.*

पृथक्त्वेन तु यज्ज्ञानं नानाभावान्पृथग्विधान्।
वेत्ति सर्वेषु भूतेषु तज्ज्ञानं विद्धि राजसम्॥ २१॥

*pṛthaktvena tu yajjñānaṁ*
*nānābhāvān pṛthagvidhān*
*vetti sarveṣu bhūteṣu*
*tajjñānaṁ viddhi rājasam*

(21) But that knowledge which perceives in all beings, the manifold entities of distinct kind, as different from one another—know that knowledge to be *rajasic.*

यत्तु कृत्स्नवदेकस्मिन्कार्ये सक्तमहैतुकम्।
अतत्त्वार्थवदल्पं च तत्तामसमुदाहृतम्॥ २२॥

*yattu kṛtsnavadekasmin*
*kārye saktamahetukam*
*atattvārthavadalapaṁ ca*
*tat tāmasamudāhṛtam*

(22) That which is confined to one single act, as if it were the whole, which is without reason, without foundation in truth and is trivial—that

is declared to be *tamasic.*

नियतं सङ्गरहितमरागद्वेषतः कृतम्।
अफलप्रेप्सुना कर्म यत्तत्सात्त्विकमुच्यते॥ २३॥

*niyataṁ saṅgarahitam*
*arāgadveṣataḥ kṛtam*
*aphalaprepsunā karma*
*yat tat sāttvikamucyate*

(23) The obligatory action which is performed without attachment, without love or hatred by the one who is not desirous of any reward—that action is called *sattvic.*

यत्तु कामेप्सुना कर्म साहङ्कारेण वा पुनः।
क्रियते बहुलायासं तद्राजसमुदाहृतम्॥ २४॥

*yat tu kāmepsunā karma*
*sāhaṅkāreṇa vā punaḥ*
*kriyate bahulāyāsaṁ*
*tad rājasamudāhṛtam*

(24) That action, however, which is performed with great strain by the one who seeks to gratify his desire or is impelled by egoism—that action is declared to be *rajasic.*

अनुबन्धं क्षयं हिंसामनवेक्ष्य च पौरुषम्।
मोहादारभ्यते कर्म यत्तत्तामसमुच्यते ॥ २५ ॥

*anubandhaṁ kṣayaṁ hinsām-*
*anavekṣya ca pauruṣam*
*mohād ārabhyate karma*
*yat tat tāmasamucyate*

(25) The action which is performed with delusion, regardless of the consequences, loss, injury and the individual's own ability—that is declared to be *tamasic.*

मुक्तसङ्गोऽनहंवादी
धृत्युत्साहसमन्वितः।
सिद्ध्यसिद्ध्योर्निर्विकारः
कर्ता सात्त्विक उच्यते ॥ २६ ॥

*muktasaṅgo'nahaṁvādī*
*dhṛtyutsāhasamanvitaḥ*
*siddhyasiddhyor nirvikāraḥ*
*kartā sāttvika ucyate*

(26) Free from attachment and the feeling of I, who is endowed with determination and enthusiasm, who

remains unaffected by success and failure—that doer is said to be *sattvic* (pure).

रागी कर्मफलप्रेप्सुर्लुब्धो हिंसात्मकोऽशुचिः ।

हर्षशोकान्वितः कर्ता राजसः परिकीर्तितः ॥ २७ ॥

*rāgī karmaphalaprepsur-*

*lubdho hinsātmako'śuciḥ*

*harṣaśokānvitaḥ kartā*

*rājasaḥ parikīrtitaḥ*

(27) The one who is swayed by passion, who eagerly seeks the fruits of his actions, who is greedy, violent, impure and who is easily moved by joy and sorrow—that doer is said to be *rajasic* (passionate).

अयुक्तः प्राकृतः स्तब्धः शठोऽनैष्कृतिकोऽलसः ।

विषादी दीर्घसूत्री च कर्ता तामस उच्यते ॥ २८ ॥

*ayuktaḥ prākṛtaḥ stabdhaḥ*

*śaṭho naiṣkṛtiko'lasaḥ*

*viṣādī dīrghasūtrī ca*

*kartā tāmasa ucyate*

(28) Who is unsteady, vulgar, stubborn, deceitful, malicious, lazy,

despondent and procrastinating—that doer is declared to be *tamasic* (ignorant).

बुद्धेर्भेदं धृतेश्चैव गुणतस्त्रिविधं शृणु।
प्रोच्यमानमशेषेण पृथक्त्वेन धनञ्जय॥ २९॥

*buddher bhedaṁ dhṛteś caiva*
*guṇatas trividhaṁ śṛṇu*
*procyamānamaśeṣeṇa*
*pṛthaktvena dhanañjaya*

(29) Now hear, O'Arjuna the threefold division of intellect and also of steadiness, according to the gunas; as I declare them fully and separately.

प्रवृत्तिं च निवृत्तिं च,
कार्याकार्ये भयाभये।
बन्धं मोक्षं च या वेत्ति,
बुद्धिः सा पार्थ सात्त्विकी॥ ३०॥

*pravṛttiṁ ca nivṛttiṁ ca*
*kāryākārye bhayābhaye*
*bandhaṁ mokṣaṁ ca yā vetti*
*buddhiḥ sā pārtha sāttvikī*

(30) The intellect which determines clearly the path of activity

and renunciation; what ought to be done and what should not be done; what is to be feared and what is not to be feared; what is bondage and what is freedom; O'Partha (Arjuna)—that intellect is *sattvic* (Pure).

**यया धर्ममधर्मं च कार्यं चाकार्यमेव च।**
**अयथावत् प्रजानाति बुद्धिः सा पार्थ राजसी ॥ ३१ ॥**

*yayā dharmamadharmaṁ ca*
*kāryaṁ cākāryameva ca*
*ayathāvat prajānāti*
*buddhiḥ sā pārtha rājasī*

(31) That which gives an erroneous understanding of Dharma and Adharma, and also of what should be done and what should not be done—that intellect O'Partha is *rajasic.*

**अधर्मं धर्ममिति या मन्यते तमसावृता।**
**सर्वार्थान्विपरीतांश्च बुद्धिः सा पार्थ तामसी ॥ ३२ ॥**

*adharmaṁ dharmamiti yā*
*manyate tamasāvṛtā*
*sarvārthān viparītānś ca*
*buddhiḥ sā pārtha tāmasī*

(32) That which perceives even Adharma to be Dharma; which is enveloped in darkness and reverses every value—that intellect O'Partha is indeed *tamasic.*

**धृत्या यया धारयते**

**मनः प्राणेन्द्रियक्रियाः ।**

**योगेनाव्यभिचारिण्या**

**धृतिः सा पार्थ सात्त्विकी ॥ ३३ ॥**

*dhṛtyā yayā dhārayate*

*manaḥ prāṇendriyakriyāḥ*

*yogenāvyabhicāriṇyā*

*dhṛtiḥ sā pārtha sāttvikī*

(33) The unwavering steadiness by which, through Yoga, one controls the activities of the mind, the life breath and the senses—that firmness O'Partha is *sattvic.*

**यया तु धर्मकामार्थान्धृत्या धारयतेऽर्जुन ।**

**प्रसङ्गेन फलाकांक्षी धृतिः सा पार्थ राजसी ॥ ३४ ॥**

*yayā tu dharmakāmarthān*

*dhṛtyā dhārayate'rjuna*

*prasaṅgena phalākāṅkṣī*

*dhṛtiḥ sā pārtha rājasī*

(34) The steadiness by which one holds fast to Dharma (duty), pleasure and wealth; desiring the fruit in consequence thereof—that firmness is *rajasic,* O'Arjuna.

यया स्वप्नं भयं शोकं विषादं मदमेव च।

न विमुञ्चति दुर्मेधा धृतिः सा पार्थ तामसी॥ ३५॥

*yayā svapnaṁ bhayaṁ śokaṁ*

*viṣādaṁ madameva ca*

*na vimuñcati durmedhā*

*dhṛtiḥ sa pārtha tāmasī*

(35) That by which a fool does not abandon sleep, fear, grief, depression and conceit as well—that firmness O'Arjuna is *tamasic.*

सुखं त्विदानीं त्रिविधं शृणु मे भरतर्षभ।

अभ्यासाद्रमते यत्र दुःखान्तं च निगच्छति॥ ३६॥

*sukhaṁ tvidānīṁ trividhaṁ*

*śṛṇu me bharatarṣabha*

*abhyāsād ramate yatra*

*duhkhāntaṁ ca nigacchati*

(36) Now hear from Me, O'Arjuna, the threefold division of happiness—that in which one comes to rejoice by long practice and in which he reaches to the end of his pain.

यत्तदग्रे विषमिव परिणामेऽमृतोपमम्।
तत्सुखं सात्त्विकं प्रोक्तमात्मबुद्धिप्रसादजम्॥ ३७॥

*yat tad agre viṣamiva*
*pariṇāme'mṛtopamam*
*tat sukhaṁ sāttvikaṁ proktam-*
*ātmabuddhiprasādajam*

(37) That which is like poison in the beginning but becomes like an elixir in the end—which is born of a clear understanding of the Self, that happiness is declared to be *sattvic.*

विषयेन्द्रियसंयोगाद्यत्तदग्रेऽमृतोपमम्।
परिणामे विषमिव तत्सुखं राजसं स्मृतम्॥ ३८॥

*viṣayendriyasaṁyogād*
*yat tadagre'mṛtopamam*
*pariṇāme viṣamiva*
*tat sukhaṁ rājasaṁ smṛtam*

(38) That which arises from contacts of the senses with their objects; which is at first like nectar and in the end like poison—that happiness is said to be *rajasic.*

यदग्रे चानुबन्धे च सुखं मोहनमात्मनः।
निद्रालस्यप्रमादोत्थं तत्तामसमुदाहृतम्॥ ३९॥

*yad agre cānubandhe ca*
*sukhaṁ mohanamātmanaḥ*
*nidrālasyapramādotthaṁ*
*tat tamasamudāhṛtam*

(39) That happiness which at the beginning as well as in the end, deludes the embodied-self, through sleep, sloth and negligence—that is declared to be *tamasic.*

न तदस्ति पृथिव्यां वा दिवि देवेषु वा पुनः।
सत्त्वं प्रकृतिजैर्मुक्तं यदेभिः स्यात् त्रिभिर्गुणैः॥ ४०॥

*na tadasti pṛthivyāṁ vā*
*divi deveṣu vā punaḥ*
*sattvaṁ prakṛtijair muktaṁ*
*yadebhiḥ syāt tribhirguṇaiḥ*

(40) There is no creature either

on earth or in heaven among the celestials, which is free from these three qualities, born of Prakriti (Nature).

**ब्राह्मणक्षत्रियविशां शूद्राणां च परन्तप।**

**कर्माणि प्रविभक्तानि स्वभावप्रभवैर्गुणैः॥४१॥**

*brāhmaṇakṣatriyaviśāṁ*
*śūdrāṇāṁ ca parantapa*
*karmāṇi pravibhaktāni*
*svabhāvaprabhavairguṇaiḥ*

(41) Of Brahmins, Of Kshatriyas and Vaisyas as well as of Sudras, O'Arjuna, the activities are divided in accordance with their own inborn qualities of nature.

**शमो दमस्तपः शौचं क्षान्तिरार्जवमेव च।**

**ज्ञानं विज्ञानमास्तिक्यं ब्रह्मकर्म स्वभावजम्॥४२॥**

*śamo damas tapaḥ śaucaṁ*
*kṣāntirārjavameva ca*
*jñānaṁ vijñānamāstikyaṁ*
*brahmakarma svabhāvajam*

(42) Serenity, self-restraint,

austerity, purity, forbearance, and straightforwardness; knowledge, wisdom and faith in religion—all these are the duties of a Brahmin; born of his inherent nature.

शौर्यं तेजो धृतिर्दाक्ष्यं युद्धे चाप्यपलायनम्।
दानमीश्वरभावश्च क्षात्रं कर्म स्वभावजम्॥ ४३॥

*śauryaṁ tejo dhṛtirdākṣyaṁ*
*yuddhe cāpyapalāyanam*
*dānamīśvarabhāvaś ca*
*kṣātraṁ karma svabhāvajam*

(43) Heroism, vigour, steadiness, fortitude, dexterity (skilfulness), and also not fleeing from battle; generosity and lordliness—are the duties of a Kshatriya, born of his inherent nature.

कृषिगौरक्ष्यवाणिज्यं वैश्यकर्म स्वभावजम्।
परिचर्यात्मकं कर्म शूद्रस्यापि स्वभावजम्॥ ४४॥

*kṛṣigaurakṣyavāṇijyaṁ*
*vaiśyakarma svabhāvajam*
*paricaryātmakaṁ karma*
*śūdrasyāpi svabhāvajam*

(44) Agriculture, cattle rearing and trade are the duties of a Vaisya, born of his nature; while the work consisting of service is the duty of a Sudra, born of his nature.

स्वे स्वे कर्मण्यभिरतः संसिद्धिं लभते नरः।
स्वकर्मनिरतः सिद्धिं यथा विन्दति तच्छृणु॥ ४५॥

*sve-sve karmaṇyabhiratah*
*saṅsiddhiṁ labhate narah*
*svakarmaniratah siddhiṁ*
*yathā vindati tacchṛṇu*

(45) Sincerely devoted to his own duty, man attains the highest perfection. How he attains the perfection, being devoted to the performance of his own inborn duty; listen to that now.

यतः प्रवृत्तिर्भूतानां येन सर्वमिदं ततम्।
स्वकर्मणा तमभ्यर्च्य सिद्धिं विन्दति मानवः॥ ४६॥

*yatah pravṛttir bhūtānāṁ*
*yena sarvamidaṁ tatam*
*svakarmaṇā tamabhyarcya*
*siddhiṁ vindati mānavah*

(46) He from whom all beings have evolved and by whom all this is pervaded—worshipping Him, through the performance of ones own duty, a man attains perfection.

श्रेयान्स्वधर्मो विगुणः परधर्मात्स्वनुष्ठितात्।
स्वभावनियतं कर्म कुर्वन्नाप्नोति किल्बिषम्॥ ४७॥

*śreyān svadharmo viguṇaḥ*
*paradharmāt svanuṣṭhitāt*
*svabhāvaniyataṁ karma*
*kurvannāpnoti kilbiṣam*

(47) Better is one's own duty, though destitute of merits, than the duty of another well performed—He, who does the duty ordained by his own inherent nature, he incurs no sin.

सहजं कर्म कौन्तेय सदोषमपि न त्यजेत्।
सर्वारम्भा हि दोषेण धूमेनाग्निरिवावृताः॥ ४८॥

*sahajaṁ karma kaunteya*
*sadoṣamapi na tyajet*
*sarvārambhā hi doṣeṇa*
*dhūmenāgnirivāvṛtāḥ*

(48) Therefore, O'son of Kunti

(Arjuna) one should not abandon one's innate duty, even though it is imperfect; for, all enterprises are enveloped by imperfections, as is the fire by smoke.

असक्तबुद्धिः सर्वत्र जितात्मा विगतस्पृहः।
नैष्कर्म्यसिद्धिं परमां संन्यासेनाधिगच्छति॥४९॥

*asaktabuddhiḥ sarvatra*
*jitātmā vigataspṛhaḥ*
*naiṣkarmyasiddhiṁ paramāṁ*
*sannyāsenādhigacchati*

(49) He, whose intellect is unattached in all respects, who is self-controlled and free from all desires—he by renunciation, attains the Supreme state of freedom from action.

सिद्धिं प्राप्तो यथा ब्रह्म तथाप्नोति निबोध मे।
समासेनैव कौन्तेय निष्ठा ज्ञानस्य या परा॥५०॥

*siddhiṁ prāpto yathā brahma*
*tathāpnoti nibodha me*
*samāsenaiva kaunteya*
*niṣthā jñānasya yā parā*

(50) Know from Me, in brief, O'Arjuna, how having attained perfection, he attains to the Brahman—The Supreme consummation of knowledge.

बुद्ध्या विशुद्धया युक्तो धृत्यात्मानं नियम्य च।
शब्दादीन्विषयांस्त्यक्त्वा रागद्वेषौ व्युदस्य च॥५१॥

*buddhyā viśuddhayā yukto*
*dhṛtyātmānaṁ niyamya ca*
*śabdādīn viṣayāns tyaktvā*
*rāgadveṣau vyudasya ca*

(51) Endowed with the purity of intellect, controlling the mind by steadfastness, relinquishing the external sounds and the other objects of senses; laying aside both attraction and aversion.

विविक्तसेवी लघ्वाशी यतवाक्कायमानसः।
ध्यानयोगपरो नित्यं वैराग्यं समुपाश्रितः॥५२॥

*viviktasevī laghvāśī*
*yatavākkāyamānasaḥ*
*dhyānayogaparo nityaṁ*
*vairāgyaṁ samupāśritaḥ*

(52) Resorting to solitude, eating but very little, controlling speech, body and mind; always engaged in Yoga of meditation and taking refuge in dispassion.

अहङ्कारं बलं दर्पं कामं क्रोधं परिग्रहम्।
विमुच्य निर्ममः शान्तो ब्रह्मभूयाय कल्पते॥५३॥

*ahaṅkāraṁ balaṁ darpaṁ*
*kāmaṁ krodhaṁ parigraham*
*vimucya nirmamaḥ śānto*
*brahmabhūyāya kalpate*

(53) Having abandoned egoism, violence, arrogance, lust and anger; who is free from the notion of 'mineness' and is totally at peace within—he becomes worthy of being one with Brahman.

ब्रह्मभूतः प्रसन्नात्मा न शोचति न कांक्षति।
समः सर्वेषु भूतेषु मद्भक्तिं लभते पराम्॥५४॥

*brahmabhūtaḥ prasannātmā*
*na śocati na kāṅkṣati*
*samaḥ sarveṣu bhūteṣu*
*madbhaktiṁ labhate parām*

(54) Settled in the identity with the Brahman, cheerful in mind; he neither grieves nor desires. Regarding all beings alike, he attains Supreme devotion to Me.

भक्त्या मामभिजानाति यावान्यश्चास्मि तत्त्वतः।
ततो मां तत्त्वतो ज्ञात्वा विशते तदनन्तरम्॥५५॥

*bhaktyā māmabhijānāti*
*yāvān yaś cāsmi tattvataḥ*
*tato māṁ tattvato jñātvā*
*viśate tadanantaram*

(55) Through devotion, he comes to know about Me, what and who I am in essence; then having known Me in truth, he forthwith enters into Me.

सर्वकर्माण्यपि सदा कुर्वाणो मद्व्यपाश्रयः।
मत्प्रसादादवाप्नोति शाश्वतं पदमव्ययम्॥५६॥

*sarvakarmāṇyapi sadā*
*kurvāṇo madvyapāśrayaḥ*
*matprasādād avāpnoti*
*śāśvataṁ padamavyayam*

(56) While performing all actions, he who always seeks refuge

in Me—by My grace, he attains the eternal, immutable state.

चेतसा सर्वकर्माणि मयि संन्यस्य मत्परः।
बुद्धियोगमुपाश्रित्य मच्चित्तः सततं भव॥५७॥

*cetasā sarvakarmāṇi*
*mayi sannyasya matparaḥ*
*buddhiyogamupāśritya*
*maccittaḥ satataṁ bhava*

(57) Consciously surrendering all actions to Me, regarding Me as the Supreme goal; resorting to the Yoga of integral wisdom (Buddhi-yoga)—focus your mind constantly on Me.

मच्चित्तः सर्वदुर्गाणि मत्प्रसादात्तरिष्यसि।
अथ चेत्त्वमहङ्कारान्न श्रोष्यसि विनङ्क्ष्यसि॥५८॥

*maccittaḥ sarvadurgāṇi*
*matprasādāt tariṣyasi*
*atha cet tvamahaṅkārān*
*na śroṣyasi vinaṅkṣyasi*

(58) Focusing thus your mind on Me—by My grace, you will overcome all the difficulties; but, if because of egoism, you will not listen to Me, thou shalt perish.

यदहङ्कारमाश्रित्य न योत्स्य इति मन्यसे।
मिथ्यैष व्यवसायस्ते प्रकृतिस्त्वां नियोक्ष्यति ॥५९॥

*yadahaṅkāramāsritya*
*na yotsya iti manyase*
*mithyaiṣa vyavasāyaste*
*prakṛtis tvāṁ niyokṣyati*

(59) If, in your self-conceit, you think "I will not fight," your resolve is in vain. Nature will compel you.

स्वभावजेन कौन्तेय निबद्धः स्वेन कर्मणा।
कर्तुं नेच्छसि यन्मोहात्करिष्यस्यवशोऽपि तत् ॥६०॥

*svabhāvajena kaunteya*
*nibaddhaḥ svena karmaṇā*
*kartuṁ necchasi yan mohāt*
*kariṣyasyavaśo'pi tat*

(60) O'Arjuna, bound by your sense of duty (karma) born of your own inner disposition; that which from delusion, you do not desire to do, even that, you will do helplessly.

ईश्वरः सर्वभूतानां हृद्देशेऽर्जुन तिष्ठति।
भ्रामयन्सर्वभूतानि यन्त्रारूढानि मायया ॥६१॥

*īśvaraḥ sarvabhūtānāṁ*

*hṛddeśe'rjuna tiṣṭhati*

*bhrāmayan sarvabhūtāni*

*yantrārūḍhāni māyayā*

(61) The Lord dwells in the hearts of all beings, O'Arjuna, causing them to revolve (bound by their karmas) by His illusive power; as if they were mounted on a machine.

**तमेव शरणं गच्छ सर्वभावेन भारत।**

**तत्प्रसादात्परां शान्तिं स्थानं प्राप्स्यसि शाश्वतम्॥६२॥**

*tameva śaraṇaṁ gaccha*

*sarvabhāvena bhārata*

*tatprasādāt parāṁ śāntiṁ*

*sthānaṁ prāpsyasi śāśvatam*

(62) Take refuge in Him alone, with all your being, O'Arjuna. By His grace, you will attain the Supreme peace and the eternal abode.

**इति ते ज्ञानमाख्यातं गुह्याद् गुह्यतरं मया।**

**विमृश्यैतदशेषेण यथेच्छसि तथा कुरु॥६३॥**

*iti te jñānamākhyātaṁ*

*guhyād guhyataraṁ mayā*

*vimṛśyaitadaśeṣeṇa*

*yathecchasi tathā kuru*

(63) Thus, this knowledge, which is the Supreme mystery of all mysteries, has been declared to you by Me. Reflect on it fully, and then act as thou wishest.

सर्वगुह्यतमं भूयः शृणु मे परमं वचः।

इष्टोऽसि मे दृढमिति ततो वक्ष्यामि ते हितम्॥ ६४॥

*sarvaguhyatamaṁ bhūyaḥ*

*śṛṇu me paramaṁ vacaḥ*

*iṣṭo'si me dṛḍhamiti*

*tato vakṣyāmi te hitam*

(64) Listen, once again to My Supreme word, the profound secret of all. Since you are very dear to Me, therefore, I shall tell you, that which is good for you.

मन्मना भव मद्भक्तो मद्याजी मां नमस्कुरु।

मामेवैष्यसि सत्यं ते प्रतिजाने प्रियोऽसि मे॥ ६५॥

*manmanā bhava madbhakto*
*madyājī māṁ namaskuru*
*māmevaiṣyasi satyaṁ te*
*pratijāne priyo'si me*

(65) Focus your mind on Me, be devoted to Me, worship Me, and prostrate thyself before Me—you will come to Me alone. I promise you certainly, because you are very dear to Me.

सर्वधर्मान्परित्यज्य मामेकं शरणं व्रज।
अहं त्वा सर्वपापेभ्यो मोक्षयिष्यामि मा शुचः ॥ ६६ ॥

*sarvadharmān parityajya*
*māmekaṁ śaraṇaṁ vraja*
*ahaṁ tvā sarvapāpebhyo*
*mokṣayiṣyāmi mā śucaḥ*

(66) Resigning all the Dharmas, seek refuge in Me alone. I shall liberate you from all sins. Grieve not.

इदं ते नातपस्काय नाभक्ताय कदाचन।
न चाशुश्रूषवे वाच्यं न च मां योऽभ्यसूयति ॥ ६७ ॥

*idaṁ te nātapaskāya*
*nābhaktāya kadācana*

*na cāśuśrūṣave vācyaṁ*
*na ca māṁ yo'bhyasūyati*

(67) This should not be told by you to the one, who is devoid of austerities and also who lacks devotion; or to the one who is unwilling to hear and also who finds fault with Me.

य इदं परमं गुह्यं मद्भक्तेष्वभिधास्यति।
भक्तिं मयि परां कृत्वा मामेवैष्यत्यसंशयः॥ ६८॥

*ya idaṁ paramaṁ guhyaṁ*
*madbhakteṣvabhidhāsyati*
*bhaktiṁ mayi parāṁ kṛtvā*
*māmevaiṣyatyasaṁśayaḥ*

(68) He, who with Supreme devotion to Me, will teach this Supreme secret to My devotees, shall come to Me, there is no doubt about it.

न च तस्मान्मनुष्येषु कश्चिन्मे प्रियकृत्तमः।
भविता न च मे तस्मादन्यः प्रियतरो भुवि॥ ६९॥

*na ca tasmānmanuṣyeṣu*
*kaścin me priyakṛttamaḥ*

*bhavitā na ca me tasmād*

*anyaḥ priyataro bhuvi*

(69) There is none among men, who does dearer service to Me than he; nor shall there be another on earth dearer to Me than he.

**अध्येष्यते च य इमं धर्म्यं संवादमावयोः।**

**ज्ञानयज्ञेन तेनाहमिष्टः स्यामिति मे मतिः॥७०॥**

*adhyeṣyate ca ya imaṁ*

*dharmyaṁ saṁvādamāvayoḥ*

*jñānayajñena tenāham-*

*iṣṭaḥ syāmiti me matiḥ*

(70) He, who will study this sacred dialogue of ours, by him I shall be worshipped through the *yajña* (sacrifice) of knowledge. Such is my conviction.

**श्रद्धावाननसूयश्च शृणुयादपि यो नरः।**

**सोऽपि मुक्तः शुभाँल्लोकान्प्राप्नुयात्पुण्यकर्मणाम्॥७१॥**

*śraddhāvānanasūyaś ca*

*śṛṇuyādapi yo naraḥ*

*sopi muktaḥ śubhāṅllokān*

*prāpnuyāt puṇyakarmaṇām*

(71) The man who listens to this with full faith and without scoffing—he too shall be liberated, and shall attain the auspicious worlds of the righteous.

कच्चिदेतच्छ्रुतं पार्थ त्वयैकाग्रेण चेतसा।
कच्चिदज्ञानसम्मोहः प्रनष्टस्ते धनञ्जय॥ ७२॥

*kaccidetacchrutaṁ pārtha*
*tvayaikāgreṇa cetasā*
*kaccidajñānasaṁmohaḥ*
*pranaṣṭas te dhanañjaya*

(72) Have you heard this gospel attentively, O'Arjuna? Has your delusion, born of ignorance been dispelled?

अर्जुन उवाच

नष्टो मोहः स्मृतिर्लब्धा त्वत्प्रसादान्मयाच्युत।
स्थितोऽस्मि गतसन्देहः करिष्ये वचनं तव॥ ७३॥

*naṣṭo mohaḥ smṛtir labdhā*
*tvatprasādān mayā'cyuta*
*sthito'smi gatasandehaḥ*
*kariṣye vacanaṁ tava*

**Arjuna said :**

(73) O'Kṛṣṇa, my delusion is destroyed and I have regained my memory (knowledge of the self) through your grace. Now I am totally integrated and free from all doubts. I shall act according to Thy word.

संजय उवाच

इत्यहं वासुदेवस्य पार्थस्य च महात्मनः।
संवादमिममश्रौषमद्भुतं रोमहर्षणम्॥ ७४॥

*ityahaṁ vāsudevasya*
*pārthasya ca mahātmanaḥ*
*saṁvādamimamaśrauṣam-*
*adbhutaṁ romaharṣaṇam*

**Sanjaya said :**

(74) Thus, I have heard this most wondrous dialogue between Srī Kṛṣṇa and the highly enlightened Arjuna, which makes my hair stand on end (genuinely thrilled and blessed).

व्यासप्रसादाच्छ्रुतवानेतद् गुह्यमहं परम्।
योगं योगेश्वरात्कृष्णात्साक्षात्कथयतः स्वयम्॥ ७५॥

*vyāsaprasādācchrutavān-*
*etad guhyamahaṁ param*

*yogaṁ yogeśvarāt kṛṣṇāt*
*sākṣāt kathayataḥ svayam*

(75) Through the grace of the sage Vyasa, I have heard this Supreme mystery of Yoga as declared in person by Srī Kṛṣṇa himself—the Lord of Yoga.

राजन्संस्मृत्य संस्मृत्य संवादमिममद्भुतम्।
केशवार्जुनयोः पुण्यं हृष्यामि च मुहुर्मुहुः ॥७६।

*rājan saṅsmṛtya-saṅsmṛtya*
*saṁvādamimamadbhutam*
*keśavārjunayoḥ puṇyaṁ*
*hṛṣyāmi ca muhur-muhuḥ*

(76) O'King, as I recall again and again the most wondrous and the sacred dialogue between Srī Kṛṣṇa and Arjuna I rejoice over and over again.

तच्च संस्मृत्य संस्मृत्य रूपमत्यद्भुतं हरेः।
विस्मयो मे महान्राजन्हृष्यामि च पुनःपुनः॥७७॥

*tacca saṅsmṛtya-saṅsmṛtya*
*rūpamatyadbhutaṁ hareḥ*
*vismayo me māhān rājan*
*hṛṣyāmi ca punaḥ-punaḥ*

(77) And remembering over and over again, that most magnificent cosmic form of Hari (Srī Kṛṣṇa); greater is indeed my amazement. O'King, I feel thrilled with joy again and again.

**यत्र योगेश्वरः कृष्णो यत्र पार्थो धनुर्धरः।**
**तत्र श्रीर्विजयो भूतिर्ध्रुवा नीतिर्मतिर्मम॥७८॥**

*yatra yogeśvaraḥ kṛṣṇo*
*yatra pārtho dhanurdharaḥ*
*tatra śrīr vijayo bhūtir-*
*dhruvā nītir matir mama*

(78) Wherever there is Srī Kṛṣṇa, the Lord of Yoga, and wherever there is Arjuna, the wielder of the bow; there are always the glory, victory, prosperity and righteousness; such is my firm conviction.

**ॐ तत्सदिति श्रीमद्भगवद्गीतासूपनिषत्सु ब्रह्मविद्यायां योगशास्त्रे श्रीकृष्णार्जुनसंवादे मोक्षसंन्यासयोगो नाम अष्टादशोऽध्यायः॥१८॥**

***'Aum' tatsaditi***
***Srīmadbhagawadgītā sūpaniṣatsu***
***brahmavidyāyām yogaśāstre***
***Srīkṛṣṇārjunasamvāde***
***mokṣasannyāsayogo nāma***
***aṣṭādaso'dhyāyaḥ***

**'AUM TAT SAT'**—Thus in the Upanishad of the glorious Bhagawad Geeta, the science of the Brahman (Absolute) the scripture of yoga, the dialogue between Srī Kṛṣṇa and Arjuna—thus ends the eighteenth chapter entitled *"Moksasannyasayoga"*.

इति श्रीमद्भगवद्गीतासु अष्टादशोऽध्यायः ॥ १८ ॥

श्रीमद्भगवद्गीता समाप्ता ॥

ॐ तत् सत् ॐ

*oṁ tat sat oṁ*

—:O:—